Microsoft® Access™ 2010
VBA Macro Programming

D1500937

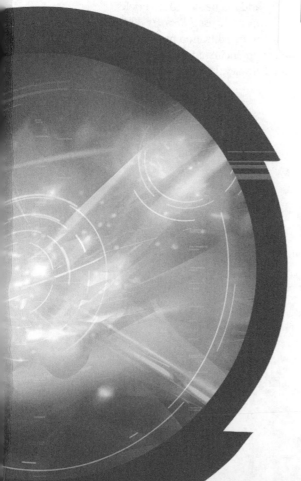

About the Author

Richard Shepherd has worked for many years for major banks and corporations in the United Kingdom creating Access databases to solve specific problems. These companies include National Grid plc (electricity distribution), Hertz Car Leasing, NatWest plc (retail banking), Schroders plc (fund management), BNP Paribas (investment banking), Lloyds TSB plc (corporate banking), The Royal Bank of Scotland plc (investment banking), and the British National Health Service

He has developed advanced databases for budgeting, business planning, trading reporting, and profit and loss reporting. He has qualified as an accountant with the Association of Chartered Certified Accountants and is now a Fellow of the Association. He is also the author of *Excel VBA Macro Programming* and *Excel 2007 VBA Macro Programming* (McGraw-Hill Professional).

Richard works as a freelance software developer and can be contacted at tollside@yahoo.com.

About the Technical Editor

Allen G. Taylor is a 30-year veteran of the computer industry and the author of 27 books, including *SQL for Dummies*, *Database Development for Dummies*, and *Crystal Reports 2008 for Dummies*. He teaches database development through a leading online education provider, and lectures internationally on astronomy, history, innovation, and entrepreneurship. His blog address is www.moontube.wordpress.com, and his web site can be found at www.DatabaseCentral.Info. You can contact Allen at allen.taylor@ieee.org.

Microsoft® Access™ 2010
VBA Macro Programming

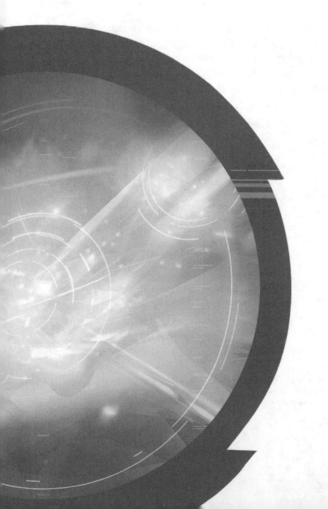

Richard Shepherd

New York   Chicago   San Francisco
Lisbon   London   Madrid   Mexico City   Milan
New Delhi   San Juan   Seoul   Singapore   Sydney   Toronto

The McGraw·Hill Companies

Cataloging-in-Publication Data is on file with the Library of Congress

McGraw-Hill books are available at special quantity discounts to use as premiums and sales promotions, or for use in corporate training programs. To contact a representative, please e-mail us at bulksales@mcgraw-hill.com.

Microsoft® Access™ 2010 VBA Macro Programming

1 2 3 4 5 6 7 8 9 0   DOC DOC   1 0 9 8 7 6 5 4 3 2 1 0

ISBN   978-0-07-173857-6
MHID   0-07-173857-6

Sponsoring Editor Wendy Rinaldi	**Technical Editor** Allen Taylor	**Production Supervisor** Jean Bodeaux
Editorial Supervisor Jody McKenzie	**Copy Editor** Michael McGee	**Composition** Glyph International
Project Manager Vipra Fauzdar, Glyph International	**Proofreader** Claire Splan	**Illustration** Glyph International
Acquisitions Coordinator Joya Anthony	**Indexer** Claire Splan	**Art Director, Cover** Jeff Weeks

To my wife, Elaine, and my son, Alexander.

Contents at a Glance

Contents

Acknowledgments

With grateful thanks to all the people at McGraw-Hill who have made this book happen. Special thanks to Joya Anthony and Vipra Fauzdar, who have managed this project and dealt with the vast numbers of e-mails it has generated. Others who deserve special mention for all the help they have given to the project include Wendy Rinaldi (who asked me to write this book), Allen Taylor, and Melinda Lyttle.

Finally, a big thank you to Elaine and Alexander for all their support on this project.

Introduction

Database macro programming has changed enormously over the last 15 years, having gone from Access Basic macros to VBA. Another major change occurred with Office 95, when macros went to VBA modules in a separate environment accessed via the Visual Basic Editor. It used to be fairly basic: code was entered into a special design window. Although the language was rather powerful in its own right, it was not a structured language and could certainly not be described as object-oriented. The number of commands was limited, and a fair amount of ingenuity was required to do certain tasks. The main advantage was that it was fairly easy to learn and understand; many programmers cut their teeth by initially writing database macros.

If anyone other than the original author examined the code, it could take days to find out exactly how it worked and what it was doing. Commercial companies frequently found that when the author of a complicated macro left the company, that macro had to be rewritten from scratch because of the time involved in assessing what it was doing.

Microsoft has introduced a new programming language called Visual Basic for Applications (VBA). VBA is a more intuitive and robust programming language, using an object-oriented design. It has many similarities with its older and larger cousin, Visual Basic (VB). Once you learn VBA, you will have a fair understanding of how Visual Basic itself operates.

VBA is extremely different from the old macro language, and if the older language is what you are used to, it will mean totally rethinking how you write and structure your code. The concepts of object-oriented programming (OOP) are as different as chalk and cheese to the old macro language, but there is a huge advantage in terms of what you can achieve on a spreadsheet. With object-oriented programming, you are dealing with the concept of objects. To use an example, the database you load is an object. The tables and queries where you access your data are other objects, and so are the printer and the screen. They have properties, events, and methods (discussed later in the book). You will start to see object-oriented programming in more detail when you reach Chapter 14.

VBA does allow a more structured and object-oriented approach to writing your macros. If this is your first foray into the world of Access macro programming, you may well find the concepts easier to grasp, since you have no knowledge of the technologies used in the past within Excel. The Access Basic macros were a completely different language in terms of how and where you entered it. The concept of VBA is unique and cannot be compared to the old Access Basic macros. Unfortunately, knowledge of the old system of writing macros can add to confusion with the new method of VBA and extend the learning curve.

Since VBA is shared by all Office applications, a great deal of the information contained in this book will help with other Office applications such as Word or Excel and also with Visual Basic itself. VBA is more powerful than the previous text macro language and enables you to extend Access in any way you choose. It lets you write code to do things that are not within the Access menu structure. It even provides a means to access and manipulate other Microsoft Office applications under software control. For example, by using the Outlook object model, you can copy address lists onto your database merely by executing VBA code. This will happen even if Outlook is not running since Outlook only needs to be installed for the object model to work.

By the same token, you can also manipulate the Access object model from another Microsoft application. For example, you can produce an Excel spreadsheet file from Microsoft Access without Excel ever appearing onscreen or being loaded. Access users know that it is very easy to write a macro to export a table into Excel, but what if you desire information from several tables and you want presentation formatting on the numbers, as well as audit trails on the figures explaining how they were calculated? VBA lets you do this.

VBA is an object-oriented language that requires a totally different viewpoint from the old text-based macro programming. All objects can have events, methods, and properties, and these can be manipulated to assist your programs. The objects are arranged in a hierarchy. This concept is explained in more detail in Chapter 12.

Whether you are totally new to macro programming in Access or simply want to update your skills, this book will show you how to use the Access object models along with VBA to learn how to program macros effectively.

The Objectives of this Book

The first objective of this book is to show you how VBA works in Access and the basics of object-oriented programming. The intricacies of the VBA programming language are explained, and specific keywords and functions are discussed. It then takes you through a number of worked examples, detailing how to set up subroutines and functions. Full source code is shown for all examples.

The book not only shows you how to do things that are on the Access menu but also describes how to do several things outside of the Access menu structure and make them all look absolutely mind-blowing in a database. People seeing them for the first time and not knowing they were done through VBA code will either be amazed and congratulate you on your knowledge, or quietly go away and study the menu structure to see if there is a way of doing it without using VBA (which, of course, there is not). Examples like this can be found in Chapter 11, which shows you how to set up your own ribbon menu structures within Access, and Chapter 35, which explores how to control the population of an Excel spreadsheet from Access.

The book is full of completed examples, all tried and tested, in which you are walked through each step of what the code is doing. Screenshots are plentiful, so you can see what your code should be producing. Personally, I have always learned programming by example and experimentation. If I can view the code and see what it produces, then I can study how it works and learn from it. Even if the examples do not do exactly what you want, you'll be able to modify them to suit your own needs.

This book assumes you already have a good working knowledge of Access from the database perspective but that you have not dealt with writing macros.

By the time you finish all the examples in this book, you should be versed in how to use VBA to solve problems. The only limiting factor will be your imagination.

You can contact the author (Richard Shepherd) with any further points at tollside@yahoo.com.

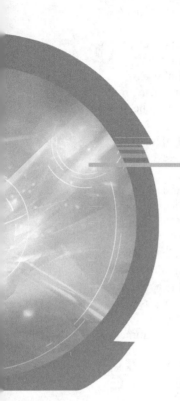

Programming in Access VBA

In this part, you will learn all about how Visual Basic for Applications (VBA) works for Access 2010. A number of new VBA features have been incorporated into the 2010 version, and the aim of this book is to show you how to use code to interact with both them and the classic features of Access.

You will learn rules for coding, how to write code, how to debug your code—looking for the inevitable errors that occur—and how to build graphical user interfaces (GUIs) so users can run your code easily. This is really all about the mechanics of code writing and is transferable to other Microsoft applications such as Excel or Word.

The final chapters of this book are made up of examples that show you how to harness VBA to deal with problems you may encounter in Access. I have always found that one of the best ways to learn a coding language is to go through examples, try them out, understand them, and modify them to suit your own requirements.

This book assumes the reader already has a basic understanding of how to create a database using tables and queries. The purpose is to educate the reader on how to make use of VBA code within the database, not to show all the steps of how to design and implement a database.

Access is frequently used in organizations to produce RAD (Rapid Application Development) applications. It has a huge advantage in that a prototype application can be written very quickly, sometimes in as little as one day, and then shown to the users.

The developer can then go through iterations with the users. In my experience, there can be a huge number of these! Although this can be a messy way of development, many organizations are so fast moving that they need the application quickly. Normally, a specification of requirements would be mapped out, but in many cases there is a danger of the application being obsolete by the time it comes to fruition. I have found this to be very much the case in investment banking.

Some organizations do not like Access applications because they can be difficult to support due to the often undocumented way in which they are developed. However, they do solve problems very quickly.

The main advantage of Access over other applications in the Microsoft Office suite is that it is multiuser. If you open up an Excel file or Word file, you have exclusive access to that file. If another user opens the file as well, they will get a message stating that they can only open it as a read-only file and cannot save changes back to that file.

If you create an application in Access, then a number of people can use it simultaneously. This turns it into a real application. However, this then opens up a whole load of security issues and audit trail issues, which we will discuss later on. Maintenance of the application is also a problem. You will need exclusive access to the database to make any changes to its structure or even make a change to VBA code in a module.

I hope you will be able to use this book to learn all about Access VBA and the immense power it can bring to your workplace.

The Basics

This chapter is intended to take you through the basic steps of using the Visual Basic Editor window and writing a simple piece of VBA code. It will show you how to use the Visual Basic Editor (VBE), and the Project Explorer and code windows. You will learn how to write a simple macro to display a "Hello World" message box.

Macros and VBA Modules in Access

You may have noticed that in Access you can create both macros and modules containing VBA code. What is the difference between these? They are both a means of creating automation procedures, but macros are more limited than modules and do not use VBA.

If you click Create on the menu bar and then click the Macro icon in the Macros and Code section of the ribbon, you will see the macro editor window shown in Figure 1-1.

If you click the Add New Action drop-down, a drop-down of various macro commands such as CloseWindow or DeleteRecord will appear. If you click one of these options, you can enter in parameters such as the name of the form to be opened or add a filter.

Basically, it is a simplistic means of building a macro, but it is nowhere near as rich and flexible as a VBA module. Everything offered in the Macro Editor can also be used in VBA modules (albeit in a different format) and the modules offer the flexibility of a real programming language. Note that many macro commands can be used directly within VBA code. Since this book concentrates on VBA modules, macros will not be discussed further.

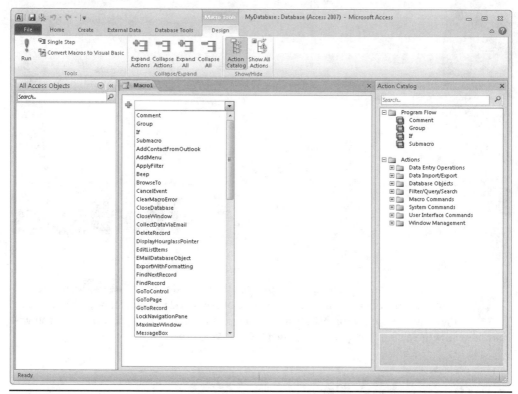

Figure 1-1   *The Macro editor window showing the Add New Action drop-down*

Exploring the Visual Basic Editor in Access

If you use Access a lot, you are familiar with its database layout. When you open Access, a standard view looks like Figure 1-2. You have the Office ribbon across the top and a window on the left-hand side that lets you define and edit various database objects such as tables, queries, forms, and reports.

Readers who have already used Access 2007 will be familiar with the new ribbon style menu, but if you are upgrading from an older version of Access, you will find that the user interface is completely different than what you are used to. In some ways, first-time users have a big advantage here because they are not looking for menu options in the old places. It can be quite frustrating if you know the old menu system and are trying to adjust to the new ribbon.

Fortunately, the Visual Basic Editor (VBE) window has stayed much the same as in older versions of Access, so if you have used Access 2003/2007 to design VBA code, you will not find too many differences.

Figure 1-2   *The standard Access database screen*

Many users are unaware that, in addition to the database application of Access, there is an extremely powerful programming language built into Access that you can use to design your own applications. You can use VBA code to write macro applications in VBA that do some very powerful things. A *macro application* is a procedure written in VBA code that performs certain tasks. This could be something like outputting a text file from a table or creating or editing a query. Whatever you decide to do with them, macros automate tasks and make life easier for you and the users of your database.

The language works in conjunction with object structures and hierarchies, and you can even create your own objects by using class modules (see Chapter 21). Some people may argue that VBA is not an object-oriented language, but it certainly has all the features of one.

These VBA projects can be accessed through a companion program called the Visual Basic Editor (VBE). Press ALT-F11 to see the window shown in Figure 1-3. You can also click Create on the Access menu bar and then use the drop-down on the Macro/Module icon in the "Other" group of the ribbon. However, this creates a new module in addition to any others you have, so you may not wish to do this.

Figure 1-3   *The standard Visual Basic Editor window*

At first glance, this window with its new menu bar, containing menus for File, Edit, View, Insert, Format, Debug, Run, Tools, Add-Ins, Window, and Help, might be confusing. It opens as a separate application window, but it is still very much a part of the Access application. In fact, this window opens up a whole new ball game in terms of what you can do with Access. In the next section, I'll explain the windows in more detail.

VBA Project Explorer and Code Windows

The Project Explorer, which shows a Project tree, is on the left-hand side of the screen, just below the menu and toolbar. It shows the VBA project for the database as it stands, displaying the details in tree form so you can easily navigate between them. Notice that it will only show modules and class modules you have created. If you are used to using VBA in Excel, you will have noticed that each workbook and worksheet has its own module and the structure of modules reflects the sheets in your workbook.

If you imagine that in Access the forms and reports take the place of dialogs and worksheets in Excel, then you can also have modules attached to these objects. Once the module is created on a form or a report, it will show up in the tree of objects on the left-hand side of the VBE window.

One of the problems in Access is that code can appear in a number of different places. Modules can be inserted via the VBE window, or they can be added to forms or reports. Provided the form or report is open, all the code modules are interactive and program flows can often cross from one module to another or, for example, from one form to another.

For example, a subroutine may call another subroutine or function that is in another module. That action will be performed and then the program flow will move back to the original procedure it was called from.

This can make it quite hard to keep track of exactly what is going on in an Access application and debugging code can become a very complex task. It is certainly more difficult to pick up an existing Access application and find out how it all works.

Remember, VBA is an object-oriented language. This means that the language works in terms of various objects. For example, the Access application is an object, a query definition is an object, as is a table definition. When using VBA, you use these objects and their various properties, methods, and events to create your code.

The first branch on the tree coming from the root of the VBA project says Microsoft Office Access Class Objects. Coming off this branch are objects for the modules that have been created in the VBE. However, as you add in forms and reports and add modules to these objects, you will see them reflected in the tree structure.

This is a very important concept to understand because all the forms and reports you create are objects that can be referred to. These are not the only objects within Access, but looking at the Project Explorer simplistically, these are the objects shown there.

On a brand new Access database that you have just created, no modules will be visible. Click Insert | Module on the menu bar to insert a module.

Initially, the module does not show a great deal, and you may wonder what to do with it. If you type something at random such as **What do I do now?** and press ENTER, you will get a compile error. This is because there are disciplines and rules about entering code. Everything you enter here goes through a Visual Basic compiler that interprets what you have written and converts it into instructions that your computer understands. Unfortunately, it does not understand plain English, which is why you get a compile error.

Click OK in the Compile Error message box and delete your statement. Notice the statement line turned red when the compile error appeared to draw your attention to the problem. Even if you do nothing about it, it will remain red as a danger signal to show there is a problem with your code.

Your screen should now look like Figure 1-4.

The first step in entering some VBA code is to enter a subroutine called MyCode. You do this by simply typing in **Sub MyCode** anywhere in the module screen and pressing ENTER. VBA will automatically add End Sub and the brackets after MyCode.

```
Sub MyCode()
End Sub
```

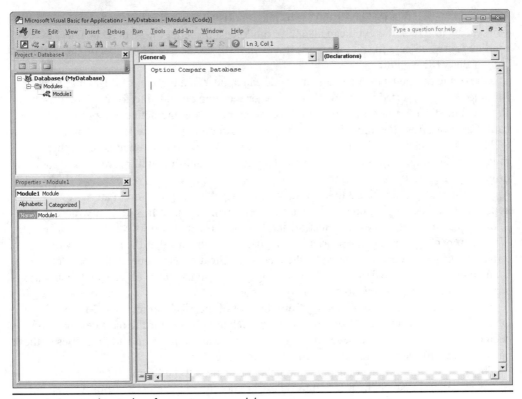

Figure 1-4 *Code window for an Access module*

This gives you a code area to write your VBA code against. Notice that in the drop-down list in the top right-hand corner of the module window that your subroutine MyCode has now been added. This is useful as a navigational facility. In complex applications where many procedures exist in a module, this gives a useful alphabetical list of them.

If you intend to write any code for the event, then you must include these two statements or you will get a compile error. Think of them as start and finish lines in a race—they tell the compiler where the code starts and stops. If you do not want to write any code for that event, you can delete them, but both must be deleted or you will get a compile error. The compiler wants your code neat and tidy, which means it must be structured properly.

Currently, you have the start and finish of an event. Although there's nothing between the **Sub** and **End Sub** statements, the routine is still live and will fire when you click the Run icon on the toolbar (green triangle pointing to the right) or press F5. However, because there is no code in the event, it will not do anything.

Your First Access VBA Macro

Programming books traditionally help direct your first steps in a program by writing a simple piece of code to display the text "Hello world," and this book is no exception. You will use the **MsgBox** statement to display the statement. This is a simple user interface showing the statement and an OK button that you have probably seen before in Windows.

Under the statement **Sub MyCode()** but before **End Sub**, type in **msgbox "Hello World"**. Be sure to be lazy and do not use the SHIFT key when typing **msgbox** and see what happens. The word "msgbox" transforms into the upper- and lowercase "MsgBox" because it is a defined statement word in VBA and is already set up to appear this way. However, you must make sure you spell it correctly—make a mistake, and you will get a compile error.

```
Private Sub MyCode()
  MsgBox "Hello World"
End Sub
```

Notice that the **MsgBox** statement is indented with the TAB key. This is a useful way to see where one set of statements begins and ends. Without this notation, it is easy to get lost and lose track of where a loop starts and finishes when complicated loops are used. For more on loops, see Chapter 4.

A **MsgBox** statement is a simple way to provide an interface to the user by displaying a message and an OK button. I'm sure you've seen message boxes like this pop up from time to time, and now you know how easy they are to create. They can be quite sophisticated, and Chapter 5 explains in more detail how to use them.

After you type in the word **msgbox**, a box containing all the parameters for this command is displayed. In this instance, you do not have to take any notice of this box since you are only displaying a text string. However, it can be extremely useful in telling you what parameters are required for a function and in what order they should appear. If, for example, you wanted to give the message box an icon or a title, the parameter box would help you do this correctly. The parameter box is a list box that appears when you reach the parameter for the icon and gives a list of optional constants for the icon of your choice. This type of help is available for all functions when using the VBA editor. Your code window should now look like Figure 1-5.

You can now run your code, which can be done in one of three ways:

► Click your mouse anywhere on your code (MyCode) and then click the Run icon in the VBE toolbar—this is a green triangle pointing to the right-hand side.

► Press F5.

► Click Run | Run Sub/UserForm from the VBE menu.

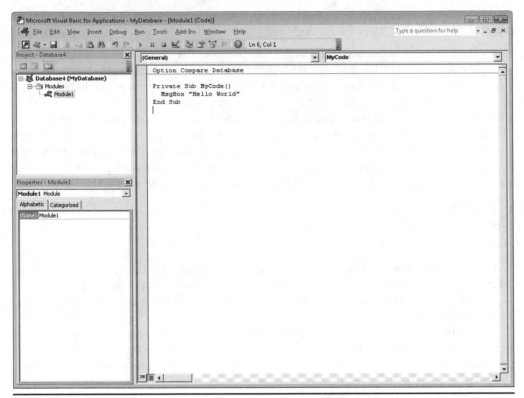

Figure 1-5 *Code to display "Hello World" message box using MyCode*

Make sure you click the cursor on the body of the subroutine before you run it so VBA knows which procedure to run. Your screen should now look like Figure 1-6. This figure assumes you did not already have a database open, because the ribbon is grayed out in it.

See, you can produce professional-looking interfaces on Access with hardly any code!

This is a simple demonstration of adding code to a module. If you have used VBA in Excel, you know there are events you can also add code to, such as Workbook_Open. Events are also available in Access VBA on Forms and Reports. A similar example in Access would be the Form Open event that is fired off every time that particular form is opened within the database. This is discussed further in Chapter 9.

Events are being fired off all the time when things happen in an Access database. You can insert code to take action on a particular event, such as a user making a selection on a form, and each time the event happens, your code will be run.

However, you cannot do any editing in the code window until you click OK on your message box and the macro finishes running. This is because the focus of the code is on your message box window, and the focus cannot be moved anywhere else within Access until the message box disappears.

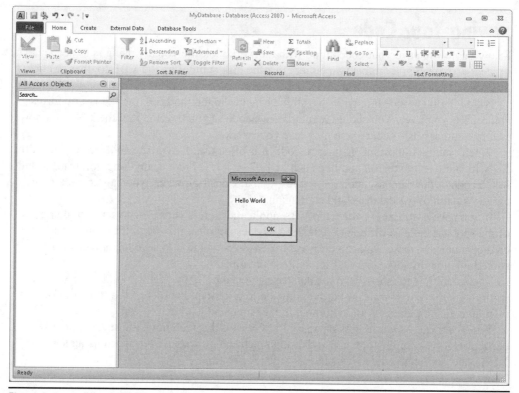

Figure 1-6   *Hello World message box*

To remove this procedure, simply delete all the lines for it or delete the line MsgBox "Hello World" by pressing the DELETE key. Another way to prevent code from running is to turn it into a comment by putting the single quote (') character in front of the line: **' MsgBox "Hello World"**. This line will then turn green and will not be used. Comments are also used to place explanations and descriptions of your code inside a macro so it can be understood at a later date.

More Exploring of the VBA Project Window

Going back to the Project Explorer and the tree showing the project (in the top left-hand corner of screen), there are also objects for forms and reports that have VBA modules attached to them. Every form and report is a separate object and is represented as such in the Project tree.

Modules that you insert via the VBE do not have events, but modules related to forms and reports do. These can range from the form being opened to the user making a data change. These events give the VBA programmer places to set code up to intercept the user's actions. This is more fully explained in Chapter 9.

Saving Your Code

Knowing how to save your code along with the workbook file you are using is important. The process is quite simple in that you either click the disk symbol on the VBE toolbar or click File | Save... on the menu bar in the VBE window.

Following this procedure will save all the changes in the modules, including any forms and reports you have. You should regularly save code as you develop it. Otherwise, if a power failure or other crisis occurs, you may lose your work.

When making important changes to code, it is often useful to create another version of the file with a different version number, such as 1.02 or 1.1. If there is anything untoward found in the code or the database, you then have a fallback position where you can go back to an earlier version of the database and start again.

If you have used Excel to develop VBA applications, it is very easy to save another copy of the spreadsheet as a different name. Access does not offer this flexibility. Once you have created a new database, you can only use the Save As function to save to another format, something you do not want to do for another version.

The solution is to close down the database and make a copy of it in Windows Explorer (right-click the Windows Start button in the bottom left-hand corner of the screen). You can then give this file a new version number in the name and load that to work on it.

When working on an Access database I always use this technique for development, particularly if the application is live. Far too much can go wrong even when using simple VBA code, so you should always have a fallback position.

Variables, Arrays, Constants, and Data Types

Although the concept of having places to store data while the program is running is fairly straightforward, variables, arrays, and constants have some fairly complicated rules. They are intrinsic to any program, so I have devoted a chapter to explaining about them.

Variables

Building up a structure of *variables* is a bit like building up a filing cabinet at home. You might have files for your job, insurance policies, taxation, and personal documents such as passports. These files can grow in size. Some may only hold a single document, such as an insurance policy, while others can carry quite a lot of information, such as a tax file.

The important thing is that each file has a particular category of document. You would not file your passport in with your tax papers, for example. You need to know which file holds which papers for quick and easy reference.

Think of a variable as being similar to a particular file holding a specific type of information. The variable may just be a single number or a piece of text that the program needs to hold and refer to while it is running. It could also be a whole array of information, almost like a spreadsheet. A spreadsheet has many cells that can hold information, and an array can be set up to have many cells or locations in exactly the same way.

A variable can have its value changed by the program when running, which is why it is called a variable. The same rules apply from the filing cabinet example, in that you do not mix the data types between the variables. If a variable has been defined as a certain type, it will not accept data specified as another type. For example, if you have defined a variable as an integer (whole) number, you cannot put text into it, or if you put a floating point number (with decimal places) into an integer, you will lose the decimal places.

As your program runs, you often need a place to store data temporarily. Use variables to store values while your code is executing. Within a procedure, you declare a variable using the **Dim** statement, supplying a name for the variable:

Dim variablename [As type]

Variable names must follow these rules:

▶ They must begin with a letter.

▶ They must contain only letters, numbers, or the underscore character—no spaces!

▶ They must not exceed 40 characters.

▶ They must not be a reserved word (see the section "Reserved Words" at the end of this chapter).

The optional **As** type clause allows you to define the data type of the variable you are declaring. If you omit the type, it defaults to the Variant data type discussed in the next section.

```
Dim MyInteger as Integer
```

Implicit Declaration

You do not have to declare a variable before using it. You can just include the statement

```
TempVal=6
```

A variable will automatically be created for **TempVal** as a variant (default type), and it will have the value of 6.

However, a problem with doing this is that it can lead to subtle errors in your code if you misspell the name of the variable in a later statement. For example, if you refer to it as **temval** instead of **tempval**, you know what you mean but VBA does not. It assumes that **temval** is a new variable and assigns it as such. The old variable, **tempval**, is still there but is no longer being used. You now have two different variables, although you think you only have one. This can lead to enormous problems that can take some time to straighten out in your code.

Explicit Declaration

To avoid the problem of misnaming variables, you can stipulate that VBA always generate an error message whenever it encounters a variable not declared. To do this, you'll need to go to the declarations section of the code module. If you look at a module within the VB Editor window, you will see a heading called (General) in the top left of the module window and a heading called (Declarations) in the top right of the module window. Click (Declarations), and you will go straight to the declarations section. Do not worry if it appears you are not typing into a defined section. Type the following statement. As soon as you type a declaration, a line will automatically appear underneath to show it is within the declarations section.

```
Option Explicit
```

This prevents implicit declarations from being used. Now you have to define **TempVal**:

```
Dim TempVal
```

If you refer to **temval** during execution, an error message will be displayed, stating that the variable has not been defined.

NOTE

Option Explicit works on a per-module basis—it must be placed in the declarations section of every code module you want it to apply to unless you define the variable as a global variable. A global variable is valid right across your project and can be used by the code in any module. See the section later in this chapter called "Global Variables."

Which method you use (implicit or explicit) depends on your personal preference. Coding is often much faster using implicit because you do not have to initially define your variables before you use them. You can simply make variable statements, and VBA will take care of the rest. However, as discussed, this can lead to errors unless you have a good memory for variables you are using and have the experience to know exactly what you are doing. Implicit can also make it more difficult for someone else to understand your code. Using Option Explicit is the best practice and helps stop runtime errors.

The Scope and Lifetime of Variables

If you declare a variable within a procedure, only code within that procedure can access that variable. The scope is local to that procedure. You will often need variables that can be used by several procedures or even the whole application. For these reasons, you can declare a variable at the local, module, or global level.

Local Variables

A *local* variable uses **Dim**, **Static**, or **ReDim** (arrays only) to declare the variable within a procedure. Several procedures can have a variable called **temp**, but because every variable is local to its procedure, they all act independently of each other and can hold different values. Local variables declared with the **Dim** statement remain in existence only as long as the procedure is executing. Local variables declared with **Static** remain in existence for the lifetime of the application. You may well wish to maintain a variable value throughout the application, and if you look at Chapter 21, you will see an example of how a static variable can make a difference to your code.

```
Dim TempVal
Static TempVal
```

You can also dimension a variable as an array of several elements, and even several dimensions. An array is almost exactly like a spreadsheet in concept. You can define an array with ten elements so it has ten pigeonholes or cells to store information. You can also give it another dimension so it is a 10 by 10 array and has 100 pigeonholes or cells to store your information. An array gives you tremendous flexibility over storing data—it is like poking the data into individual spreadsheet cells. For example, if you recursively searched a disk drive for all subdirectories on it, the way Windows Explorer does, then you would need an array to store all the pathnames as they were found so you could easily find and refer to them within your program.

```
Dim A()
ReDim A(10)
ReDim Preserve A(12)
```

To use **ReDim**, you must define the variable initially as an array (see the section "Arrays" later in this chapter). **Dim A(3)** creates a small array with four elements (0–3), so there are effectively four **A** variables. **ReDim A(10)** then makes it an 11-element array but loses all the data in it. **ReDim A(12) Preserve** makes a 13-element array but keeps all existing data. Note all subscripts start at 0 by default.

ReDim is useful when you need an array to store data but you do not know how many elements you will need. For example, if you are recursively searching directories, you have no idea how many will be on a disk device, so you start by specifying a small array of ten elements. As this fills up, it can be resized using **ReDim** and **Preserve** to retain the data already in it.

Module-Level Variables

A *module-level* variable is declared for a particular module. It is available to all procedures within that module but not to the rest of the application. Module-level variables remain in existence for the lifetime of the application and preserve their values.

```
Dim TempVal
```

This would be placed in the declarations section of the module instead of an actual procedure on that module.

Global Variables

Global variables are declared in the declarations part of a module with the **Global** statement, but they can be accessed by any code within the application. Global variables exist and retain their values for the lifetime of the application.

```
Global TempVal
```

Again, this would be placed in the declarations section of any module. Because you have specified that it is global, it can be accessed for any part of your code.

Name Conflicts and Shadowing

A variable cannot change scope while your code is running. However, you can have a variable with the same name in a different scope or module. You can have a global variable called **temp** and also a local variable in a procedure called **temp**. References to **temp** within the procedure would access the local variable **temp**, and references outside the procedure would access the global variable **temp**. In this case, the local variable *shadows* (that is, is accessed in preference to) less local variables. The only way to use the global variable over the local variable is to give it a different name. Shadowing can be confusing and can produce subtle errors that are difficult to debug. The best way is to use unique names for all variables.

  The names of module-level and global variables can also cause conflicts with procedure names. A procedure (a subroutine) has global scope unless it is declared privately, as you will see in Chapter 3. A global variable cannot have the same name as any public procedure in any code module.

Static Variables

Variables also have a lifetime based on their scope. Module and global variables are preserved for the lifetime of the application, which means they hold their values while the application is executing until the user closes the application. Local variables declared with **Dim** exist only when the procedure is executing. When it stops, the values are not preserved and the memory is released. The next execution reinitializes the variables for the lifetime of the procedure. You should only use local variables to hold values that are being used during that procedure. If you expect to access them from other modules, they need to be global. However, you can use the **Static** keyword to declare and preserve a local variable:

```
Static Temp
```

  You can make all local variables static by placing the **Static** keyword at the beginning of a procedure heading:

```
Static Sub Test_MyProc()
```

Data Types

A variable can be given a data type that determines the type of data it can store. This can have an effect on the efficiency of your code. If there is no data type, the default type is Variant.

Variant

A *variant* can store all kinds of data, whether it is text, numbers, dates, or other information. It can even store an entire array. A variant variable can freely change its type at runtime, whereas one that has been specified as, say, a string cannot. You can use the function **VarType** to find out the type of data held by a variant:

```
Sub TestVariables()
stemp = "richard"
MsgBox VarType(stemp)
stemp = 4
MsgBox VarType(stemp)
End Sub
```

The message box will first display 8, which means it is a string. It will then display 2, which means it is an integer.

Table 2-1 shows the return values for specific data types.

VBA always uses the most efficient means of storing data in a variant. As you can see from the preceding example, it automatically changes to suit the data stored in it.

If you perform a mathematical operation on a variant that is not a numeric value, you will get a Type MisMatch error. This means you are trying to put a data type into a variable not set up to hold that data type—a bit like banging a square peg into a round hole. In this case, it may be that you are trying to perform a mathematical operation on a variant holding a string of text.

ReturnValue	Type
0	Variant
1	Null
2	Integer
3	Long
4	Single
5	Double
6	Currency
7	Date/Time
8	String
11	Boolean
17	Byte

Table 2-1   *VarType Return Values*

You can use the **IsNumeric** function to test if the value of a variant is a number—it returns true or false (nonzero or zero).

```
Sub TestNumeric()
temp="richard"
MsgBox IsNumeric(temp)
End Sub
```

This will give the result False.

Date/Time Values Stored in Variants

Variant variables can also contain Date/Time values. This is a floating point number—the integer part represents the days since 31-Dec-1899, and the decimal part represents the hours, minutes, and seconds expressed as a proportion of 24 hours. For example, 37786.75 represents 14-June-2003 at 18:00. The difference between 31-Dec-1899 and 14-June-2003 is 37,786 days, and 0.75 of 24 hours is 18 hours.

Adding or subtracting numbers adds or subtracts days. Adding decimals increases the time of day—for example, adding 1/24 (0.0416) adds one hour. A number of functions handle date and time, as explained in Chapter 5.

Note that the interpretation of day and month is dependent on the Regional Options settings within the Windows Control Panel. If you set your date to mm/dd/yy in Regional Options, this will be the default interpretation of day and month.

Just as you can use **IsNumeric** to determine if there is a numeric value, you can use the **IsDate** function to determine if there is a date value.

```
temp = "01-Feb-2009"
MsgBox IsDate(temp)
```

This will return True (nonzero).

Empty Value

A variant that has not had a variable assigned to it will have an empty value. You can test for this using the **IsEmpty** function.

```
MsgBox IsEmpty(MyTest)
```

This example will return True (nonzero) because MyTest has not been assigned a value.

Null Values

A variant can contain a special value of Null. The Null value is used to indicate unknown or missing data. Variables are not set to Null unless you write code to do this. If you do not use Null in your application, you do not have to worry about Null.

NOTE

Null is not 0. This is an easy but incorrect assumption to make when you're starting to learn VBA.

The safest way to check for a Null value in your code is to use **IsNull**. Other methods, such as the statement **Is Null**, may not give correct results.

```
Sub TestNull()
temp=Null
Msgbox IsNull(temp)
End Sub
```

The result here will be True (nonzero).

Other Data Types

Why use data types other than Variant? Because Variant may not use the best data type for the purpose. If you want to create concise fast code, you need other data types. For example, if you are doing lots of mathematical calculations on relatively small integer numbers, you can gain an enormous speed advantage by using the data type Integer instead of Variant. You can use Variant by default, but Variant will not necessarily assume it is an integer being used. It could assume it is a floating point number, in which case calculations will take far longer, although the same result will be produced.

Memory considerations should also be taken into account. Each double number takes up 8 bytes of memory, which may not seem like a lot. However, across a large array it can use a large amount of RAM, which would slow the process down. This will use up memory in the computer, which Windows could be using as virtual memory for its graphical display.

VBA Data Types

A number of data types can be used in VBA. The details of these are set out in Table 2-2.

Numeric Types

If you only work with whole numbers, then you declare your variables as Integer or Long, depending on size. Mathematical operations are much faster and memory demands are less for these types.

If you are working with fractions of numbers, use Single, Double, or Currency. Currency (fixed decimal point) supports up to 4 digits to the right of the decimal point and 15 digits to the left. Floating point (Single and Double) have larger ranges but can produce small rounding errors.

```
Dim temp1 as Integer
Dim temp2 as Long
Dim temp3 as Currency
Dim temp4 as Single
Dim temp5 as Double
```

Name	Description	Type-Declaration Character	Range
Integer	two-byte integer	%	−32,768 to 32,767
Long	four-byte integer	&	−2,147,483,648 to 2,147,438,647
Single	four-byte floating point number	!	−3.402823E38 to 1.401298E-45 (negative values) 1.401298E-45 to 3.402823E38 (positive values)
Double	eight-byte floating point number	#	−1.79769313486232E308 to −4.94065645841247E-324 (negative values) 4.94065645841247E-324 to 1.79769313486232E308 (positive values)
Currency	eight-byte number with fixed decimal point	@@	−922337203685477.5808 to 922337203685477.5807
Fixed Length String	String of characters— fixed length	$	0 to approximately 65,400 characters
Variable Length String	String of characters— variable length	$	0 to approximately 2 billion characters
Variant	Date/Time, floating point number, or string	None	Date Values: January 1, 0000 to December 31, 9999; numeric values: same range as double; string values: same range as string

Table 2-2   *Data Types Within VBA*

String Types

If your variable will always contain text, you can declare it to be of type **String**:

```
Dim temp as String
```

You can then use string handling functions to manipulate it. You can take sections from it, search for a particular character, or turn it all into uppercase characters. For a more detailed description, see the section "Functions" in Chapter 5.

A string is of variable length by default. The string grows or shrinks according to the data in it. If you do not want this to happen, you can declare a fixed-length string by using **String * size**:

```
Dim temp as String * 50
```

This forces a string to be fixed at 50 characters in length. If your string is less than 50, it is padded with spaces. If it is greater than 50 characters, the excess characters are truncated and lost. So, although you do get control over the amount of memory being used because there is always a fixed length to each element, there is a risk of data loss if a user manages to input a longer string than you originally envisioned.

Arrays

Up to now I have discussed individual variables. You can set up a variable and give it a value such as a number or a string. A simple example is the name of an employee. You can set up a variable called **employee** and give it a string with the employee's name. However, what about other employees? Suppose you are writing a program that needs to refer to 26 employees. You would have a great deal of difficulty referring to them in your program using simple variables. You would have to do something like this:

```
Dim employee1 as String, employee2 as String, employee3 as String,.......
```

This would be extremely cumbersome and inefficient. What would you do if new employees had to be added? Your program would no longer work!

Fortunately, a variable can be dimensioned as an *array*. All you need to specify is

```
Dim employee(25) as String
```

As mentioned previously, an array is effectively like a block of pigeonholes or cells in a spreadsheet that you can read and write data to by using the index of that array. You use the subscript number in brackets to indicate which element you are referring to. You can also **ReDim** the array at runtime to enlarge it if your program requires.

This example sets up a 26-element array numbered from 0 to 25, with 26 strings to put your names into. Each element can be referenced from your code by using the index number. A For..Next loop can easily be used to list out all names within the array:

```
Dim employee(25) as String
For n = 0 To 25
    employee(n)  = Chr(n+65)
Next n
For n = 0 To 25
    MsgBox employee(n)
Next n
```

In this macro, you first dimension an array called **employee** as a string with 26 elements.

The first For..Next loop puts data into the array. The ASCII (American Standard Code for Information Interchange—see Appendix A) code for the letter *A* is 65, and this is added to the value of *n*, which starts at 0. The **Chr** function converts this into a character, which is inserted into the appropriate element of the array. On the first loop, the character *A* is inserted into the first element of the array because *n* is 0 at this point. The value of 65, which is the code for *A*, is added to it.

The second For..Next loop displays each element of the employee array in turn. When you run this example, it gives the letters *A* to *Z*.

Arrays follow the same rules as ordinary variables. They can be local, module, or global and can be any data type, including Variant. The size of the array in terms of elements is limited to an integer (in the range –32,768 to 32,767). The default lower boundary is always 0, but this can be altered by placing an Option Base statement in the declarations section of the module:

```
Option Base 1
```

All arrays in that module start at 1.

You can also specify the lower limit for an array by using the **To** keyword:

```
Dim temp (1 To 15) as String
```

Multidimensional Arrays

I have only discussed one-dimensional arrays, but you can have several dimensions to an array. Think of it as being like a spreadsheet. You have rows and columns that give a reference; you can also have several different sheets so that a cell reference is made up of the sheet name plus the cell column and row:

```
Dim temp(10,4) as String
```

If this was a spreadsheet, it would have 11 columns and five rows, giving you a total of 55 pigeonholes or cells to place your data into and refer to it.

A three-dimensional array would be as follows:

```
Dim temp(10,4,3) as String
```

Imagining this again as a spreadsheet, it would have 11 columns and five rows, but they would span across four worksheets, giving you a total of 220 pigeonholes. If you remember that each one of these elements can take a string up to 65,400 characters, you begin to see how much memory can be used by a simple array and how much data can be stored.

Dimensioning an array immediately allocates memory to it—this is an important consideration when planning your program. Taking up large chunks of memory can cause your program and Windows to run inefficiently. Because Windows itself is a graphical application, it uses large amounts of RAM (random access memory) to hold information. You may find that using a large array slows Windows down, and other applications run more slowly and take longer to process information. This may be all right on your home computer, but a professional application needs to take this into account.

Further dimensions are possible, but these become difficult to keep track of and manipulate. Five dimensions is considered the safe maximum to use. If you go back to thinking of an array as being like a series of spreadsheets, think how complicated a five-dimensional spreadsheet would be!

ReDim can still be used to resize the array, but you cannot use it to change the number of dimensions in the array, nor can you use it to change the type of the array—for example, from string to integer.

Dynamic Arrays

Sometimes you do not know how large an array needs to be. A good example is if you are recursively storing pathnames from a disk device in each array element. You do not know how many subdirectories there are and how long a branch will extend. You could set your array to 1,000 elements, taking up valuable memory in the process, and then find that you only needed 500 elements. Alternatively, there could be 2,000 subdirectory pathnames, so you would run out of room.

You create a *dynamic* array in exactly the same way as a normal array—using the **Dim** statement at the global, module, or local level, or using **Static** at the local level. You give it an empty dimension list:

```
Dim temp()
```

You then use the **ReDim** statement within your procedure to resize the number of elements within the array. The **ReDim** statement can only be used within a procedure, and you cannot change the number of dimensions:

```
ReDim temp(100)
```

You could write code to check the number of values collected and then resize the array if it is getting close to the upper boundary. Two functions are helpful when working with arrays—**LBound** and **UBound**. These functions can be used to return the lower and upper limits of the dimensions of an array by specifying the array number as a subscript:

```
Dim temp(10)

MsgBox LBound(MyTemp)

MsgBox UBound(MyTemp)
```

LBound will return the value of 0; **UBound** will return the value of 10.

ReDim will automatically clear all values in the array unless you use the **Preserve** keyword:

```
ReDim Preserve temp(100)
```

Data already held in **temp** will now be preserved.

User-Defined Types

You can also define your own type of variable by employing existing variable types using the **Type** keyword. This must be entered in the declarations section of a module:

```
Type Employee
     Name as String
     Salary as Currency
```

```
      Years as Integer
End Type
```

This creates a new type called **Employee**, which holds information for Name, Salary, and Years of Service.

You can then use this type in exactly the same way as the built-in variable types. It is even automatically included in the drop-down lists within the VBA editor. You can use these as normal variables, as seen in the following:

```
Dim temp As employee
temp.Name = "Richard Shepherd"
temp.Salary = 10000
temp.Years = 5
MsgBox temp.Name
MsgBox temp.Salary
MsgBox temp.Years
```

Note that the variable name has a list box showing the properties or fields for this data type as you type in the variable name within the code.

You can also create an array of this type and effectively use it as an object in its own right. Notice that after specifying the name of the array and the subscript index that will receive the data, a dot is used so **Name** appears as a property:

```
Dim temp(10) as employee
temp(0).Name = "Richard Shepherd"
```

Constants

Constants are, in effect, variables that do not change. They hold values that are used repeatedly within your code and effectively provide shorthand for that particular constant value.

You use the same rules to create a constant as you do to create variables, but you cannot assign a new value to that constant from within your code as you can with a variable.

```
Const Path_Name = "C:\temp\"
```

The preceding code sets up a constant called **Path_Name**, which here always has the value: **C:\temp**. Thus, you can use this in your program every time you want to use that particular path.

The Access object model also has predefined constants, which you can see by using the Object Browser (covered in Chapter 12). In the Access object model, all constants begin with the letters "xl" to denote that they are part of the Access object model—for example, **xlSaveChanges** or **xlDoNotSaveChanges**. The Object Browser also shows the actual value of the constant at the bottom of the browser window.

Reserved Words

You probably noticed that there are a number of keywords within VBA that make up the language—for example, **For**, **Next**, **Do**, and **Loop**. These cannot be used within your program for the purpose of naming variables, subroutines, or functions because they are *reserved words*. This means they are part of the VBA language itself, and it would cause enormous confusion if you were allowed to go ahead and use these for random purposes within your own code. Fortunately, VBA checks what you are typing in instantly and puts up an error message—usually "Expected Identifier," which means you have used a reserved word and VBA thinks you are entering it as a program statement. Try entering

```
Dim Loop as String
```

Loop is, of course, part of VBA and is used in **Do** loop statements. It is impossible to enter this statement. Instantly an error message appears, and the line of code turns red to warn of a problem. Of course, you can ignore the warning, but as soon as you try to run the code, you will get an error again. Try entering

```
Sub ReDim()
```

You will get an error message, and the code will turn red because **ReDim** is a keyword within VBA.

Strangely enough, you *can* use words from the Access object model. You can call a subroutine Application or Worksheets, and it will work. However, this is not advised. I have seen problems of code not exiting cleanly when the application is closed down because it used words from the object model. It certainly causes confusion within VBA and should be avoided.

Generally, any VBA keyword or function cannot be used as a variable name, subroutine name, or function name.

Modules, Functions, and Subroutines

Modules are containers where you write your code. Functions and subroutines are the two different ways of creating a piece of working code.

Modules

Modules are code sheets that are specific to your application. They are not fired off directly by events in the database, but have to be called directly. They are a means of creating procedures in a general manner, rather than specifically running in an object like a form or a report. You can call them in a number of ways:

▶ Use a custom ribbon command or a custom toolbar command. See Chapter 11 for more on customizing the ribbon.

▶ Insert a VBA control from the Control toolbox into the form or report directly and attach your code to this. For example, you might enter code for a user's actions on a command button or a combo box.

▶ Run the code from a form. In Chapter 9, you will learn how to define your own forms, which the user can employ to make selections and take options. When the user clicks the OK button on the form, your macro runs and picks up the user preferences.

▶   Call your code from another VBA procedure. Code can form subroutines or functions that can then be used within other macros written on the same spreadsheet. For example, say you have to search a string of text for a particular character and you write a subroutine to do this, using a parameter to pass the text string to the subroutine. You can use this subroutine as a building block by calling it from anywhere else within other procedures in exactly the same way you would a normal VBA keyword.

▶   Click directly on your code and press F5. This is for development work only. For example, if you are working on a subroutine in isolation, you may wish to run it only to see how it works.

All these methods are dealt with in further detail later in the book.

A VBA project normally uses at least one module to store the necessary functions and subroutines known as procedures. To insert a new module, simply select Insert | Module from the VBE menu, and the new module will appear. Note that this contains only a general area initially. It has no events, as with the form and report code sheets.

You can enter subroutines or functions here and make them public or private. The distinction between public and private is to decide whether other modules within the same workbook can access the procedure. If the code is private, it can only be used in the current module where it resides. If it is public, it can be used by any other procedure in any other module in the database. Should you have a subroutine you do not want used elsewhere in the code, make the subroutine private. The default is always public.

The Difference Between Subroutines and Functions

Subroutines and functions are two types of code procedures. On casual inspection, they appear to be the same. In truth, however, they are different.

A *subroutine* is a piece of code that performs a set of actions or calculations, or a combination of the two. It can form a "building block" within a program and may sometimes need to be repeated. It can be called by several different routines. The programmer has to write a subroutine only once, and it can be called from anywhere within the program as many times as needed. However, it does not directly return a value; if it performs a calculation, there is no direct way of finding the result. It can alter values of variables if you pass parameters using the ByRef methodology, which is explained later in this chapter. It is called by inserting a **Call** instruction into the code, as shown here:

```
Sub Main()
     Call MySub      'Calls another macro/procedure called MySub
End Sub
```

You do not have to use the word **Call** to utilize the subroutine **MySub**. The following example also works:

```
Sub Main()
     MySub           'Calls another macro/procedure called MySub
End Sub
```

A *function* is exactly like a subroutine except that it returns a value. Functions start with **Function** (instead of **Sub**) and end with **End Function** (instead of **End Sub**). This means that, generally speaking, functions should be called using a variable, as discussed in Chapter 2, to accept the return value:

```
x=Now()
```

The variable **x** will contain the value of today's date. This is a very simple example of calling a built-in function.

Both subroutines and functions can have parameters or values passed to them. These are passed inside parentheses (more on this in the next section).

Writing a Simple Subroutine

A subroutine is different from a function in that it does not return anything directly and so cannot be used directly in the code the way a function can. A subroutine is usually a building block that forms a piece of code that will be called many times, possibly from different points within your program. This is one of the great flexibilities of a subroutine. When it is called, the return address (from where the subroutine was called) is stored. When the subroutine finishes running, control is passed back to the return address. You can still pass parameters to it, but these are used internally within the code itself.

Click back to Module1 and add the following code:

```
Sub Display(Target)
    MsgBox Target
End Sub
```

Note that this subroutine has an argument parameter for a variable called **target**. This is because you are going to call the subroutine from another procedure and pass a variable across.

A line is drawn to differentiate the new subroutine, and the subroutine you have written is automatically added to the drop-down in the top-left corner. Now return to the initial Hello World example from Chapter 1 and add the following code:

```
Sub MyCode()
'MsgBox "Hello World"
x = 3 * 5
MsgBox x
Call Display("my subroutine")
End Sub
```

Make sure you have already defined the function called "Display," otherwise you will get an error when you try to run MyCode.

Click the mouse cursor anywhere on the MyCode procedure and then click the Run icon on the VBE toolbar or press F5. You will see the message box showing 15, followed by a message box showing "my subroutine."

The **Call** command calls your subroutine and passes any required parameters to it. It then executes the code in the subroutine and returns to the next instruction following the **Call** statement. In this particular case, it passes the string "my subroutine" into the variable called **target**.

If the subroutine you have written does not use parameters (arguments), you can run it from the code page by selecting Run | Run Sub/UserForm from the VBE (Visual Basic Editor) menu, pressing F5, or clicking the Run symbol on the toolbar. The cursor must click on the subroutine you intend to run. This is a useful way of testing the code you have written and seeing if it has any bugs.

Subroutines are a useful way of breaking large projects down into manageable pieces so you do not end up with enormous and cumbersome routines. It is far easier to break a problem into constituent parts and work separately on each section, making sure you get that section working properly before moving onto others. The alternative is to write a large chunk of code, which inevitably leads to unnecessary duplication.

Writing a Simple Function

The object of this exercise is to create a function to accept two numbers, which then multiplies them together and returns the result. The function will have the name **Multiply**. The following table cites the four main mathematical operators you will use when writing functions and subroutines in VBA.

Add	+
Subtract	−
Multiply	*
Divide	/

The code for this function is as follows:

```
Function Multiply(a, b)

        Multiply = a * b

End Function
```

It should look like Figure 3-1. As with the subroutine, you must have at a bare minimum the function line and the end function line (header and footer). Note that it must be entered in a module you have inserted, not a module belonging to a form or report.

The header introduces two parameters, **a** and **b**, by showing them in parentheses after the title of the function. A comma separates the two arguments. These arguments represent the two numbers to be multiplied—they could be called anything, as long as the variable name is consistent throughout the function.

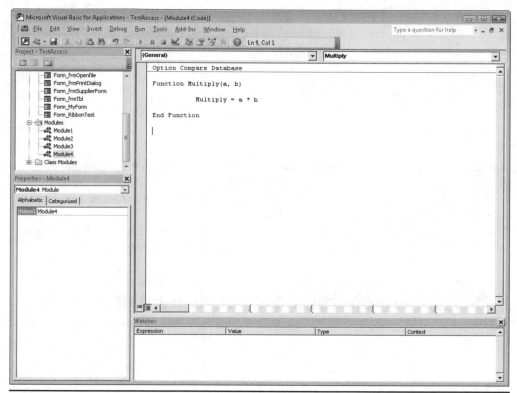

Figure 3-1   *Creating a simple multiply function*

The name of the function is **Multiply**, and this is used as a variable to return the answer. This is the only way to return the answer to the routine that called the function. Note that the name of the function now appears in the drop-down at the top right of the code window. This is because it is now an official function within both your VBA code and Access.

You can now use this function in two ways: by calling it directly from within a SQL query as a function, or by using it within your VBA code. To call it directly from within a SQL query, use "select Multiply(3.4) from MyTable;". Having your own custom functions opens up interesting possibilities as to what you can now build into your queries.

However, a word of warning when running custom function queries over large amounts of data. Close down the VBE window before you run the query, otherwise this window will keep being updated as the query is run, meaning the query will take considerably longer to run than normal.

Now, for the second way to use the function: calling it from within your VBA code. For the sake of simplicity, you will next call your new function using the same event from which you called the Hello World example.

Return to the initial Hello World example in Chapter 1. Turn the "Hello World" statement into a comment by putting a single quote (') character before it and enter the following code so it looks like this:

```
Sub MyCode()
      'MsgBox "Hello World"
      x = Multiply(3, 5)
      MsgBox x
End Sub
```

Note that when you type the word **Multiply** and open the brackets, VBA automatically displays the parameters it is expecting by name. By inserting the function into the code, you are forcing a call to that function using the parameters **3** and **5** to replace **a** and **b** in your function. The result is returned in the variable **x**.

Click the cursor anywhere on the MyCode procedure and run the code by clicking the Run icon in the VBE toolbar or pressing F5. You will see a message box displaying 15.

Public and Private Functions and Subroutines

VBA allows you to define your functions or subroutines as public or private using the keyword **Public** or **Private**. For example:

```
Private Sub PrivateSub()
End Sub
```

Any subroutines or functions you create are public by default. This means they can be used throughout the modules within your application, and database users will find the subroutines available to use in any VBA code that may write in the database. They will also be able to access public functions in your code and either use them in their own code or their own SQL queries.

The one exception to this is forms/reports. As will be discussed in Chapter 9, forms represent dialog forms and have their own modules. Reports also have modules. A public subroutine or function on a form can be called from other modules within your code by referencing the form object—for example, **Form_Form1.MysubRoutine**. If you do not reference the subroutine to the form name as shown earlier, or the subroutine is made private, you will get a compile error when this is run.

Using private declarations, you can have procedures that have the same names but are in different modules. That procedure is private to that module and cannot be seen by other modules. More importantly, it cannot be seen and run by the Access user in SQL queries. This can cause confusion both for the programmer and for VBA. Which one does VBA choose to invoke if you call that procedure? Fortunately, VBA has a set of rules it uses for this. It first looks in the current module where the code is executing. If it cannot find a procedure of that name there, it scans all modules for the procedure. Calls within the module where the private procedure is defined will go to that procedure. Calls outside that module will go to the public procedure.

Argument Data Types

When you specify arguments for a procedure, they always default to Variant, which is the default variable type in VBA. You can also declare your parameters as other data types, choosing from the data types you saw in the last chapter.

The advantage of declaring with data types is that they introduce a discipline to your code in terms of what information the procedure is looking for. If you do not specify a type but use the default Variant, your procedure will accept anything, be it a number or a string. This can have unfortunate consequences within that procedure if you are expecting a string and a number gets passed across, or vice versa. If you specify the parameter as a string, an error will occur if you do not pass a string:

```
Function Myfunction(Target as String)
```

This can also be useful if you are writing a custom function for use in a SQL query. When users enter your function into their query, they must give the parameters according to the data type specified. If a string is specified, they must put the value in quotes or they can request the user input a value by using [Input Value] as a parameter in the function.

Optional Arguments

You can make specific arguments optional by using the **Optional** keyword:

```
Function Myfunction (Target as String, Optional Flag as Integer)
```

In this example, the user must specify the parameter **Target** as a string, but the parameter **Flag** will appear with square brackets around it and need not be specified. All optional parameters must come after the required ones.

Passing Arguments by Value

You can also use the **ByVal** or **ByRef** keyword to define how parameters are passed to your procedure. The important distinction is that ByVal takes a copy of the variable that is being passed and does not alter the original value of the variable within the subroutine or function. ByRef uses the original variable itself and any changes to the value that are made within the subroutine or function are reflected through the entire scope of the variable. The ByRef methodology can often lead to bugs that are hard to track down. Your function may alter the value of your variable, but this may not be apparent when you are looking at the chain of your code.

It is generally accepted by programmers that ByRef is not a good idea unless you know exactly what you are doing.

```
Function MyFunction (ByVal Target as String)
```

The **ByVal** keyword ensures that parameters are passed by value rather than by a reference to a value from a variable. Passing a value by reference can easily allow bugs to creep into your code. To demonstrate this, if you pass by reference using a variable name, the value of that variable can be changed by the procedure that the variable is passed to—for example,

```
x = 100
z = Adjust(x)
Function Adjust(ByRef Target as Integer)
```

The variable **x** will be modified by what is going on within the function **Adjust**. However, if you pass by value, as shown here, only a copy of the variable is passed to the procedure:

```
x = 100
z = Adjust(x)
Function Adjust(ByVal Target as Integer)
```

If the procedure changes this value, the change affects only the copy, not the variable itself. The variable **x** will always keep its value of 100.

Normally, you would not expect a function to modify an argument, but it can happen and can lead to hard-to-find bugs within the code. Sometimes you do require the function to modify the value of a variable, which is when it would be appropriate to use ByRef, but generally ByValue is used the most.

Programming Basics: Decisions and Looping

hen writing programs, it's important to understand how programs make decisions and perform looping. Looping is the process of carrying out the same set of instructions until certain conditions are met.

I'm sure you're familiar with decisions. After all, you have to make them every day. For example when you wake up, which shirt do you decide to put on? You make this decision based on various facts such as what the weather is like outside and what you are doing today. Your life would be very dull if you never had to make any decisions—think what it would be like if it was already decided what shirt you wore each day!

Programs also have to make decisions based on the parameters to which they have access. The computer program would also be very dull if it never made a decision. For example, if a program tries to load a text file and the file is not found, a decision needs to be made as to what to do next. Should the program simply display an error message and crash, or should it show some intelligence and alert the user that the file is missing and offer an alternative action?

Artificial intelligence is something that is frequently discussed in computing circles. By having your programs make decisions, you are introducing some primitive intelligence into your program. Admittedly, it is your intelligence that goes into the code, but it tells the program what to do in the event of different circumstances happening. You are effectively writing a set of rules to deal with various situations.

Looping is also something everyone does daily without thinking about it. When you eat a meal, you perform the same routine of taking food from a plate and putting it into your mouth. Computer programs frequently loop around the same piece of code a number of times until a certain condition is met.

Decisions

Programs, unless they are extremely simple, usually have to make *decisions* according to data retrieved or input from the user. Decision making is one of the most important areas of programming, because it specifies what will happen when different events occur.

A good example of a common programming decision is IF something is true, THEN do *action1*, or ELSE do *action2*. In everyday life, this might be the statement "IF it is raining, THEN carry an umbrella, or ELSE (if the condition is not met and it is not raining) carry sunglasses."

The following is some sample code to show how the conditional If..Then..Else statement works and how it produces different results. Enter this in the module you created in Chapter 2 (this must be in a module that you have inserted yourself). See Figure 4-1 for an example of what your code window should look like.

```
Sub Test_If()
If CurrentDb.Name= "C:\Temp\MyDB.accdb" Then

      MsgBox "Database path and name are correct"
Else

      MsgBox "Database has been re-named/moved"
End If
End Sub
```

This example refers to the current database name in the line **CurrentDb.Name**. In Access, this will give the full path and name of the Access file. Run this code, replacing "C:\Temp\MyDB .accdb" with the path and name of your own file. You will get the message that the database path and name are correct.

Save the code and then go into Windows Explorer and make a copy of the database file. Load the file in and re-run the code again in the new file and you will get the message box saying that the database has been renamed/moved.

You can see that a simple piece of code like this checks where the database was loaded from and checks that it has not been renamed. This might seem straightforward, but there are times when the integrity of the database relies on this information being correct.

Notice in Figure 4-1 that I have indented the code to separate the main parts of the conditional statement—this makes it easier to read and easier to debug because you can instantly see the groups of statements and where they start and finish. It is possible for If statements to be nested inside each other, so you can have an If statement within an If statement; this frequently happens in more complicated programs. (See the section "Looping," later in this chapter, for more on how this works.) It is convenient to be able to see at a glance where one If statement starts and ends. If others are in between your start and stop point, you can frequently get lost when debugging code.

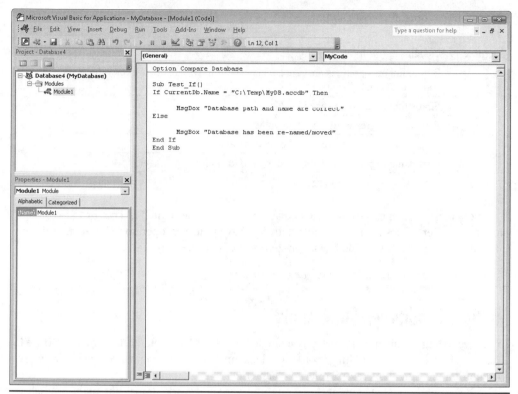

Figure 4-1   *Code for a conditional If statement*

The End..If statement shows where the conditional statements finish, or you can put the entire If statement onto one line, which then would not require an End..If, as shown here:

```
If CurrentDb.Name= "C:\Temp\MyDB.accdb" Then MsgBox  _

"Database path and name are correct"
```

However, note that a continuation character (space and underscore) has been used to get all the code in, and you cannot use the continuation character between quotes (as part of a string).

If you have multiple instructions to be executed, you can place the statements on a single line as long as you separate each statement with a colon. However, this can become very difficult to read and debug, and often several instructions must be carried out that preclude putting everything on one line.

Conditional operators that can be used are as follows:

Operator	Meaning
=	Both numbers or values are equal. This condition will also work for values, such as "dog" and "cat."
<	First value is less than second value.
>	First value is greater than second value.
<=	First value is less than or equal to second value.
>=	First value is greater than or equal to second value.
<>	First value is unequal to second value.

An expression such as **x=1** is evaluated as a Boolean value, which is True or False or Non-zero or Zero. This means you do not always have to use an operator. If you are only interested in whether a variable has a non-zero value in it, then you can use

```
If MyVar Then MsgBox "MyVar has a value"
```

Multiple Conditional Statements

In the preceding statements, I used only a single conditional statement in the form of **If x=1 Then...**. You can also use multiple conditional statements using a logical operator. For more information on logical operators, refer to Chapter 6.

Multiple conditional statements are straightforward and work almost like plain English. They use the operators **And** and **Or** and, for the purposes of this example, mean exactly what they mean in English.

If you have two conditions that you want to test, you write the If statement in the following form:

```
If x = 1 And y > 5 Then
      MsgBox "x=1 and y>5"
End If
```

The message box will be displayed only if both conditions ($x = 1$ and $y > 5$) are met. If, for instance, $x > 1$, but y has a value of 4, the message box will not be displayed. Similarly, you could use the following statement:

```
If x = 1 Or y > 5 Then
      MsgBox "x=1 or y>5"
End If
```

In the case of the preceding **Or**, the message box will be displayed if either one of the conditions is met. For example, if $x = 1$ or $y > 5$, the message box will be displayed. Therefore, x could be 0 and y could be 6, or x could be 1 and y could be 4, and the message box would still be displayed in either case.

You can put in several **And**s or **Or**s within the condition, although it gets complicated with more than three. It all depends on what you are trying to achieve in your decision statement and what the procedure is trying to do. You may be writing something very simple such as **If x=1 Then**, or you may be working on a more complicated conditional statement.

Select Case Statements

Another statement available in VBA for conditional processing is the **Select Case** statement. If you have a variable and you want different actions to occur depending on the value of that variable, you can use a series of If statements as follows:

```
If x=1 then MsgBox "x=1"
If x=2 then MsgBox "x=2"
If x=3 then MsgBox "x=3"
```

However, this is a good example of where a **Select Case** statement makes the code much cleaner:

```
x = 23
Select Case (x)

    Case (1)
       MsgBox "x=1"
    Case (23)
       MsgBox "x=23"


End Select
```

The **Select Case** statement provides a simple means to interrogate a specified variable and take action accordingly. The statement **Select Case (x)** defines the variable to be interrogated as **x** and is the start of the block of code for this procedure. **Case (1)** gives the action for if the value is 1—show a message box showing "x=1." **Case (23)** gives the action for if the value is 23—show a message box showing "x=23." Because **x** has been set to **23** at the start of the code, the message box will show "x=23."

You can also include the statements **To** and **Is** in the **Case** statement:

```
Sub Test_Case (Grade)
    Select Case Grade
        Case 1
             Msgbox "Grade 1"
        Case 2, 3
             Msgbox "Grade 2 or 3"
        Case 4 To 6
             Msgbox "Grade 4, 5 or 6"
```

```
        Case Is > 8
                MsgBox "Grade is above 8"
        Case Else
                Msgbox "Grade not in conditional statements"
    End Select
End Sub
```

Looping

Without looping facilities, programs would be extremely tedious and difficult to maintain. *Looping* allows a block of code to be repeated until a condition or a specified value is met. Suppose, for example, you wanted to display the numbers from 1 to 5. You could write the program as follows:

```
MsgBox "1"
MsgBox "2"
Msgbox "3"
Msgbox "4"
MsgBox "5"
```

This would work, but it is very inefficient and does not make use of the functionality of VBA. If you wanted to display more numbers, you would have to write more code. If you wanted to display all the numbers up to 1,000, it would require you to add an additional 995 lines of code! This would not be very efficient.

For..Next Loops

This code can be reduced and made easier to maintain by using the For..Next looping statement as follows:

```
For n = 1 to 5
    MsgBox n
Next n
```

The message box will appear five times showing the values of **n** from 1 to 5.

The variable used can be anything. Although I used **n** here, it could be a word such as **num**, but it must be consistent throughout the looping process. You could not use **For n = 1 to 5** and then try to use an index called **m**. If you changed the line "Next n" with "Next m," you would get an error because it does not match your original loop. Also, you must not use a reserved word for the variable name. You can put as many instructions as necessary between For and Next and even call subroutines or functions. The start and end values in the For..Next loop can also be different—they do not have to start at 1 or end at 5.

Step gives extra functionality. You may have noticed that the variable **n** is incremented by 1 each time in the loop—this is the default. You can change this behavior by using the

Step option. **Step** allows you to specify the size of the increment and also the direction by using the following code:

```
For n = 3 to 12 Step 3

    MsgBox n
Next n
```

You will get the results 3, 6, 9, and 12, because it works in increments of 3.

To see how **Step** works backward, try this example:

```
For n= 10 to 1 Step -1
    MsgBox n
Next n
```

You will get the results 10, 9, 8, 7, 6, 5, 4, 3, 2, and 1.

For..Next loops can also be nested inside each other. For example, if you want to look at each value in a spreadsheet, you can use one For..Next to go across a multidimensional array and a second For..Next to go down the multidimensional array.

Following is an example that loops through values for **n** and **m**. Notice the indentation of the code; it makes the nesting of the For..Next clear. The **m** loop has been nested inside of the **n** loop so it will perform the first **n** value, then all values of **m**, then the next **n** value, then all values of **m** again. Indenting helps prevent you from getting lost in your code when you look at it in a month's time.

```
Sub test_loop()
  For n = 1 To 4

    For m = 1 To 5

      MsgBox "n= " & n
      MsgBox "m= " & m
    Next m
  Next n
End Sub
```

For Each Loops

The For Each loop is very similar to a For..Next loop, but it is specifically for use on collections or arrays. For Each allows you to step through each item within the collection or array. You do not use an index (such as **n** in the previous example) because it automatically moves through each item within the collection. This is very useful if you need to search through a collection for a certain object and then delete it because the position in the collection after deletion is maintained in your loop. If you use a For..Next loop with an index and delete the object, the index will be moved up one and your routine will go through one loop too many, causing an error message.

The following example iterates through all the query names in the current database using a For Each loop:

```
Sub ShowName()
      Dim oQry As QueryDef
      For Each oQry In CurrentDb.QueryDefs
            MsgBox oQry.Name
      Next oQry
End Sub
```

Do Until Loops

The **Do Until** loop keeps looping until a specified condition is met. Often this means waiting for a variable to contain a particular value. When the condition is met, the loop stops, and the program continues executing on the next instruction after the loop. You can also use a While statement so that while a certain condition is met, the code will carry on looping. Here is a simple example:

```
Sub test_do()
x = 0
Do Until x = 100
    x = x + 1
Loop
MsgBox x
End Sub
```

First a variable **x** is set to the value 0. The condition of x = 100 is then supplied as the criterion for when the **Do** loop should stop. The variable (**x**) is then incremented by 1 each time through the loop, so it loops 100 times until x = 100. At this point, it displays a message box giving the value of **x** that is 100.

While..Wend Loops

Finally, there is the While..Wend loop. This continues to loop while a specified condition is true. It stops as soon as the condition is false. The following is a simple example that is very similar to the previous Do Until loop:

```
Sub test_do()
x = 0
While x < 50
    x = x + 1

Wend
MsgBox x
End Sub
```

Again, a variable, **x**, is set to 0. The condition that **x** must be less than 50 is supplied, and **x** is incremented by 1 each time the loop is run. When x=50, it is no longer less than 50, so a message box is displayed showing the value of **x** at 50.

Early Exit of Loops

Under some circumstances, you may want your procedure to exit a loop early before it has worked all the way through and satisfied its criteria. An example might be where you are searching for a particular string of characters within an array. You may have 25 instances of that string to look through, but once the procedure has found what it is looking for, there is no point in further looping until the final condition is met. You could have an array of several thousand records you are searching through, and much time could be wasted carrying on to the bitter end when the instance has already been found. In the case of a For..Next loop, the value of the index is also preserved, which means you can use it to locate where your condition was correct. Here is an example:

```
Sub test_exit()

    For x = 1 To 100
        If x = 50 Then
            Exit For
        End If
    Next x
    MsgBox x
End Sub
```

You exit a loop by using an **Exit For** statement in a For..Next loop or a For Each loop. Use an **Exit Do** within a **Do Until** loop. In the case of a For..Next loop, the value of the index is preserved. If the loops are nested, your code will only exit from the loop it is actually in. It will not exit from the outer loop unless you put another **Exit** statement in. The statement **Exit Do** and **Exit For** will stop execution of the loop and go on to the next instruction after the end of that loop.

Strings, Functions, and Message Boxes

T his chapter covers how to handle strings of text, how to use the built-in functions of
VBA, and how to design professional message boxes.

Strings

If you already use Access frequently, you will know that a string is not something that you
cut off from a ball of string and use around the house. It is instead a stream of consecutive
characters. They are not limited to the alphabet but can be any character within the character
set (0 to 255). This covers all alphanumeric and control characters. These can be different
according to what language code page you are using, but there are still only 256 characters.
A string is useful for displaying a message to the user or providing a caption. A string could
be "Richard", or it could be "1234".

VBA provides a number of functions for concatenating (joining) strings together, removing
sections, searching, and changing case (to upper- or lowercase). For example, if you have a
string "Your answer" and another " is wrong", you can join these together into one string:
"Your answer is wrong". You can also use a function to change the entire string to uppercase
characters so it reads "YOUR ANSWER IS WRONG", or you can search for a particular
word or set of characters within the string.

Concatenation

Concatenation is how you join strings together, generally using the & sign. It is extremely useful when you want to display messages. Suppose you are writing a program to display the number of tables in a database. Your program counts up the tables and stores the number in a variable. You could easily display the variable to the user, but what would it mean to that user?

When writing software, you want a clear message displayed to the user, such as, "There are *n* tables within the database." You do this by concatenating the string "There are", the variable **n** (which contains the number of databases), and the string "tables within the database". You can also introduce code that changes the first string to read "There is" when **n** has a value of 1, so that it is always grammatically correct.

```
MsgBox "There are " & n & " tables within the database "
```

Consider the simple example of a For..Next loop from the section titled "Looping" in Chapter 4. The code is as follows:

```
For n = 1 to 5
    MsgBox n
Next n
```

The message box gives the value of **n** as it increments, but it is just a message box with a number and does not give the number any meaning. By adding a string, you can make a more user-friendly message:

```
For n = 1 to 5
    MsgBox "The value of n is " & n
Next n
```

The message box will now show the text "The value of *n* is 1." This will be displayed five times in all with the value of **n** incrementing each time. Don't forget to leave a space after the word "is," or your message will look peculiar and may be difficult to read.

There is no limit to how many strings and values you can concatenate in this way. Note that, although **n** is numeric, VBA automatically turns it into a character string for concatenation.

Splitting Strings

You may need only a part of a string in your code. For example, say you have a two-figure reference number at the beginning of the string that you need to use elsewhere in your program, but you wish to show only the name:

```
"12Richard"
```

To pull out the name only, you can use the **Mid** function:

```
x=Mid("12Richard",3)
```

This code will start at the third character and continue to the end of the string and place the result in the variable **x**, which will then contain the string "Richard". The **Mid** function has an optional length parameter so that you can specify the length of your substring. If you leave this out, you will get everything from your start point to the end of the string.

Note that in all these situations you can also use a variable that contains a string:

```
temp="12Richard"

x=Mid(temp,3)
```

You can also use this function to extract the number portion of the string at the front:

```
x=Mid("12Richard",1,2)
```

This code will start at the first character and take the next two characters from the string and place them in the variable **x**, which will contain a string with the value of 12, although this is not actually a number but a string. VBA is quite forgiving—if you want to do further calculations with this, you do not need to change it back to a number.

However, if you are putting it back into a field in a table, you may need to change it to a number from a formatting point of view. You do this by using the **Val** function:

```
Dim iValue as Integer
iValue = Val("12")
```

The variable **iValue** will then be an actual number rather than a string.

VBA also includes **Right** and **Left** string functions. The **Left** function can also be used to separate the number 12:

```
x=Left("12Richard",2)
```

The variable **x** will have the value 12.

If the **Right** function is used, **x** will have the value rd:

```
x=Right("12Richard",2)
```

The **Left** and **Right** functions grab from the side of the string, as indicated by the function name.

VBA also contains functions to change the case of a string, as discussed next.

Changing the Appearance of Strings

UCase changes everything in the string to uppercase:

```
x=UCase("Richard")
```

The variable **x** will have the value RICHARD.

LCase changes everything to lowercase:

```
x=LCase("Richard")
```

The variable **x** will have the value richard.

In both of these examples, any nonletter characters such as numbers will be left as they are.

Searching Strings

Another function can search a string for a specified substring. This function is called **Instr**, which stands for "in string." The syntax for this is fairly complicated because two of the arguments are optional:

```
InStr([start, ]string1, string2[, compare])
```

Start is an optional parameter and shows where in the string the search should start from. If it is omitted, the search starts from position 1. **Start** must not contain a null value, and if **start** is used, then the **Compare** parameter must be used.

String1 is the string being searched (for example, "Richard Shepherd"). **String2** is the string being sought (for example, "shepherd").

Compare is the technique used to compare the strings. The possible values are **vbBinaryCompare** and **vbTextCompare**. In simple terms, this determines whether the search is case sensitive or not. Binary compare uses the actual binary value, so *A* equals *A*, but *A* does not equal *a*. Text compare ignores case, so *A* will equal *a*. A null value here will produce an error. The default for **Compare** is binary, which means it is case-sensitive.

Table 5-1 lists the values the **Instr** function produces. Here is a simple example:

```
x=Instr("Richard Shepherd","Shepherd")
```

This will give an answer of 9.

Note that the default compare flag is binary/case sensitive:

```
x = Instr("Richard Shepherd","shepherd")
```

Value Returned by Instr	Meaning
0	**String1** is zero length.
Null	**String1** is null.
Start Value	**String2** is zero length.
Null	**String2** is null.
0	**String2 not found**.
Position	Position of **String2** within **String1**.
0	Start is greater than length of **String1**.

Table 5-1   *Values of the Instr Function*

This will give the answer 0 because the string "shepherd" is not found due to the difference in case. The following will give the answer 9:

```
MsgBox InStr(1, "Richard Shepherd", "shepherd", vbTextCompare)
```

The next example uses the two optional parameters. Notice the use of the start position:

```
MsgBox InStr(10, "Richard Shepherd", "shepherd", vbTextCompare)
```

This will give the result 0 (string not found) because the start search position is after where the search string is found.

The **InstrRev** function can be used to do a reverse search through a string. This means that it begins the search from the end of the string instead of the beginning.

Functions

This section is intended to give an overview of the most commonly used functions in VBA. Many others are available, but you will find that these are the major ones used.

Len

Len returns the number of characters in a string. The following will return the value of 3:

```
MsgBox Len("abc")
```

This example will return the value 8:

```
Msgbox Len("shepherd")
```

This function is useful in conjunction with the other string-handling functions. For example, if you want the last four characters of a string that is variable in length, you would need to know the string's length.

Abs

Abs stands for *absolute value* and returns a value of the unsigned magnitude. The following examples both will give the value of 1:

```
MsgBox Abs(1)
MsgBox Abs(-1)
```

Int

Int is short for *integer* and truncates a number to an integer. It does not round to the nearest whole number. This will give the value of 1:

```
MsgBox Int(1.2)
```

The following will also give the value of 1 despite being so close to 2:

```
MsgBox Int(1.99)
```

Sqr

Sqr returns the square root of a number. This example will result in the value 2:

```
MsgBox Sqr(4)
```

The following will result in the value 1.732:

```
MsgBox Sqr(3)
```

The following will give the value 10:

```
MsgBox Sqr(100)
```

Asc

Asc gives the ASCII (American Standard Code for Information Interchange) code for a given character. Values are from 0 to 255. The following will give the value of 65:

```
MsgBox Asc("A")
```

The following will give the value of 105:

```
MsgBox Asc("i")
```

Note that this only works on the first character of the string:

```
Asc("richard")
```

This will give 114, as this is the ASCII code for "r".

Chr

Chr is the reverse of **Asc**; it takes an ASCII code number and converts it to a character. This example will give the string "A":

```
MsgBox Chr(65)
```

The following will give the string "i":

```
MsgBox Chr(105)
```

Because this deals with the entire character set, it also includes nonprintable characters. For example, ASCII code 13 is a carriage return, which can be useful if you want to force a carriage return on something like a message box:

```
MsgBox "This is " & Chr(13) & "a carriage return"
```

Conversion Functions

Conversion functions are used to convert a value from one format to another. An example would be converting a numeric value into a string or converting the string back into a numeric value. These functions are extremely useful for switching values between various formats. For example, you may have a four-figure number where you want the second digit on its own. One of the easiest ways to do this is to convert the number into a string and then use the **Mid** function to separate out that digit. You can then convert it back to a numeric for the purposes of performing further calculations.

CStr

Cstr converts a value to a string. The following example will produce the string "1234":

```
Cstr(1234)
```

CInt

CInt converts a value or a string to an integer (two bytes). No decimal places are shown. Both of the following examples will give the value 123:

```
CInt (123.45)
CInt("123.45")
```

CInt does not work like the **Int** function but instead rounds to the nearest whole number in lieu of truncating. If the expression has any nonnumerical characters, you will get a Type Mismatch error.

CLng

CLng converts a value or a string to a long integer (four bytes). No decimal places are shown. Both of the following examples will return the value 123456789:

```
CLng(123456789.45)
CLng("123456789.45")
```

Note that **CLng** does not work like the **Int** function but rounds to the nearest whole number instead of truncating. If the expression has any nonnumerical characters, you will get a Type Mismatch error.

CDbl

CDbl converts a value or a string to a double-precision floating point number (eight bytes) where decimal places are allowed:

```
CDbl("123.56789")
```

This will return the value 123.56789.

If the expression has any nonnumeric characters, you will get a Type Mismatch error.

Val

Val converts a string to a value. It is more forgiving than **CInt** or **CLng** because it will accept nonnumeric characters:

```
Val("123")
```

This will give the value 123. The following will give the value 123.45:

```
Val("123.45")
```

The next example will give the value 12:

```
Val("12richard")
```

The following will give the value 0, meaning there are no numeric characters to evaluate:

```
Val("richard")
```

Format Function

The **Format** function is one of the most useful and complex functions within VBA. It allows you to format numbers to a chosen output format, similar to the way Access formats a cell, where you can select from a number of options designating how a number will appear in a cell.

The **Format** function does exactly the same thing as formatting a number or a date within a cell in a spreadsheet, except it does so from within the code itself. If you wish to display a number in a message box or on a user form, this function is very useful for making it readable, particularly if it is a large number:

```
MsgBox Format(1234567.89, "#,###.#")
```

This will give the displayed result 1,234,567.9.

In the format string, each # represents a digit placeholder. The comma indicates that commas are used every three numeric placeholders. Only one numeric placeholder is shown after the decimal point, which means that the number is shown rounded to one decimal place.

Format Name	Description
General Number	Display the number as is.
Currency	Display the number with currency symbol. Use thousand separator. Enclose in brackets if negative. Display to two decimal places.
Fixed	Display at least one digit to the left and two digits to the right of the decimal point.
Standard	Display number with thousand separator. Display to two decimal places.
Percent	Display number multiplied by 100 with a percent sign (%) appended after. Display to two decimal places.
Scientific	Use standard scientific notation.
Yes/No	Display No if number is 0; otherwise, display Yes.
True/False	Display False if number is 0; otherwise, display True.
On/Off	Display Off if number is 0; otherwise, display On.

Table 5-2   *Predefined Formats*

You can also use the predefined format names as the format string, as shown in Table 5-2. This example uses the format "Currency":

```
MsgBox Format(1234567.89, "Currency")
```

This will give the displayed result of $1,234,567.89, depending on the currency symbol in the Windows settings. Other settings could be a pound sign for England or a euro sign for Europe.

A number of characters can be used to define a user-defined format, as shown in Table 5-3.

The format string can have up to four sections separated by semicolons (;). This is so different formats can be applied to different values, such as to positive and negative numbers. For example, you may wish to show brackets/parentheses around a negative value:

```
MsgBox Format(-12345.67,"$#,##0;($#,##0)")
```

The following table provides section details depending on the number of sections included.

Section	Details
One section only	Applies to all values
Two sections	First section for positive values, second section for negative values
Three sections	First section for positive values, second section for negative values, third section for zeros
Four sections	First section for positive values, second section for negative values, third section for zeros, fourth section for null values

Predefined date and time formats can also be used, as shown in Table 5-4. These are controlled by the time and date settings in the Windows Control Panel.

Character	Description
Null String	No formatting.
0	Digit placeholder. Displays a digit or a zero. If there is a digit for that position, then it displays the digit; otherwise, it displays 0. If there are fewer digits than zeros, you will get leading or trailing zeros. If there are more digits after the decimal point than there are zeros, then the number is rounded to the number of decimal places shown by the zeros. If there are more digits before the decimal point than zeros, these will be displayed normally.
#	Digit placeholder. This displays a digit or nothing. It works the same as the preceding zero placeholder, except that leading and trailing zeros are not displayed. For example, 0.75 would be displayed using zero placeholders, but this would be .75 using # placeholders.
.Decimal point.	Only one permitted per format string. This character depends on the settings in the Windows Control Panel.
%	Percentage placeholder. Multiplies number by 100 and places % character where it appears in the format string.
,	Thousand separator. This is used if 0 or # placeholders are used and the format string contains a comma. One comma to the left of the decimal point means to round to the nearest thousand (e.g., ##0,). Two adjacent commas to the left of the thousand separator indicate rounding to the nearest million (e.g., ##0,,).
E- E+	Scientific format. This displays the number exponentially.
:	Time separator—used when formatting a time to split hours, minutes, and seconds.
/	Date separator—this is used when specifying a format for a date.
- + £ $ ( )	Displays a literal character. To display a character other than listed here, precede it with a backslash (\).

Table 5-3   *User-Defined Formats*

Format Name	Description
General Date	Display a date and/or time. For real numbers, display date and time. Integer numbers display time only. If there is no integer part, then display only time.
Long Date	Displays a long date as defined in the international settings of the Windows Control Panel.
Medium Date	Displays a date as defined in the short date settings of the Windows Control Panel, except it spells out the month abbreviation.
Short Date	Displays a short date as defined in the International settings of the Windows Control Panel.
Long Time	Displays a long time as defined in the International settings of the Windows Control Panel.
Medium Time	Displays time in a 12-hour format using hours, minutes, and seconds and the AM/PM format.
Short Time	Displays a time using 24-hour format (e.g., 18:10).

Table 5-4   *Predefined Date and Time Formats*

You can use a number of characters to create user-defined date and time formats, as listed in Table 5-5.

The following is an example of formatting the current time to hours, minutes, and seconds:

```
MsgBox Format(Now(), "hh:mm:ss AM/PM")
```

Character	Meaning
c	Displays the date as ddddd and the time as ttttt.
d	Displays the day as a number without a leading zero.
dd	Displays the day as a number with a leading zero.
ddd	Displays the day as an abbreviation (Sun–Sat).
dddd	Displays the full name of the day (Sunday–Saturday).
ddddd	Displays a date serial number as a complete date according to Short Date in the International settings of the windows Control Panel.
dddddd	Displays a date serial number as a complete date according to Long Date in the International settings of the Windows Control Panel.
w	Displays the day of the week as a number (1 = Sunday).
ww	Displays the week of the year as a number (1–52).
m	Displays the month as a number without a leading zero.
mm	Displays the month as a number with leading zeros.
mmm	Displays month as an abbreviation (Jan–Dec).
mmmm	Displays the full name of the month (January–December).
q	Displays the quarter of the year as a number (1–4).
y	Displays the day of the year as a number (1–366).
yy	Displays the year as a two-digit number.
yyyy	Displays the year as a four-digit number.
h	Displays the hour as a number without a leading zero.
hh	Displays the hour as a number with a leading zero.
n	Displays the minute as a number without a leading zero.
nn	Displays the minute as a number with a leading zero.
s	Displays the second as a number without a leading zero.
ss	Displays the second as a number with a leading zero.
ttttt	Displays a time serial number as a complete time.
AM/PM	Uses a 12-hour clock and displays AM or PM to indicate before or after noon.
am/pm	Uses a 12-hour clock and uses am or pm to indicate before or after noon.
A/P	Uses a 12-hour clock and uses A or P to indicate before or after noon.
a/p	Uses a 12-hour clock and uses a or p to indicate before or after noon.

Table 5-5   *Date/Time Formats*

Character	Definition
@	Character placeholder. Displays a character or a space. If there is a character, it is displayed; otherwise, a space is displayed.
&	Character placeholder. Display a character or nothing. If there is a character, display it; otherwise, display nothing.
<	Force lowercase.
>	Force uppercase.
!	Force placeholders to fill from left to right.

Table 5-6   *Additional Format Characters*

A number of characters can be used to create a user-defined format

Date formats, like number formats, can use sections. One section only applies to all data; two sections means that the first section applies to all data and the second to zero-length strings and null. For examples, look at the following table:

Format String	Definition
mm/dd/yy	01/03/03
dd-mmm-yyyy	01-Mar-2003
hh:mm	a.m./p.m.

You can also use certain characters within your format string to create formatting, as shown in Table 5-6.

Some examples of using the **Format** function on numbers and strings are shown here:

```
MsgBox "This is " & Format("1000", "@@@,@@@")
MsgBox "This is " & Format("1000", "&&&,&&&")
MsgBox Format("richard", ">")
```

Date and Time Functions

A number of functions deal specifically with date and time. These are included in this section.

Now

The **Now** function returns the current date and time:

```
MsgBox Now
```

This displays the short date and time formats from the Windows Control Panel.

Date

Date returns the current date in short format as defined in the Windows Control Panel:

```
MsgBox Date
```

Time

The **Time** function returns the current system time:

```
MsgBox Time
```

The preceding line is an example of setting the time to 11 minutes past one in the afternoon.

DateAdd

DateAdd allows the addition and subtraction of a specified time interval to a date. This function is dealt with in more detail in Chapter 28. The syntax is as follows:

```
DateAdd (interval, number, date)
```

Interval is a string that expresses the interval of time you want to add.

The following table provides a list of interval types:

Time Period	Interval
Year	Yyyy
Quarter	Q
Month	M
Day of Year	Y
Day	D
Weekday	W
Week	Ww
Hour	H
Minute	N
Second	S

Number is a numeric that determines the number of intervals you want to add. A negative value is allowed and will prompt subtraction from the date.

Date is the date being added to, or the name of a variant containing, the date. This example will add one month to January and return 1-Feb-03:

```
MsgBox DateAdd ("m",1,"1-Jan-03")
```

The following will add two weeks and return 15-Jan-03 (depending on your date format):

```
MsgBox DateAdd ("ww",2,"1-Jan-03")
```

The following will subtract two days from 1 January 2003 and return 30-Dec-02:

```
MsgBox DateAdd ("d", -2, "1-Jan-03")
```

See Chapter 28 for more information on this very useful function.

DateDiff

The **DateDiff** function returns the number of time intervals between two specified dates:

```
DateDiff (interval, date1, date2)
```

Interval is a string expression based on the following table to show the type of interval. The **date1** string indicates the start date, and **date2** the end date.

Time Period	Interval
Year	yyyy
Quarter	q
Month	m
Day of Year	y
Day	d
Weekday	w
Week	ww
Hour	h
Minute	n
Second	s

The following is an example of **DateDiff**:

```
MsgBox DateDiff("m", "1-jan-03", "15-mar-03")
```

This will return the result 2 because there are two months between 1-jan-03 and 15-mar-03. Note that it truncates to the lower month. If **date2** was 30-mar-03, it would still return 2. Only when **date2** is 1-apr-03 will it return 3.

DatePart

The **DatePart** function returns a specified part of a given date:

```
DatePart (interval, date)
```

Interval is the time period based on the following table, and date is the date you want to inspect.

Time Period	Interval
Year	yyyy
Quarter	q
Month	m
Day of Year	y
Day	d
Weekday	w
Week	ww
Hour	h
Minute	n
Second	s

The **DatePart** syntax is as follows:

```
MsgBox DatePart("q", "1-mar-03")
```

This will return the result 1 because 1-Mar-03 is in quarter 1.

The following will return the result 3 because March is the third month:

```
MsgBox DatePart("m", "1-mar-03")
```

DateSerial

DateSerial returns the date serial for a specific year, month, and day entered as integers. The date serial is the actual number representing that date:

```
DateSerial (year, month, day)
```

where **year** is a number between 100 and 9999 or a numeric expression; **month** is a number between 1 and 12 or a numeric expression; and **day** is a number between 1 and 31 or a numeric expression.

For example, the following will return the value 37686, which is the date 6-Mar-2003:

```
MsgBox CDbl(DateSerial(2003, 3, 6))
```

You need to use CDbl (convert to double) in this code, or the message box will display the date per the format in the Windows Control Panel rather than as an actual number.

DateValue

This function converts a date into a value. For example, the following will return the value 37686, which is the date 6-Mar-2003:

```
Msgbox CDbl(DateValue("06-Mar-2003"))
```

You need to use **CDbl** (convert to double) in this code or the message box will display the date per the format in the Windows Control Panel rather than as an actual number.

Day

This will return an integer between 1 and 31, representing the day of the month for the date expression given, as seen here:

```
Day (dateexpression)
```

Dateexpression can be a date string or it can be a numeric expression representing a date.

Both of the following return the value 6 for the sixth day of March because they represent the same date:

```
Msgbox Day(37686)
Msgbox Day("6-Mar-2003")
```

Hour

Hour returns an integer between 0 and 23, representing the hour of the day for the date expression:

```
Hour(dateexpression)
```

An example of a **dateexpression** could be "31-Dec-2002 12:00" or could be a time without the date, such as "09:00":

```
MsgBox Hour("17:50")
```

This will return a value of 17 for the 17th hour.

The following will return a value of 16 because 4:30 in the afternoon is the 16th hour:

```
MsgBox Hour("6-Mar-2003 4:30pm")
```

The following will return the value of 11; 11 divided by 24 is equal to .458333, which is the time value for 11:00 a.m.:

```
MsgBox Hour(11 / 24)
```

Month

Month returns an integer between 1 and 12, based on the date expression:

```
Month (dateexpression)
```

An example of a **dateexpression** could be "31-Dec-2002 12:00" or could be a time without the date, such as "09:00."

The following will both return the value of 3 because both date expressions represent 6-Mar-2003:

```
Msgbox Month(37686)
Msgbox Month("6-Mar-2003")
```

Second

The **Second** function returns an integer between 0 and 59 based on the **timeexpression** representing the seconds of a minute:

```
Second(timeexpression)
```

An example of a **timeexpression** could be "31-Dec-2002 12:00" or could be a time without the date, such as "09:00."

The following will return the value 48:

```
Msgbox Second("4:35:48pm")
```

Minute

The **Minute** function returns an integer from a time expression representing the actual minute of that time.

```
Msgbox Minute(11.27 / 24)
```

This will return the value 16, since 11.27 is 11:16:12 a.m. This may look confusing because we are dealing with decimal parts of an hour. The expression 11.27 is a decimal of an hour, so .27 is just over a quarter of an hour.

Following are two examples of the **Minute** function:

```
Msgbox Minute("4:35pm")
Msgbox Minute(11.25 / 24)
```

Year

The **Year** function returns an integer from a date expression representing the actual year value of that date:

```
Msgbox Year(37686)
Msgbox Year("6-Mar-2003")
```

Weekday

The **Weekday** function returns an integer between 1 (Sunday) and 7 (Saturday) that represents the day of the week for a date expression:

```
Weekday (dateexpression)
MsgBox WeekDay("6-Mar-2003")
```

This will return the value 5, which is Thursday.

This function can be useful if you want a date to always default to a particular day of the week. For example, if you always want a date to show the week ending Friday for the current week, you could use the following formula:

```
MsgBox Now - WeekDay(Now) + 6
```

The **Weekday** function starts from Sunday, so it reduces **Now** back to the last Sunday and then adds 6 to get to Friday. You can also use it to calculate the number of working days between two dates:

```
For n = DateValue("1-Jan-03") To DateValue("18-Jan-03")

    If Weekday(n) <> 1 Or Weekday(n) <> 7 Then



        WorkDay = WorkDay + 1

    End If
Next n

MsgBox WorkDay
```

WorkDay will return the value of 13, which is the number of working days between the two dates.

The SendKeys Command

The **SendKeys** command is not really a function but rather a command statement. A command statement like this can be used in a function or a subroutine. It allows you to command another application by sending keypresses to it, exactly the same as if you were typing at the keyboard into that application. It effectively simulates keypresses on the keyboard and can be used for low-level automation of programs that do not support OLE automation.

All the applications in the Microsoft Office Suite support OLE automation in that you can load in a reference to a particular object model and then manipulate that application from inside your code. See Chapter 17 on how to use other Microsoft applications from within your code.

Other applications do not support this; a good example is the calculator application that is supplied with Microsoft Windows. There is no access to an object model, but you can use **SendKeys** to manipulate it.

SendKeys sends one or more keystrokes to the active window as if they had been entered at the keyboard:

```
SendKeys keytext [,wait]
```

In this example, **keytext** is the string of keys to be sent to the active window; **wait** is a Boolean value (True or False). If **wait** is True, then the keys must be processed first before control is returned to the procedure. If **wait** is False, then control is returned to the procedure immediately after the keystrokes are sent. If **wait** is omitted, then False is assumed as the default.

The value of **wait** can be extremely important when sending keys to another application. If the application is running quickly, it may have moved on in execution by the time the key statement comes across, so the **SendKeys** statement gets ignored. You set **wait** to True so that the keystrokes are processed first, preventing the application from moving on ahead.

Generally, the keyboard keys themselves are used in the **SendKeys** statement most of the time. For example,

```
SendKeys "A123"
```

sends A123 to the current window.

Of course, this is assuming you have the relevant application running and that it is the active window!

Two other commands will help with this. The first is the **Shell** function. This allows your code to launch another application and transfer control to it:

```
Shell (commandstring [,windowstyle])
```

The **commandstring** parameter is the command line to call the application. If you look at the shortcuts on your desktop, you will see there is a text box called Target that holds the pathname and filename of the application plus any necessary parameters. This is used as the **commandstring parameter**.

The **windowstyle** parameter dictates how the application will be opened, whether it will be opened as a normal window and icon or hidden.

Before you can send your keypresses to the application, you need to open it. The following example opens the Windows Calculator:

```
x = Shell("calc.exe",1)
```

This opens the Windows Calculator application in a standard window with focus. Since it is now the active window, you can use **SendKeys** to send keypresses to it.

The other command to use before you send keys is **AppActivate**. If the application is already loaded, you do not need to use the **Shell** function to load it in again, but you do need to switch the focus over to that application so it can send the keys. This allows your code to activate another application already loaded by use of the title in the header bar:

```
AppActivate "Microsoft Word"
```

In this way, you can perform simple automation of other applications:

```
Sub test_sendkeys()

x = Shell("calc.exe")

For n = 1 To 10

    SendKeys n & "{+}", True

Next n

MsgBox "Press OK to close calculator"

AppActivate "calculator"

SendKeys "%{F4}", True

End Sub
```

In this example, the Windows Calculator is loaded, and then a For..Next loop makes it add up the numbers from 1 to 10.

The message box will appear on the Access application, because that is where the code is running from. The Access icon will flash on the Windows toolbar. Select Access and click OK, and the calculator will close.

The plus sign (+), caret (^), percent sign (%), tilde (~), and parentheses (( )) have special meanings to **SendKeys**. To specify one of these characters, enclose it in braces ({}). For example, to specify the plus sign, type {+}. Brackets ([ ]) have no special meaning to **SendKeys**, but you must enclose them in braces.

To specify special characters that aren't displayed when you press a key, such as ENTER or TAB, and keys that represent actions rather than characters, use the codes shown in Table 5-7.

To specify keys combined with any combination of the SHIFT, CTRL, and ALT keys, precede the key code with one or more of the following codes:

Key	Code
SHIFT	+
CTRL	^
ALT	%

Key	Code
BACKSPACE	{BACKSPACE}, {BS}, or {BKSP}
BREAK	{BREAK}
CAPS LOCK	{CAPSLOCK}
DEL OR DELETE	{DELETE} or {DEL}
DOWN ARROW	{DOWN}
END	{END}
ENTER	{ENTER}or ~
ESC	{ESC}
HELP	{HELP}
HOME	{HOME}
INS OR INSERT	{INSERT} or {INS}
LEFT ARROW	{LEFT}
NUM LOCK	{NUMLOCK}
PAGE DOWN	{PGDN}
PAGE UP	{PGUP}
PRINT SCREEN	{PRTSC}
RIGHT ARROW	{RIGHT}
SCROLL LOCK	{SCROLLLOCK}
TAB	{TAB}
UP ARROW	{UP}
F1	{F1}
F2	{F2}
F3	{F3}
F4	{F4}
F5	{F5}
F6	{F6}
F7	{F7}
F8	{F8}
F9	{F9}
F10	{F10}
F11	{F11}
F12	{F12}

Table 5-7   *Special Keys Not Normally Displayed*

To specify that any combination of SHIFT, CTRL, and ALT should be held down while several other keys are pressed, enclose the code for those keys in parentheses. For example, to specify to hold down SHIFT while E and C are pressed, use **+(EC)**. To specify to hold down SHIFT while E is pressed, followed by C without SHIFT, use **+EC**.

If you use **SendKeys** to drive another application, be aware that the keyboard is still active and can have disastrous results if it is touched while **SendKeys** is running.

Some years ago, I wrote a **SendKeys** program for a major bank in the UK to work with a time-recording application. The program ran overnight and generated timesheets for use on Friday morning. One Friday morning, there were no timesheets because the program had gone haywire. The reason for this was that during the evening, a cleaner had been dusting and managed to press the RIGHT ARROW key on the keyboard, throwing off my careful sequence of keystrokes. This meant that instead of going down one particular column, it went down the next one, and the keystrokes had no effect. After that incident, when the program was run on a Thursday evening, the keyboard was always placed behind the monitor out of harm's way.

SendKeys is not the most elegant way of doing things, but in this particular case it was the only option available given the application involved. Because of thousands of users on the application, it put immense pressure on the server on a Friday morning with people logging on and generating timesheets, and it certainly led to the server going down and a lot of unhappy project managers.

The **SendKeys** option saved the day in this particular case and allowed the timesheets to be generated overnight. Managers were pleased and the servers stayed up!

Message Boxes

In many of the examples in this book, I have used the **MsgBox** function to communicate results to the user. You can write code to place the result into a particular cell on the spreadsheet, but the message box is an extremely easy way to send data back to the user. It only needs one command, along with the line of text you wish to display to provide a professional-looking message box onscreen. So far it has only been used in its simplest form:

```
MsgBox "Hello World",vbInformation
```

Figure 5-1 shows the result of this. It does look slightly different from the message boxes that you see in other programs. The caption in the title bar says "Microsoft Access." In addition, there is no icon and there is only one option button.

You can very easily customize the message box's title bar and icon to suit your needs.

```
MsgBox "Hello World", vbInformation
```

This will cause the message box to look more professional, with a proper icon and a meaningful title. When you typed this line of code, you probably noticed that when you get

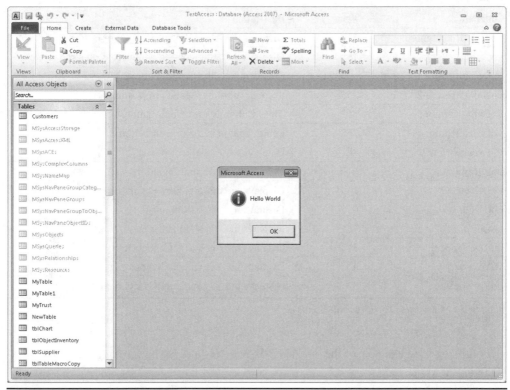

Figure 5-1   *A simple message box*

to the **type** parameter, you get a nice list box showing all your options. Four icons can be used, depending on circumstances, as shown in the following table:

Constant	Definition
vbCritical	Stop. A white cross on a red circular background. Use this to tell users they are attempting to do something they should not.
vbExclamation	Exclamation mark. Use this as a warning, for example, "This may lead to loss of data."
vbInformation	Information sign. Use this to indicate that the message box is supplying information that the user may find useful at this point in the program.
vbQuestion	Question mark. Usually associated with multiple buttons, for example, "Are you sure you wish to take this action: Yes or No?"

This is all quite straightforward, but what happens if you want to add more or different buttons, such as Yes and No? Microsoft has built in a number of constants to allow for different button combinations and icons. These are detailed in Table 5-8.

Constant	Value	Description
vbAbortRetryIgnore	2	Displays the Abort, Retry, and Ignore Buttons.
vbCritical	16	Displays the Stop icon—a white cross on a red circle.
vbDefaultButton1	0	First Button is the default button.
vbDefaultButton2	256	Second Button is the default button.
vbDefaultButton3	512	Third Button is the default button.
vbDefaultButton4	768	Fourth Button is the default button.
vbExclamation	48	Displays the Exclamation icon.
vbInformation	64	Displays the Information icon.
vbOKCancel	1	Displays the OK and Cancel buttons.
vbOKOnly	0	Displays the OK button only.
vbQuestion	32	Displays the Question icon.
vbRetryCancel	5	Displays the Retry and Cancel Buttons.
vbYesNo	4	Displays the Yes and No buttons.
vbYesNoCancel	3	Displays the Yes, No, and Cancel buttons.

Table 5-8 *Constants for Message Boxes*

Following is an example of the message box with Yes and No buttons and a defined caption:

```
MsgBox "Test message", vbYesNo, "My message"
```

This will display Yes and No buttons.

You can combine icon and button constants with the **Or** operator:

```
x = MsgBox("Test Message", vbAbortRetryIgnore Or vbCritical)
```

This will display a message box with the Abort, Retry, and Ignore buttons and a Critical message icon.

Displaying the buttons is relatively easy, but how do you detect when the user clicks a particular button? You still need to write code to deal with the button that has been clicked. You do this by collecting the response in a variable:

```
x = MsgBox ("Test Yes No",vbYesNo,"Test")
Msgbox x
```

Note that in this instance you use **x =** and put parentheses around the parameters. Without the parentheses, you will get an error because you are calling a function, which needs the parentheses to show the parameters.

This example will show a two-button message box (Yes and No). If Yes is clicked, the following message box will show 6 (**vbYes**). If No is clicked, the message box will show 7 (**vbNo**). You can then write your code to specify what will happen according to which action is taken:

```
If x = vbYes Then Action1 Else Action2
```

The following table lists the return values for a message box:

Constant	Value	Description
vbOK	1	OK button clicked
vbCancel	2	Cancel button clicked
vbAbort	3	Abort button clicked
vbRetry	4	Retry button clicked
vbIgnore	5	Ignore button clicked
vbYes	6	Yes button clicked
vbNo	7	No button clicked

Operators

Operators perform mathematical functions, comparison functions, or logical operations between two numbers or numerical expressions within your program. A simple example of an operator is the plus (+) or minus (–) sign. You will have already come across many operators when using formulas within Access.

Operators have orders of precedence that determine the order in which the calculations take place. Within individual categories (arithmetic, comparison, and logical), operators are evaluated in the order of precedence, as shown in the following table from the top down.

Arithmetic	Comparison	Logical
Exponentiation (^)	Equality (=)	Not
Negation (–)	Inequality ()	And
Multiplication and division (*, /)	Less than (<)	Or
Integer division (\)	Greater than (>)	Xor
Modulo arithmetic (Mod)	Less than or equal to (<=)	Eqv
Addition and subtraction (+, –)	Greater than or equal to (>=)	Imp
String concatenation (&)	Like / Is	

These orders of precedence can be changed by using parentheses within the formula.

The formulas within the innermost nested set of parentheses will always be evaluated first.

The use of parentheses to change the order of precedence can end up giving different results than you expect, so it is important to understand how they work. Try the following code examples in a subroutine on a module:

```
MsgBox (10 + 6) / 3
```

This gives the answer 5.3333.

```
MsgBox 10 + 6 / 3
```

This gives the answer 12.

In the first example, the parentheses force **10 + 6** to be evaluated first before division by 3. In the second example, the division of **6/3** takes precedence followed by the addition of 10.

Arithmetic Operators

The following operators—plus (+), minus (–), multiply (*), and divide (/)—do arithmetical work.

* Operator

The * operator is used to multiply two numbers.

```
MsgBox 6 * 3
```

This gives the answer 18.

The numbers can be any numeric expressions. The data type of the result is that of the most precise operand, ranging from Integer (least precise), Long, Single, Double, to Currency (most precise). See Chapter 2 for more details on these data types. If one operand is Null, then the result will be Null.

+ Operator

The + operator is used to add two numbers or expressions together.

```
MsgBox 4 + 2
```

The answer will be 6.

This operator can both add numbers and concatenate strings. String concatenation can cause confusion, so it is best to use the **&** operator because you cannot always determine if string concatenation will occur with +. See the example at the end of this section showing how string concatenation can be affected by use of the + operator.

The numbers can be any numeric expressions. The data type of the result is that of the most precise operand, ranging from Integer (least precise), Long, Single, Double, Currency (most precise). If one operand is Null, then the result will be Null.

Here are some general rules of addition and concatenation:

▶ Add if both operands are numeric.
▶ Concatenate if both operands are strings.
▶ Add if one operand is numeric and the other is a variant (not Null).
▶ Concatenate if one operand is a string and the other is a variant (not Null).

A Type Mismatch error occurs if one operand is numeric and the other is a string, as shown here:

```
MsgBox 1 + " Richard"
```

Note this does not happen if you use the **&** operator to concatenate, as shown here:

```
MsgBox 1 & " Richard"
```

– Operator

The – operator subtracts one number from another or shows a negative value. The following will give an answer of 2:

```
MsgBox 6 - 4
```

The following will display –5:

```
MsgBox -5
```

The numbers can be any numeric expressions. The data type of the result is that of the most precise operand, ranging from Integer (least precise), Long, Single, Double, Currency (most precise). If one operand is Null, then the result will be Null.

/ Operator

The / operator divides two numbers and returns a floating point result.

```
MsgBox 6 / 3
```

The result is 2. If there were a remainder, it would be displayed as decimal places.

The numbers can be any numeric expressions. The data type of the result is that of the most precise operand, ranging from Integer (least precise), Long, Single, Double, Currency (most precise). If one operand is Null, then the result will be Null.

\ Operator

The \ operator divides two numbers and returns an integer result.

```
Msgbox 6 \ 4
```

The answer is 1.

The numbers can be any numeric expressions. The data type of the result is Integer or Long. If one operand is Null, then the result will be Null.

^ Operator

The ^ operator raises a number to the power of an exponent.

```
MsgBox 2 ^ 3
```

The answer is 8 (2 to the power of 3).

The operands can be any numeric expression.

Mod Operator

The **Mod** operator divides one number by another and returns only the remainder.

```
MsgBox 6 Mod 4
```

This returns 2, which is the remainder of 6 divided by 4.

This is often used when testing to see if a number is odd or even. If the modulus is True (nonzero) when divided by two, then the number is odd.

Comparison Operators

Comparison operators compare two expressions, as you found out in Chapter 4 when we discussed making decisions in VBA.

```
MsgBox 3 > 1
```

This returns True because 3 is greater than 1.

Comparison operators always return a Boolean value of True or False except when Null is included, in which case the result is always Null. The following is a list of comparison operators:

Operator	Meaning
<	Less than
<=	Less than or equal to
<	Greater than
>=	Greater than or equal to
=	Equal to
<>	Not equal to

If both expressions are numeric, then a numeric comparison is performed. If they are both string expressions, then a string comparison is performed. If one is numeric (the variable is a numeric type containing a number) and one is a string (a variable containing a string of characters), then a Type Mismatch error will occur.

Concatenation Operator

The concatenation operator (**&**) concatenates two operands together.

```
MsgBox "Richard " & "Shepherd"
```

This gives the result "Richard Shepherd." Note that a space was left at the end of "Richard " to give the space in the final string.

You can also concatenate numbers and strings, but remember that the result will be a string. The following gives the result "12 Twelve":

```
Msgbox 12 & " Twelve"
```

While this works because VBA is intelligent enough to work out that you are combining a number and a string and converts the number (12) to a string, it is not best practice to concatenate two different data types without converting them to the same data type.

The following gives the result 34, but as a string, not a number:

```
Msgbox 3 & 4
```

Logical Operators

Logical operators perform a logical bit-by-bit conjunction on two expressions. They use pure binary math to decide the result.

And Operator

The **And** operator works on the basis that both values have to be True (nonzero). The value of True in VBA is actually -1. The following will give the result False because both values have to be True for an overall True value when the **And** operator is used:

```
Msgbox True And False
```

Numbers can also be **And**ed together. This is done on a binary basis. The top row of the following table represents the value of each binary bit going from bit 7 to bit 0. The two rows below it represent the binary equivalents of the numeric numbers on the right of the table (column n). The final row shows both the binary and numeric equivalents when the two numbers are **And**ed together. Each bit pair uses an **And** operator to achieve the final result on the bottom row.

128	64	32	16	8	4	2	1	n
0	1	0	1	0	1	0	0	84
1	0	0	1	0	0	0	1	145
0	**0**	**0**	**1**	**0**	**0**	**0**	**0**	**16**

Each column of this table shows a binary bit based on an eight-bit number. The bit values are shown in bold across the top. The right-hand column (*n*) contains the actual decimal values.

Bits are counted from the right to left, starting at bit 0 and ending at bit 7 for a single-byte number. Notice that the values of each bit increase in powers of 2. Bit 0 is represented by the value of 1, and bit 7 is represented by the value of 128. The first number is 84, so bit 6, bit 4, and bit 2 are all set. If you add 64 + 16 + 4, this comes to 84. The second number is 145, so bit 7, bit 4, and bit 0 are set. If you add 128 + 16 + 1, this comes to 145.

When a logical **And** is done on the two numbers, the result is 16. This is because the only bit where both numbers have a value is bit 4. This can be shown with the following example:

```
MsgBox 84 And 145
```

This will give the result of 16.

This strange binary arithmetic is generally used for testing whether bits are set within a number or for masking purposes. Masking sets the values of certain bits to True or False within a number. To do this, a "mask" number is **Or**ed with the target number, and the bit in the mask will be set to the mask value. For example, if you want bit 7 to be set to 1, then you Or your target number with 128 (bit 7 value) and bit 7 in the target number is then set to True, regardless of what values the other bits have.

Also, for example, you could have a variable that uses eight bits to hold various information on something, almost like properties. Each bit may represent a certain setting. If bit 4 represents a certain value and you want to see if it is set, all you do is **And** it with 16, which is the binary number for bit 4. If the bit is set, it will give a value of 16; otherwise, it will give a value of 0. This acts totally independently of values that the other bits are set to.

Not Operator

The **Not** operator performs a logical **Not** on two numbers or expressions. It basically inverts the bits within a number. If a bit is set to 0, then it becomes 1; if it is set to 1, it becomes 0.

```
MsgBox Not (2 = 3)
```

This will give the result True because 2 does not equal 3 (which is False), but the Not statement then inverts the bits and makes it True.

Or Operator

The **Or** operator works on the basis that either two values can be True (nonzero) or one can be True and the other False (zero). The following returns True because one of the values is True (True and False are built in variables within VBA):

```
MsgBox True Or False
```

The following returns False because there is no True value:

```
MsgBox False Or False
```

It works using binary arithmetic, on the basis that 1 or 1 make 1, 1 or 0 make 1, 0 or 1 make 1, and 0 or 0 make 0.

The top row of the following table represents the value of each binary bit going from bit 7 to bit 0. The two rows below it represent the binary equivalents of the numeric numbers on the right of the table (column *n*). The final row shows both the binary and numeric equivalents when the two numbers are **Or**ed together. Each bit pair uses an **Or** operator to achieve the final result on the bottom line.

128	64	32	16	8	4	2	1	*n*
0	1	0	1	0	1	0	0	84
1	0	0	1	0	0	0	1	145
1	**1**	**0**	**1**	**0**	**1**	**0**	**1**	**213**

Each column of the preceding table shows a binary bit based on an eight-bit number. The bit values are shown in bold across the top. The right-hand column contains the actual decimal numbers.

Bits are counted from right to left, starting at bit 0 and ending at bit 7 for a single-byte number. Notice that the values of each bit increase in powers of 2. The first number is 84, so bit 6, bit 4, and bit 2 are all set. If you add 64 + 16 + 4, this comes to 84. The second number is 145, so bit 7, bit 4, and bit 0 are set. If you add 128 + 16 + 1, this comes to 145.

When a logical **Or** is done on the two numbers, the result is 213 (128 + 64 + 16 + 4 +1). This can be shown using the following VBA example:

```
MsgBox 84 Or 145
```

This will give the result of 213.

The **Or** operator is often used for masking purposes in graphics and also for combining two parameters. In Chapter 5, I discussed the message box you had to combine with **vbExclamation** and **vbYesNo** in order to get the correct icon and the correct buttons on the message box. Using a simple + operator to add **vbExclamation** and **vbYesNo** together will result in the wrong value being set for the required flag. It is only by using **Or** that the correct result is achieved.

You also see use of **Or** in If statements, as in Chapter 4:

```
If  x = 1  Or  y = 1 Then
```

Xor Operator

Xor is very similar to **Or**, except that True and True make False. Only True and False make True, but there must be one True and one False. False **Xor** True makes True, and True **Xor** False makes True.

Xor stands for *Ex*clusive *Or*—thus, both values cannot both be True or False. The following gives the value True:

```
MsgBox True Xor False
```

The following gives the value False:

```
MsgBox True Xor True
```

The **Xor** operator works on binary arithmetic on the basis that 1 **Xor** 1 make 0, 1 **Xor** 0 make 1, 0 **Xor** 1 make 1, and 0 **Xor** 0 make 0.

The top row of the following table represents the value of each binary bit going from bit 7 to bit 0. The two rows below it represent the binary equivalents of the numeric numbers on the right of the table (column *n*). The final row shows both the binary and numeric equivalents when the two numbers are **Xor**ed together. Each bit pair uses an **Xor** operator to achieve the final result on the bottom line.

128	64	32	16	8	4	2	1	*n*
0	1	0	1	0	1	0	0	84
1	0	0	1	0	0	0	1	145
1	**1**	**0**	**0**	**0**	**1**	**0**	**1**	**197**

Each column of the preceding table shows a binary bit based on an eight-bit number. The bit values are shown in bold across the top. The right-hand column contains the actual numbers.

Bits are counted from the right to left, starting at bit 0 and ending at bit 7 for a single-byte number. Notice that the values of each bit increase in powers of 2. The first number is 84, so bit 6, bit 4, and bit 2 are all set. If you add 64 + 16 + 4, this comes to 84. The second number is 145, so bit 7, bit 4, and bit 0 are set. If you add 128 + 16 + 1, this comes to 145.

When a logical **Xor** is done on the two numbers, the result is 197 (128 + 64 + 4 +1). This can be shown with the following VBA example:

```
MsgBox 84 Xor 145
```

This will give the result of 197. This result has an interesting property. If you **Xor** the result with one of the numbers used, you will get the other number that was used to create the result. The following will return the value 145:

```
MsgBox 84 Xor 197
```

The following will return the value 84:

```
MsgBox 145 Xor 197
```

This operator is often used in simple encryption routines. You use a string of random characters. The string you want to encrypt is then **Xor**ed character by character against your random string. This produces another apparently random string with no discernible pattern in it (and patterns are what code breakers look for).

To decrypt the string, all you have to do is **Xor** character by character against the original random string.

Other Operators

There are a number of other operators that can be used within Access VBA.

Is Operator

Is compares two object reference variables to see if they are the same. The following returns True because the two expressions are both the same—sheet1 is the same as sheet1:

```
MsgBox Worksheets(1) Is Worksheets(1)
```

The following returns False because the two expressions are not the same:

```
MsgBox Worksheets(1) Is Worksheets(2)
```

Here, sheet1 is not the same as sheet2 because it has a different name. There may be other differences, but if the two sheets are totally new, the name will be the only difference.

Like Operator

Like compares two string expressions that are similar to each other to see if they match a pattern. Their first few characters may be the same or they may simply be in uppercase and lowercase.

```
Option Compare Text
Sub test()
    MsgBox "RICHARD" Like "richard"
End Sub
```

If the **Option Compare** statement in declarations is set to Text, then this will return True. If it is set to **Binary**, then it will return False. This works the same way as the **Compare** parameter used in the **Instr** function in Chapter 5 in that it sets whether a binary or a text compare (case-sensitive) will happen.

You can also use wildcard characters. A **?** denotes a single character and a ***** denotes a string of characters. It is exactly the same as doing a file search when you use wildcard characters. A table of pattern characters is shown here:

Character	Meaning
?	Any single character
*	Zero or more characters
#	Any single digit (0–9)
[*charlist*]	Any single character in *charlist*
[*!charlist*]	Any single character not in *charlist*

The following examples will return True:

```
MsgBox "RICHARD" Like "ri?hard"

MsgBox "RICHARD" Like "ric*"
```

7

Debugging

In any code you write, bugs may exist that can cause a program failure, cause the program to hang, or simply create unexpected results. In my opinion, this area separates the true analytical programmers from those who just type in code and hope it works.

Many reports have been written about "computer rage," where users of an application get upset because the results are different from what they expected. All I can say to those people is wait until you work on code for an application like Access! You will then realize how straightforward and well organized this application is. Once you have tried your hand at fixing a few bugs in what appears to be a simple program, you will appreciate what goes on behind the scenes when you click a menu selection or press an OK button.

Types of Errors

Errors occur very easily when you are writing code. This section gives you examples of the types of errors you can expect to see.

Compile Errors

Compile errors result from incorrectly constructed code. You may have used a property or method that does not exist on an object, or put in a For without a Next or an If without an End If.

When you run code, the compiler goes through the code first and checks for these types of errors. If any are found, the code will not be run, but an error message will be displayed referring to the first error found. Note that there could be several compile errors in a procedure, but only the first one will be flagged. You might correct the error and think, "I've fixed it now," and then rerun the procedure, and up comes another one! This can be very frustrating, but the best answer to fixing it is to obey the rules of coding in the first place.

The following types of errors appear when the code is compiled, and are often referred to as design-time or compile-time errors.

Runtime Errors

Runtime errors occur when your program is running. You could, for example, try to open a file that does not exist, or attempt a division by zero. Such actions would create an error message and halt execution of the program. They would not show up at compile time because they are not breaking any programming rules, but they will prevent the code from running.

Logic Errors

Logic errors occur when your application does not perform the way you intended. The code can be valid and run without producing any errors, but what happens is incorrect. These are by far the most difficult errors to locate. They can require a lot of painstaking searching to find, even using all the debugging tools at your disposal. It is very easy to keep looking at a few lines of code and thinking, "There is nothing wrong with this. It should give the right answer." It is only by looking at each line in turn that you will see what has gone wrong, and often suddenly realize what a simple mistake it was. You may also run into a situation you did not envisage when first designing your code.

Design Time, Runtime, and Break Mode

When working on an application in VBA, you can be in three modes:

- ▶ **Design time**   When you are working on the code for the application or designing a form.

- ▶ **Runtime**   When you run your code or your form. The title bar of the VBA screen will contain the word "running," and at this point you can view code but you cannot change it.

- ▶ **Break**   If you press CTRL+BREAK (pressing the CTRL key at the bottom left of the keyboard and PAUSE BREAK at the top right of the keyboard simultaneously) during runtime, it will stop execution of your code. You can also insert a breakpoint by pressing the F9 Key. Pressing it again removes it. You can insert a breakpoint from the VBE menu by selecting Debug | Toggle Breakpoint. A dialog box will appear with the error message, "Code execution has been interrupted," displaying several buttons. Clicking the Debug button will take you into the code window.

When you click Debug, you go into instant watch mode, also known as debug mode. You'll be able to see your code, and the line it has stopped at will be highlighted in yellow. This is the line that is causing the problem. You can place your cursor on any variable that is in scope (meaning it is used within the procedure you are running), and it will give you the value of it instantly. You can also move the point of execution by dragging the yellow arrow to the line of code to be executed.

Try this simple program:

```
Sub TestDebug()
x = 2
Do Until x = 1
     x = x + 1
Loop
End Sub
```

When you run this, the program never finishes because **x** will never equal 1. Press CTRL-BREAK, and the error window will appear. Click Debug, and you will be in instant watch mode in the code window. Move your cursor across any instance of **x** and its value will appear (see Figure 7-1).

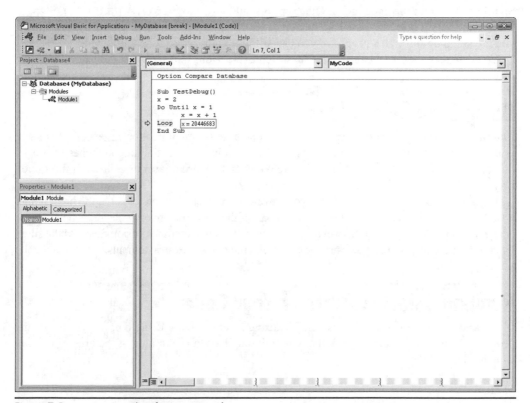

Figure 7-1   *An example of instant watch*

You can restart your code by clicking the Run symbol on the toolbar (the triangle symbol pointing to the right) or pressing F5; it will start from the point where it was stopped. A yellow arrow will appear to the left of the code, indicating the current execution point. Try dragging the yellow arrow to a new start point, such as **x = 2**, and then rerun the code. This is useful if you want to restart a loop or an If condition after you have changed code due to a bug.

Breakpoints

You can add a breakpoint to your code so it will halt at that line. You can then use step commands by pressing F8 to move through one line at a time and use instant watch to examine variables as the code steps through.

Breakpoints can be toggled on and off by using F9 or by selecting Debug | Toggle Breakpoint from the menu. They appear as a solid brown circle in the leftmost column of the code window.

If you run the preceding loop example and place a breakpoint on the **Loop** statement, you will see that every time you click the Run symbol or F5, it stops on the **Loop** statement.

You can step through the program one line at a time by clicking F8 or by using Debug | Step Into (F8) from the code menu. Other options allow you to Step Over (SHIFT+F8), Step Out (run program normally), or Run to Cursor (run code down to where the cursor is). While you are stepping through a program, you can still use your cursor to examine values.

You can also open a Debug window to watch expressions and see what they are doing.

Using Stop Statements

Entering a **Stop** statement in your code is the same as entering a breakpoint, except it is in your code. When VBA encounters a **Stop** statement, it halts execution and switches to break mode. Although **Stop** statements act like breakpoints, they are not set or cleared in the same way.

If you set breakpoints using F9, when you leave your project and then reload it, the breakpoints are all cleared. However, **Stop** statements form part of the code and are only cleared when you delete them or put a single quote (') character in front to change them into a comment. Make sure that once you have your code working properly, you remove all **Stop** statements.

Running Selected Parts of Your Code

If you know where the statement is that is causing an error, a single breakpoint will locate the problem. However, it's more likely that you will only have a rough idea of the area of code causing the problem.

You can insert a breakpoint where you want to start checking the code and then single-step the procedure to see what each statement is doing. You can also skip a statement or start execution from a different place.

Single Stepping

Single stepping allows you to execute one statement at a time. You can place your cursor on variables anywhere in the code to see the state of variables, and you can also use the Debug window to view values of variables.

You can single-step by using Debug | Step Into from the menu or pressing F8. You can also run the code to the position of the cursor. Click the mouse on a line of code and then press CTRL+F8. The code will only execute as far as where you have clicked the mouse. Note that the cursor must be on an executable line of code, not a blank line. You can also step between individual statements if they are on the same line but separated by the : character.

```
temp = 4: If temp = 3 Then Exit Sub
```

Procedure Stepping

If you have a subroutine or function that is being called, you may not wish to step through the whole procedure line by line. You may have already tested it and be satisfied with its performance. If you use F8 to step through (Single Step), you will be taken all through the subroutine's code one step at a time. This could be extremely time-consuming for something that you know already works. If you use SHIFT+F8 (Step Over), then your subroutine will be treated as a single statement but without stepping through it.

Call Stack Dialog

The Call Stack dialog box, shown in the following illustration, displays a list of active procedure calls—that is, calls that have been started but not completed. You can display this dialog by using CTRL+L, but it is only available in Break mode. It can help you trace the operation of calls to procedures, especially if they are nested where one procedure then calls another procedure.

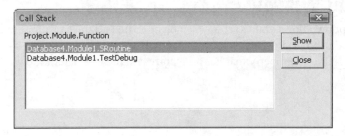

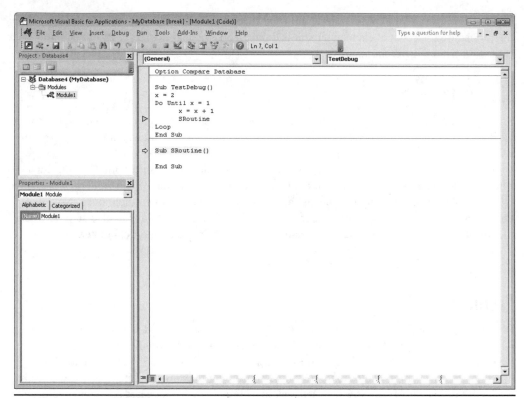

Figure 7-2   *How to call a subroutine and show which procedure called it*

The earliest active procedure call is shown at the top of the list, and any subsequent procedure calls are added to the top, as shown in Figure 7-2. By highlighting the procedure in the figure and clicking Show, you can view the statement calling that procedure. This is indicated with a green arrow.

The Debug Window

The Debug window allows you to set a watch on specific variables or properties to see what values they hold as your program executes. This will aid you in debugging by allowing you to analyze a variable or property that has an incorrect value and determine where the problem is coming from.

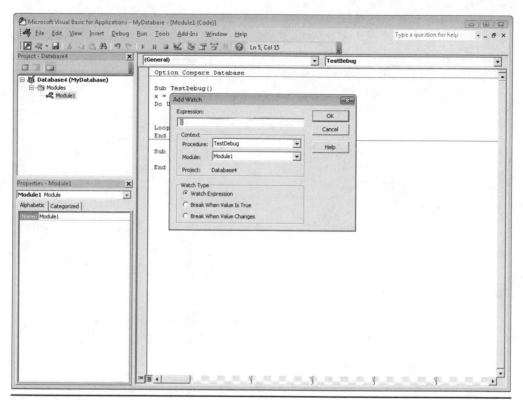

Figure 7-3   *Adding a watch on a variable*

You can set the Debug window, as shown in Figure 7-3, by using Debug | Add Watch from the menu.

Enter the variable or expression you wish to monitor in the Expression box. For example, if you have a variable **x** and wish to keep track of its value, enter **x** in the box. The context details are entered automatically but can be amended. You can also specify whether you want the code to break when the value of the variable is True (nonzero) or when the value changes.

Click OK and the Debug window will appear with details of your variable in it, as shown in Figure 7-4.

When the program reaches a breakpoint, the value in the Debug window is updated. As you step through, it will also be updated. You can delete a watch expression by highlighting the expression in the watch window, clicking it, and then pressing the DELETE key.

To edit the watch expression, right-click the selected expression and select Edit Watch.

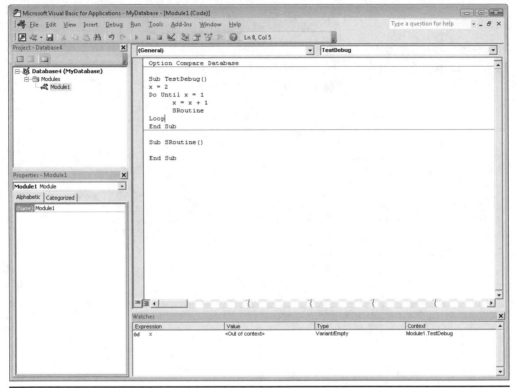

Figure 7-4   *Monitoring the value of a variable from within a watch window*

Events That Can Cause Problems When Debugging

Certain events in windows can pose problems for the debugger by complicating and confusing the debugging process. These events are discussed in the next sections.

Mouse Down

Mouse down is the event fired off when the user presses any mouse button down. This is before the button comes back up. If you break the code at this point, you will not get a mouse up event. A mouse up event occurs only when you press the mouse button and release it.

Key Down

Key down is the event fired off when the user presses any keyboard key down. This is before the key comes back up. If you break the code at this point, you will not get a key up event. A key up event occurs only when you press the key and release it.

Got Focus / Lost Focus

A got focus / lost focus event occurs when a user clicks your form or a particular control on the form to get the focus on that control. If you break the code at this point, you may get inconsistent results. Whether you do or not depends on if your control had the focus at the point that the BREAK key was pressed.

Using Message Boxes in Debugging

Some methods besides those already discussed can isolate bugs in code. They may be considered somewhat crude, but they do work. For example, message boxes are always useful for letting you know what is going on. They can display the value of a variable or even several variables by concatenating them together. They are extremely useful when you have a large procedure and you do not know the region the bug is in. For example, a large piece of code appears to run but hangs and will not respond to CTRL+BREAK. Perhaps it ran perfectly up to now but has hit certain circumstances that cause it to hang.

The question is, how far into the code do you get before the issue occurs? You could try stepping through it, but this is very time-consuming if it is a large procedure. Placing message boxes at strategic points throughout the code will give you an idea of where it stops. Make sure all the message boxes display something meaningful, such as "Ok1," "Ok2," and "Ok3." You can then see what stages the program has covered before it hangs. Be sure you clear all the extra message boxes out once you have found the bug! You can also concatenate variables together.

```
Sub test_for()
For n = 1 To 4
    For m = 2 To 8

        MsgBox m & " xxxxx " & n

    Next m

Next n

End Sub
```

This message box will display the values of **m** and **n** separated by a line of x's. The purpose of the x's is to prevent null values or spaces from being hidden. Although it would not happen in this example, variables can sometimes end up with Null values or be spaces if they are string variables, in which case you would only see one number appearing. In such instances, how would you know whether it is the value of **m** or **n**? The row of x's distinguishes this.

If you want a continuous readout of variables while the program is running, there are ways to get one. Debug does not offer this option, but with a little ingenuity it can be accomplished.

You can change the caption properties on a **UserForm** object using code. This assumes you have already defined **UserForm1** and that it is open in View mode. See Chapter 9 for how to create a user form for use with VBA.

```
Sub test_for()
For n = 1 To 4

    For m = 2 To 8


        Forms("UserForm1").Caption = n & " xxxx " & m
    Next m


Next n
End sub
```

This will display the variables in the caption of the window as the program is running. Depending on how fast the variables change and how long the procedure is, you will be able to see patterns occurring and see what is happening live at each stage. In terms of patterns, you will be able to see sequences of numbers, how they ascend and descend, what the maximum values they get to are, and so on. If a major error occurs, you can see at what value it is occurring.

Avoiding Bugs

Careful design and planning of the application is important and will help reduce bugs. Often it is best to break the application down into smaller component parts that are easier to code and test. It is easier to think of a small portion of code than to try to tackle an entire project in one thought. Make sure you document and comment your code using the single quote (') character. The comments will turn green within your code. If the application is complicated, it is often difficult to go back even after just a few days to determine what the code is doing. Even professional programmers find that if they go back to code they wrote only a few months before, they have difficulty understanding what the code was doing. Comments may provide the help needed. Also, if a programmer leaves an organization, it can be difficult for a new or different programmer to pick up where the former employee left off without any documentation about the intent of the code.

It is important to know what all your variables represent and what each function does. Once your application starts growing and begins to get complicated, its documentation becomes more important. Without such documentation, you will need a good memory to keep track of what every variable means!

Errors and the Error Function

Runtime errors can creep into code very easily, through no fault of the programmer. The user does something outside the scope of the code and causes an error message to occur that stops all execution of code. This may occur when you are accessing an external data source such as a database. The user may also take an action that the programmer never envisaged.

No matter how carefully you try to provide for all conditions, there is always a user who does something you never thought of and effectively breaks the set of rules you wrote. It may be as simple as including a name with an apostrophe, such as O'Brien. If you use this name in a SQL query string, it will cause problems in the way it is handled.

Another example is reading a file in from a disk device. The programmer may allow the user to select the drive letter for the file to be read. You assume that the files will mainly come from network drives, and a D: CD/DVD option is just nice to have, but it will probably never be used. However, if the user selects D: (CD/DVD drive), it is possible there will be no disk in the drive. This will create an error that will stop execution of your program. The user will then be very unhappy and lose a great deal of faith in your application. Thus, the error needs to be trapped, and an appropriate action needs to be taken from within the VBA code.

Error handling is also used on common dialog forms (see Chapter 10) to show that the Cancel button has been clicked. In order to test whether the user clicked the Cancel button, you must have first set the **CancelError** property to True and then put in an **On Error** statement to direct the code where to go for an error.

Try this simple example *without* a disk in drive D. Place the code into a code module and then run it by pressing F5:

```
Sub Test_Error()

    temp = Dir("d:\*.*")

End Sub
```

This will produce an error message saying that the D drive is not ready. In normal terms, your program has crashed and will not work any further until this error is resolved. Not very good from the user's point of view!

You can place a simple error-trapping routine as follows:

```
Sub Test_Error()
    On Error GoTo err_handler
            temp = Dir("d:\*.*")
    Exit Sub
    err_handler:
    MsgBox "The D drive is not ready" & "   " & Err.Description
End Sub
```

The first line sets up a routine to jump to when an error occurs using the **On Error** statement. It points to **err_handler**, which is a label just below the **Exit Sub** line further down that will deal with any error condition. The purpose of a label is to define a section of your code that you can jump to by using a **GoTo** statement.

The line to read the D drive is the same as before, and then there is an **Exit Sub** line, because if all is well you do not want the code continuing into the **err_handler** routine.

If an error happens at any point after the **On Error** line, the code execution jumps to **err_handler** and displays a message box that says drive D is not ready. However, you may have noticed that the code execution jumps to **err_handler** when *any* error occurs, not just the drive not ready error. An error could occur because you made a mistake typing in this code.

Fortunately, you can interrogate the error to find out what went wrong. You can also use the **Err** object to give the description of the error and concatenate it into your message so it also says "Drive not ready." You do this using the **Err** function. This will return the number associated with the runtime error that happened. You can add this into the previous example as follows:

```
Sub Test_Error()
    On Error GoTo err_handler
    temp = Dir("d:\*.*")
    Exit Sub
    err_handler:
```

```
    If Err.Number = 71 Then
        MsgBox "The D drive is not ready"
    Else
        MsgBox "An error occurred"

    End If
End Sub
```

You saw from the first example that the number for "Drive not ready" came up in the error message box as 71. The program looks at **Err** (a system variable that holds the last error number) and checks to see if it is 71. If it is, it displays the message box, "The D drive is not ready"; if it is not, it displays the message box, "An error occurred."

The Resume Statement

The **Resume** statement can be added to make the code execution branch back to the statement where the error occurred. This gives the opportunity for the user to intervene—for example, to put a CD into drive D and for the code to then reinterrogate drive D. You can include this in your error-handling routine so the line that created the error will be tried again following user intervention:

```
Sub Test_Error()
    On Error GoTo err_handler
    temp = Dir("d:\*.*")
    Exit Sub
    err_handler:
    If Err.Number = 71 Then
        MsgBox "The D drive is not ready"
    Else
        MsgBox "An error occurred"

    End If
    Resume
End Sub
```

You can also add the statement **Next** to **Resume**. This will skip over the statement that created the error and thus ignore it.

```
Sub Test_Error()

    On Error Resume Next

    temp = Dir("d:\*.*")

End Sub
```

If there is no disk in drive D, the code will still run perfectly because of **On Error Resume Next**—it skips over the line of code creating the error.

Resume Next can be useful for dealing with errors as they occur, but it can make debugging code very difficult. In a later stage of your program, you may have incorrect or nonexistent data being produced due to the fact that an error condition earlier was ignored. You can end up with a program that appears to run okay, but in fact does nothing because it has some hidden bugs or incomplete data. This is because every time an error is encountered, the execution just skips over it. This can give a false impression of what is actually happening, so if you do use **On Error Resume Next**, make sure you check all inputs and outputs to the code to ensure that everything is working as it should. Make sure your **On Error Resume Next** statement cannot cover up an error in a read from a table or from a file. This can be disastrous for your program because the **On Error Resume Next** statement will make it appear to work perfectly.

Implications of Error Trapping

When you use an **On Error** statement in your code, that error trap remains throughout the procedure unless it is disabled. As you just saw, you can set up a routine to check whether the D drive has a disk in it and take action accordingly. However, it is important to turn this off once the possibility of the error has taken place. If you do not do this, then all subsequent errors within that procedure will use the same error-handling routine. This gives extremely confusing results to the user, as the error message is likely to be totally meaningless in relation to the error generated. A subsequent error could relate to division by zero, but the error message will come up saying "Drive D not ready."

If **On Error Resume Next** has been used and not switched off, all sorts of errors could be taking place without the user being aware of them. You disable the error-trapping routine as follows:

```
On Error Resume Next
On Error GoTo 0
```

The **On Error Resume Next** statement that you saw previously ignores all errors. The **On Error GoTo 0** cancels any error handling and allows all errors to be displayed as they normally would. This cancels out the **On Error Resume Next** and puts everything back to normal error handling.

Generating Your Own Errors

Why would you want to generate your own errors? After all, you want to achieve error-free code, right? Well, sometimes this is useful when you are testing your own applications or when you want to treat a particular condition as being equivalent to a runtime error.

You can generate an error in your code with the **Error** statement:

```
Sub Test_Error()

    Error 71

End Sub
```

This simulates the "Drive not ready" error. You can also use **Err.Raise(71)** to do this. In addition, you can regenerate the current error by using the following:

```
Error Err
```

The purpose of this is to raise the "Drive not ready" error message as if the drive really is not ready and this is the current error found. If another error message is then created, this becomes the current error.

Forms and Reports

Forms and reports are the means by which your application interfaces to the user and communicates the information within the database. In a relational database, the data is held within tables that can be viewed simply by double-clicking the table name, but those tables are very unlikely to provide the user with anything meaningful.

This is because the data is stored in a number of tables that have relationships between them. An example might be customer orders. The customer details would be stored in a separate customer table and each order would relate to the customer table using an internal ID number.

If you looked at the customer orders table, all you would see for the customer detail would be a reference number pointing to a record within the customer details table. To get the full story, a query is necessary to join the two tables together and present the full information to the user.

Forms and reports use underlying queries and tables to present the information to the user in an understandable form. There is plenty of scope for using VBA to enhance both forms and reports.

The examples in this chapter will use the Northwind database as the source of data. To load this, click Sample in the central pane (Available Templates) when Access first loads, and then double-click the Northwind icon.

Forms

A form is based on a table or a query and allows the user to scroll through records, view specified fields, and use filtering methods. According to how the form properties are set, the user may be able to edit, update, or delete records on the form.

Creating a Simple Form

To create a form, click the Create tab in the ribbon and then click the Form Design icon in the Forms group of the ribbon. This will give you a blank form. You can resize the form by placing the mouse on the right-hand or bottom border and dragging the border to where you need it.

To give the form a name, click the Save icon in the toolbar or press CTRL+S. Give the form a name such as **frmMyForm**.

You now need to link the form to a table or query as a data source. To do this, right-click anywhere on the form and select Properties in the pop-up. At the top of the Properties window is a drop-down showing Selection Type. Select Form in this drop-down.

Choose the All tab on the Properties window and go to the first property shown, called Record Source. The drop-down on this property will display a list of all tables and queries in the Access database. You can select one of these as the source for the form, or you can enter in a SQL query string such as **select * from orders**. If you click the button with the three dots next to the drop-down, you can use the query builder window to create a query for your form.

For the purposes of this example, select Orders as the record source. This form will be referred to later in this chapter as the Orders form.

Now that you have a data source for the form, you can add controls and bind them to that data source. Click the Design tab in the ribbon if it is not already selected and then select a control from the Controls group of the ribbon. The text box control is one of the most widely used, so try this one initially. Drag it on to the form. You will notice that it automatically adds in a label box so you can enter a heading to describe the text box. Your form should now look like Figure 9-1.

If you want to delete either the label or the text box, simply select it with the mouse and press the DELETE key. You can also drag the text box to a new position (the accompanying label box will follow as well), and you can resize both the controls by selecting the handles on a particular control and dragging the borders to the size you want.

Once you have the text box as you want it, you can bind it to a field within the record source. To do this, right-click the control and click Properties in the pop-up. In the Properties window, make sure the All tab is selected, and then select Control Source in the properties list. Click the drop-down and a list of fields will be displayed according to what was entered as the Record Source property for the form.

Select the field you want to display in the text box and this will bind the field to that text box. Select a field that will display as text, not an ID number relating to another table. Choose fields like Ship Name or Ship City, not Employee ID or Customer ID since these are relational fields.

Repeat this process for some other fields so you have a form that has a reasonable population.

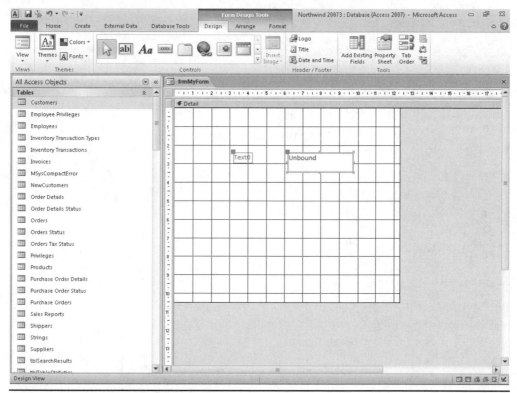

Figure 9-1   *A new form in Design mode with a text box*

To display your form, click the Design tab in the ribbon and then click the Form View icon in the Views group of the ribbon. Your form should look like Figure 9-2, depending on the fields you selected from the customer table for display purposes.

At the bottom of the form, you can see record selectors that allow the user to navigate backward and forward through the records. You will also see the number of records displayed.

You can easily apply filters and sorts to the form by clicking the Home tab on the ribbon and then using the Sort and Filter icons in the Sort & Filter group of the ribbon. This assumes that the "Allow Filters" property for the form is set to Yes. There is also a search box next to the record selectors at the bottom of the form that allows search text to be entered.

If you have chosen a record source that is updatable—such as a query that does not have a many-to-many relationship, or a table—then the record selector group of buttons will also contain a blank record icon that allows a new record to be added. This is also dependent on the "Allow Additions" property on the form being set to Yes.

If the "Allow Edits" and "Allow Deletes" properties are also set to Yes, then the user can also make changes to records or delete a record using this form, which is where there can be dangers. It is very easy when viewing a form such as this to inadvertently change a field. As

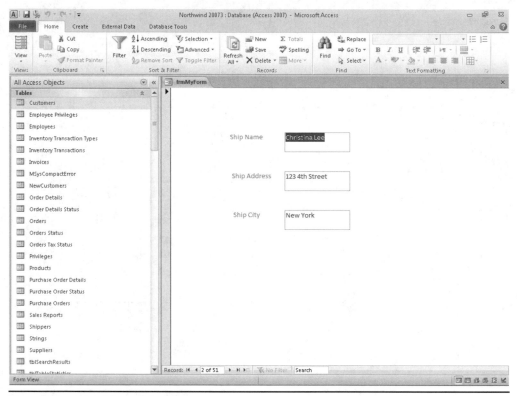

Figure 9-2 *Form View of the form*

soon as the user moves to another record or closes the form, that change is saved back to the underlying tables and there is no warning that a change has been made. If the user deletes a record, there is a confirmation message provided that you have not switched the warnings off.

When a form is created, all the Allow properties are set to Yes by default. It is well worth ensuring that changes to records can only be made by users with permission, and this is where VBA can be of help.

However, you now have a simple form that will act as a simple user interface on the Orders table of the Northwind database.

Using Relational Fields in Your Form

You will have noticed that in the Orders table of the Northwind database, relational fields such as Employee ID and Customer ID are used in the Orders table. These fields link the record to data in the Employee and Customer tables using a unique internal ID number for each record.

In order to display the name of an employee instead of the ID number, you could make the record source of your form a query joining the Orders table and the Employee table using the Employee ID to join on.

This will work fine if all the user wants to do is browse the records and view them, but if the user wants to edit a record or add a new record, they will encounter problems. If they go to choose a new employee for a specific order, they need to see the employee name (and to be restricted to that list of names), but the relevant ID number for that employee will need to be inserted into the orders table to maintain the integrity of the database.

This is where you can use a Combo Box control on your form. This is the control that you frequently see that provides a drop-down list for the user to select a value from. It is used very frequently when the user changes a field value or inserts a new record because it can be set so that only the values in the list can be used, which maintains data integrity within the database.

View the form in Design mode and click the Design tab on the ribbon.

When the Form Design ribbon appears, click Controls in the Controls section. A menu of icons will pop up. From the menu of icons, drag the Combo Box icon onto your form.

The Combo box wizard then appears to assist you in setting up your combo box. If you do not wish to use it, click Cancel, and then change the properties manually if desired.

As we are using a relational field, the wizard will not cover this, so click Cancel to exit the wizard.

Right-click the combo box control and select Properties from the pop-up. You need to make a number of changes in the Properties window for the combo box to work correctly with the relational field. The following property values will need to be changed:

▶ **Control Source** This needs to be set to Employee ID, which is the relational field supplying the actual ID number. This is based on the RecordSource property that you set earlier on the form. Click the drop-down, not on the three-dot icon, and you will see a drop-down showing the fields available based on the RecordSource property for the form. Choose Employee ID from the list.

▶ **Column Count** This defines the number of columns that will be in the drop-down. This needs to be set to 2. The first column will be the ID number of the employee and the second column will be the employee name.

▶ **Column Widths** Type in the value **0;4**. This will automatically appear as 0 cm;4 cm in the property window. This defines the widths of the two columns within the combo box. Because the first column is the ID number and is totally meaningless to the user, we do not want this to be visible, so the column width is set to zero. We want the user to be able to see the actual names column for selection, so the width of that is set to 4cm.

▶ **Row Source** This property defines where the combo box will get the list of values for the drop-down. Enter this property as:

SELECT id, [first name] & " " & [last name] FROM employees;

This is a standard SQL select statement. Notice that first name and last name are concatenated together using a space in the middle, and also notice the use of square brackets because the field names have a space in the middle. You can test this out by creating a normal query in Access. It should return a two-column result of ID number and the concatenated name of the employee.

▶ **Row Source Type**   This property must be set to Table/Query.

▶ **Bound Column**   This property is set to 1, indicating that the first column in the combo box will be bound to the underlying table. This is the hidden column holding the ID number. When the user edits an employee name or adds a new record, the ID number in the first column is written back to the Employee ID field in the Orders table.

▶ **Limit To List**   This property must be set to Yes so that users are restricted to the employees within the database and do not start inventing their own!

If you now view your form in Form View mode, you will see that the combo box is automatically populated with the full name of the employee, although this is made up of two separate fields from the Employees table.

If you click the drop-down, you will see a list of full names of employees, but what you do not see is that each employee has a hidden ID number within the list.

Try amending an employee on a record. Move to the next record to save the change and then move back to your original record. You will see that your change has taken effect and a different employee is showing on that record.

This methodology has the advantage that when new employees are added to the Employees table, they will automatically appear in the drop-down together with their relevant ID number. This preserves the integrity of the database and ensures that any queries using the relationship between orders and employees will still return the correct results.

Subforms

So far we have designed a user interface based on the user browsing through a table and looking at a single record each time. This works well on the Orders table, since each record forms a single meaningful chunk of data. However, you are only looking at a particular order and cannot see any details as to what products and quantities were included in the order.

Even though several rows of products may exist, effectively you are only looking at the order header record. This is where a subform can be used to display the multiple detail associated with a single record in the parent form. To do this, create a new blank form and call it **subfrmOrderDetails**. It is a good idea to distinguish subforms from parent forms by using a simple naming convention.

Change the Record Source property for the form to Order Details. Place a text box on the form by clicking the Text box icon in the Controls group of the Design ribbon and dragging it onto your form. Change its Control Source to Quantity. Set the corresponding label control caption to read Quantity. Add three text box controls onto the form by dragging the text box control from the Controls group of the ribbon. Set the Control Source properties for the three text boxes to Quantity, Unit Price, and Discount.

Take a look at the form in Form View mode. As before in the Orders form, you will see the Quantity, Unit Price, and Discount for each order. However, the problem is that you have the order details for every single order with no distinction as to which order is which.

Return to your original Orders form. Go into Design View and add a Subform control. This control icon is the fifth control from the left on the third row of icons in the Controls group of the ribbon. It looks like a box with four bars and two rectangles inside it. If you hover the cursor over it, it will display Subform/Subreport. You may need to enlarge your form by dragging the borders before you add this control.

A Subform wizard will appear. You can use this, but it is often better to set the properties manually, so click Cancel on the initial wizard screen.

On the Source Object property is a drop-down with a list of available forms. Select subfrmOrderDetails (or whatever you called your subform when you prepared it). You must have already made sure that both the main form and the subform have been bound to a control source by setting the control source property on each form.

Click the Link Master Fields property and click the button with three dots on it. This will display a form allowing you to choose how your subform will be linked to the main form. You can have up to two links.

Access will attempt to create a logical link between the two forms, but it is well worth checking this first.

The link is based on the relational fields within the record sources in the two forms, not the actual fields displayed. In this particular example, the Order ID field in the Orders form (which is the Master Field) is linked to the Order ID in the subform for Order Details (which is the Child Field).

On the corresponding label box for the subform, you can provide a meaningful title such as **Order Details**.

Look at the Orders form in Form View mode. It should resemble Figure 9-3.

Notice that your Order Details subform sits in a window of its own within the main form and has its own record selectors and record count.

Use the main record selectors at the bottom of the Orders form to browse through the records. The main form shows each order in turn, but the subform window will show all the products and quantities for that particular order. You can then use the record selector buttons on the subform to browse through the various products for that order, and even add or delete rows in the Order Details table.

You may wish to show your subform as a datasheet view (see next section) so that the user can see several detail rows at once. To do this, close the main Orders form, since you cannot make changes to the subform while it is open in the parent form.

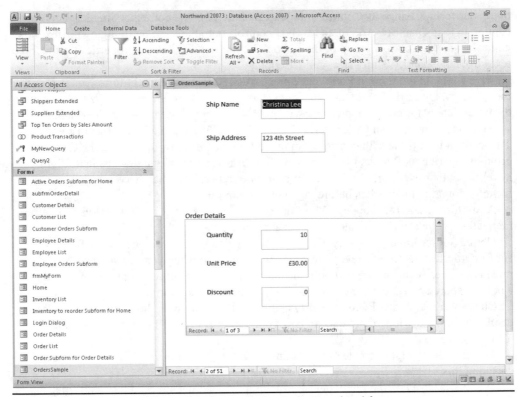

Figure 9-3 *Form View of the Orders form with the Order Details subform*

Open the Order Details subform in Design View. Set the Default View property to Datasheet View. Look at the form in Datasheet View mode to see how it looks. You can adjust the column widths by clicking the heading of the column and dragging the vertical border to one side. Make sure the Selection type of the Property Sheet is set to Form before looking at the Default View property.

Notice that the drop-down for products still works as before. Save the subform and close it. Open the Orders form again and you will see that your subform has now become a datasheet, as shown in Figure 9-4.

Users may find it easier to view the order details this way, since it is immediately apparent how many rows there are on each order.

Datasheet View

The Form view is ideal for a small number of records, such as the customer table, where the user is browsing from one customer to another.

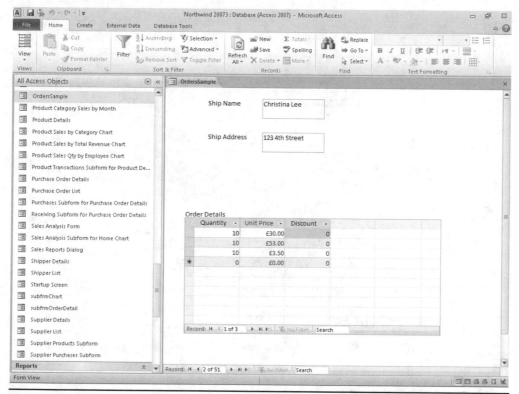

Figure 9-4   *Form View of the Orders form with the Order Details subform shown as a datasheet*

However, when the record source has many records, this can become tedious. If the form is displayed as a datasheet view, it will show the records in a columnar format, almost as if the user was looking at a table or spreadsheet of the data. See Figure 9-5 to see how this appears.

To make your form display as a datasheet, set the Default View property to Datasheet. There is also scope for preventing users seeing other views by setting properties like "Allow Form View" to No.

This format allows the user to see many records at once and to easily scroll through them. A further advantage is that the user can select all the records and copy and paste them into another application such as a spreadsheet.

If using a datasheet view, there is no need to align the text boxes and other controls on the form. The datasheet view uses the caption of the label control for each column heading. If the label control has been deleted, it will then use the name of the control itself.

The datasheet view uses the Tab Index property to order the columns. If you want to change the order, alter the Tab Index property to the number position. This will automatically renumber the other controls.

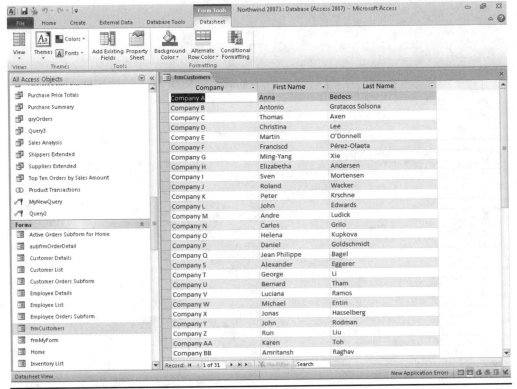

Figure 9-5   *Datasheet View of the form*

The Allow Datasheet View property on the form must be set to Yes for this view to be available.

Datasheet views are often used in subforms where the user browses through a set of main records and can then view the detail relating to an individual record.

Making Your Form Look Professional

You can make your form look cleaner by removing the record selector bar on the left-hand side of the form but keeping the navigation buttons at the bottom of the form. You do this by setting the Record Selector property on the form to No, but keeping the Navigation Button property set to Yes. Make sure the Selection type is Form before looking for the Record Selector. It is easy for the focus to jump to another object.

You will also find that it is quite difficult when dragging and sizing controls on the form to get the alignment and size uniform. Frequently, you end up with two text boxes, one of them slightly taller than the other.

Although this is very much cosmetic, users tend to home in on this kind of thing, and they expect all controls to be nicely aligned and uniformly sized! Fortunately, Microsoft provided some tools to help you with this.

View the form in Design View. Select all the controls you want to set to a uniform size and alignment by dragging a box across them with your mouse. Make sure that only the controls you want to resize are selected. They will all be shown with a colored outline and handles.

Click the Arrange tab in the ribbon. In the Sizing & Ordering group on the ribbon, you have an icon called Align to allow you to align all your controls to left, right, top, or bottom. This provides a drop-down of options. For example, if we have several text boxes that are displayed in a vertical row but do not line up vertically with each other, selecting them all and clicking the Left option of the drop-down will line them all up on the control that is furthest left within the selection.

This sorts out the alignment, but you may also have a situation where some are different widths or heights compared to others. In the same ribbon as for alignment is a Size/Space icon containing a drop-down for To Tallest, To Widest, To Shortest, To Narrowest. Click this and all the controls in the selection will be set to the same height or width according to the icon you clicked.

The Spacing options of the Size/Space drop-down allow you to set the gaps between controls using the Equal Horizontal and Equal Vertical icons. Controls can be easily moved in minute increments in any direction by selecting the control and holding down the CTRL key. If you then press any of the arrow keys while the CTRL key is held down, your control will slowly move in the desired direction. I have found this a really useful feature of Access in tidying up a form and making it look more presentable to the users.

You can also change the background color of the form and individual controls by setting the Back Color property. If you click the button with the three dots on it, you will see a palette of colors to choose from.

If you like, you can add a picture to the background of the form as well. The Picture property will allow you to upload a picture, which then becomes embedded in that form. This could be a picture associated with that form or a company logo. Remember, however, that pictures take up memory and too many can make your database unwieldy. Make sure the Selection type is Form before having the reader look for the Picture property in the Property Sheet.

If you need other text on the form, use a label control and change the Caption property to your text. As in all the controls, you can change the font, color, point size, and so on to suit your needs.

You can set the Close Button property to No in order to stop the user from using the Close button to exit your form. Bear in mind that you will need to provide them with another means of exiting if you do this. You can also use the Min Max Buttons property to prevent the user from changing the size of the form and you can do the same thing with the Control Box property.

Using a Custom Ribbon on the Form

When you design a form, it always looks like you are stuck with the standard Access ribbon, but this is far from the case. See Chapter 11 on how to design custom ribbons for particular forms. Once you have your ribbon designed, simply use the Ribbon Name property on the form to integrate it into your form. You can even remove the ribbon totally from a form using this methodology.

Other Controls

Many other controls can be used on a form, but the following are the main ones.

Button

The Command button control is very useful for directing the user to take a particular action. You may want to use the form as an opening form of options using command buttons, or you may want to allow the user to open another form on top of the existing one.

If you have disabled the Close button, you will need to place a Command button with an Exit command on the form. This could be because you wish to make certain updates before the user exits the form, and if they clicked the Close button they would circumvent your code.

To add a button to a form, you need to be in the form's Design view. Click the Design tab on the ribbon and drag the button icon onto the form. This will take you into the Command Button Wizard, as shown in Figure 9-6.

If you do not want to use the wizard to set up your button, click Cancel and you can change the properties, such as Caption, manually. However, the wizard does provide buttons

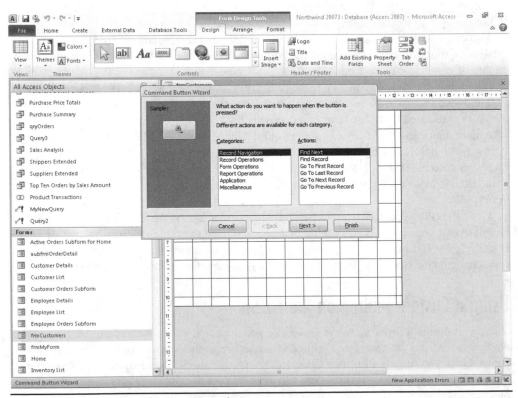

Figure 9-6 *The Command Button Wizard*

with some very nice icons on them, such as Close Form, and if you choose the wizard approach, you do not even have to write the code!

You can access the code behind the button by right-clicking the control and selecting Build Event from the pop-up. Select Code Builder in the next window. This will take you to the Visual Basic Editor window. Once you have done this, if you go back to your form and look in the Properties window for your new button, you will see that the On Click event property now reads [Event Procedure]. You can revisit the code by right-clicking the On Click property value and then clicking Build in the pop-up.

The sample code to close the current form would be:

```
Private Sub Mybutton_Click()
   DoCmd.Close

End Sub
```

List Box

The list box control works in a similar way to the combo box, but it displays a list of options that is never hidden. It is not as popular as the combo box because it can take up more room on the form.

It can be used in exactly the same way as the combo box by manipulating the same properties described earlier in this chapter. The advantage is that you do not have a Limit To List property since the user has no scope for input.

Image

The image control allows you to insert a picture into your form. If used, the picture becomes embedded in the form and the application, thus increasing the size of the file. This control can be very useful for displaying a company logo on each form to provide a corporate flavor.

Check Box

The check box control allows the user to check or uncheck a check box. You can easily find out what action the user has taken by reading the value property (which returns True or False):

```
Private Sub Detail_Click()
If Me.MyCheckBox.Value Then
    MsgBox "Box is checked"
Else
    MsgBox "Box is unchecked"

End If

End Sub
```

You can also set the Default Value property for the control to 0 or −1 to give it a starting value. This can also be changed by setting the value property using VBA.

Option Buttons

Option buttons are sometimes known as radio buttons because as you click one in a group of option buttons, the others are deselected and lose their black buttons. These are more complicated to set up and code than the simple check box. Their advantage is that the user can only select one option.

First, you must put an Option Group control onto your form. To do this, put the form into Design View mode and drag the Option Group icon from the Controls Group of the ribbon. This icon is found on the top row, third icon from the left. Size it to what you need for the number of options and provide a title for it in the corresponding label box, which is added automatically.

It is very important that you add the Options Group control first before you add the Option Button controls. This is because you cannot add an Option button that was added prior to the Options Group into an Option Group. Seems rather strange, but that is the way it is.

You can now add in the Option buttons. To do this, use the Option Button icon in the Controls Group of the ribbon, which is on the bottom row, third icon from the left.

If you view your form in Form View mode, you will see that as you click each button, the others go out. Thus, it is only possible to have one button in the group set.

To use VBA to interpret which option button is live, you can use the following code:

```
MsgBox MyOptionGroup.Value
```

This will return 1 if the first button is set, 2 if the second button is set, and so on.

You can set a default button by setting the Default Value of the Option Group control to the number of the button. If you want the second button in the group to be the default, set the Default Value property to 2.

Tab Control

The Tab Control allows you to use tabbed pages on a form and is very useful if you are running out of space on a form. I have certainly written applications where there has been so much information displayed on a form that the tabbed sheets were the only answer.

The Tab Control icon is on the top row of the Controls Group in the ribbon, fifth icon from the left in Full Screen mode. It is a case of populating it with controls as if it was a form. However, one problem is that you cannot use drag-and-drop to do this. If you do, in the Design window it looks as if your control has ended up on the Tab Control page, but when you look at the form in Form View mode, you will not see it because it is sitting behind the Tab Control.

To put controls onto the Tab Control, you must first drag them onto an empty part of your form. You then use cut and paste to move them from the form and to the Tab Control.

You can select the tabs in Design mode by clicking them. To insert and delete pages, right-click the Tab Control and select the appropriate option from the pop-up menu. To change the name of the tab, right-click the selected tab and choose Properties. You can now give the Caption property its new name. The controls on the tabbed control can be used in VBA just as if they were on the form itself.

Using VBA on Forms

Up till now, this chapter has looked at how to build forms and bind the controls to the underlying data. Although this is not directly connected with VBA, it is a very necessary part of building an Access application.

However, forms also have their own modules and there is a whole event-driven structure both for the form and the controls on it. As you have already seen, the form and controls have a rich collection of properties, which allows an enormous amount of manipulation, letting you change what the user sees according to certain circumstances.

Opening Your Form in VBA

The initial form in an Access application is usually opened by setting the Display form property of the Current Database. You do this by clicking the File tab in ribbon and clicking the Access Options button at the bottom of the pop-up.

In the next pop-up, select Current Database in the pane on the left-hand side. In the Application options section, there is a drop-down for Display Form that lists all the available forms. Select your opening form, and this will automatically load when the database opens.

To load other forms, use the OpenForm method of the DoCmd object (see Chapter 16 for more information on this object).

```
DoCmd.OpenForm _
(FormName,View,FilterName,WhereCondition,DataMode,WindowMode,OpenArgs)
```

The FormName is a required parameter, but the others are optional:

▶ **View**   An acFormView constant that specifies the view that the form will open in. This is acNormal by default.

▶ **FilterName**   The name of a query in the current database.

▶ **WhereCondition**   An SQL WHERE clause without the word WHERE.

▶ **DataMode**   An acFormOpenDataMode constant that specifies the data entry mode for the form.

▶ **WindowMode**   An acWindowMode constant that specifies the window that the form opens in.

▶ **OpenArgs**   This sets the form's OpenArgs property.

You can also use the Close method of the DoCmd object to close the form when it is finished.

Using Events

When a user opens your form, browses through it, deletes records, edits records, adds records, and closes the form, they are constantly firing off events that can be put to use in VBA. Some of these events can be confusing when they are fired off and sometimes it is a good idea to put a simple message box into each event so you can see when it actually happens.

You can view the events by right-clicking the form in Design mode and then clicking Build Event in the pop-up. Click Code Builder and this will take you into the module for that form.

In the drop-down in the top left-hand corner of the module pane (that usually reads Detail), select Form. In the drop-down in the right-hand corner of the module pane, you will be able to access all the events. The following are the main events you are likely to use:

Activate

The Activate event happens when the user activates the form by putting the focus onto it. It is not the same as the Open or Load event, since the form may already be displayed but does not have the focus.

After/Before Delete Confirm

After Delete Confirm and Before Delete Confirm events are fired off before and after a user deletes a record on the form. A Confirm message box is displayed automatically before the record deletion is confirmed.

Strangely enough, the Delete Record icon is not shown in the standard ribbon when a form is displayed. You need to customize the toolbar to show this, or write your own routine using a command button on the form.

You can disable the warnings by using:

```
Docmd.SetWarnings False
```

You can then use these events to display your own warning messages if required and take your own action:

```
Private Sub Form_BeforeDelConfirm(Cancel As Integer, Response As Integer)
x = MsgBox("Are you sure that you wish to delete this record?")
If x = vbNo Then Cancel = True
End Sub
```

You can also use the Before event to validate the deletion. In one application I wrote, there was a rule that the user could not delete the only record in a particular table. If there was only one record left, a message had to be displayed and the action canceled.

If the user deletes a record in a particular table, you may also want to delete related records in other tables that are orphaned by the first deletion. You can write code in the After Delete Confirm event to do this. For example, if the user deletes an order, you would also want to delete the order details that went with it.

After/Before Insert

After Insert and Before Insert events are fired off before and after an insert of a new record. No warning message is provided, such as in the case of a deletion. So you may wish to provide an "Are you sure message" on the Before Insert event:

```
Private Sub Form_BeforeInsert(Cancel As Integer)
x = MsgBox("Are you sure that you wish to create a new record?")
If x = vbNo Then Cancel = True
End Sub
```

You may want to use the After Insert event to create a child record in another table that is related to the new record being created.

After/Before Update

After Update and Before Update events are fired off before and after the update of a record. No warning message is provided, such as in the case of a deletion, so you may wish to provide an "Are you sure message" on the Before Update event:

```
Private Sub Form_BeforeUpdate(Cancel As Integer)
x = MsgBox("Are you sure that you wish to amend this record?")
If x = vbNo Then Cancel = True
End Sub
```

You may want to use the After Update event to amend child records in another table related to this parent record.

Click

A Click event is fired off when the user clicks the mouse somewhere on the form. Do not forget that controls also have their own on-click events so you need to guard against where the user is clicking.

Close

The Close event happens when the form is closed, either by the user clicking the Close button, or through your own code. You may use this event to open another form by using:

```
Private Sub Form_Close()
DoCmd.OpenForm ("MyForm")
End Sub
```

Current

The On Current event occurs when the user moves to a record, which then becomes the current record, or when the form is re-queried or refreshed. From its name, it is easy to confuse it with the Load event.

Load

The Load event occurs when the form is opened and its records are displayed.

Open

The Open event differs from the Load event in that the Open event does not occur until the form query has been run. At this point, your form has data on it and your code can interact with it, whereas when a load event occurs, the controls have not been populated.

Timer

The Timer event is useful if you want to run a procedure at a fixed time interval, such as re-querying the form so that the data is not stale due to the actions of other users:

```
Private Sub Form_Timer()
Me.Requery

End Sub
```

The Me object used here refers to the current form. This is explained in more detail in Chapter 15.

You need to set the Timer Interval in the form properties sheet. It is set to 0 by default (which means it never runs). It is measured in milliseconds and the maximum value is 65536 which equates to about a minute. Do not set this to a very low figure (below 1000) since your timed procedure will then be constantly running and no one will be able to use the form.

Reports

A report is very similar in some ways to a form in that it is based on a table or query. It contains controls similar to the form—usually text boxes and labels.

You define a single row in the report using controls and add in sorting, grouping, headers, and footers. When the report is run, your single row definition then repeats throughout the report giving the user a means of viewing and printing data. Reports are different from forms in that they do not usually form a user interface.

Creating a Simple Report

This section will show you how to create a simple report, similar to the form we created earlier based on the orders, order detail, and products tables in the Northwind database.

First, you need to create a query to drive the report. Click the Create tab in the ribbon and then click the Query Design icon in the Macros & Code group of the ribbon.

For the query, select the tables for Orders, Order Details, and Products. Access will automatically make the joins between the key fields in the tables. You may need to edit the join between Orders and Order Details so it shows a straight join instead of a left join.

Include the fields Order ID, Ship Name, Ship Address, Product Name, and Quantity in the output of the query. Your Query Design window should now look like Figure 9-7.

Make sure the query runs correctly and returns records. Save the query and close the Query Design window.

Select the Create tab on the ribbon and click the Report Wizard icon in the Reports group of the ribbon. I am personally not a great fan of wizards because they can often end up doing something you do not want to do. However, for me, the Report Wizard is the exception, and I have found that it can produce very professional looking results quickly with sorting and grouping all arranged. Once you have the report produced in this way, you can then easily amend it to what you need.

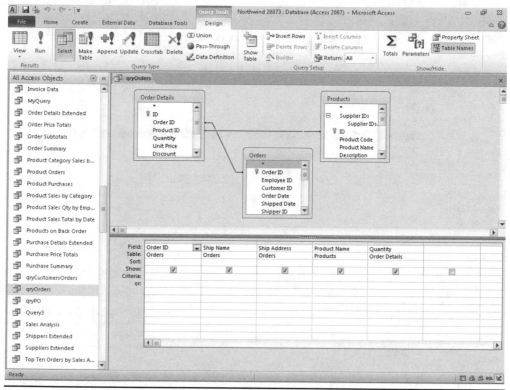

Figure 9-7   *Query Design window for a report query*

On the opening screen of the wizard, select your new query on the drop-down. You should have four possible fields showing (Ship Name, Ship Address, Product Name, and Quantity). Include all of these in the report. Then, do the following:

1. On the next screen, accept the default of Orders by which to view the data.
2. On the next screen, group by Ship Name.
3. On the next screen, use the drop-down to select Product Name for the sort order.
4. Click the Summary Options button and note that you can have a calculation on the Quantity field since this is the only numeric field on the report. For the purposes of this example, we will not use a calculation here, so close this window.
5. On the layout and style screens of the wizard, accept the defaults.
6. Preview the report, which should now look like Figure 9-8.

The wizard has produced a very professional looking report, probably better than if you had tried to do it manually.

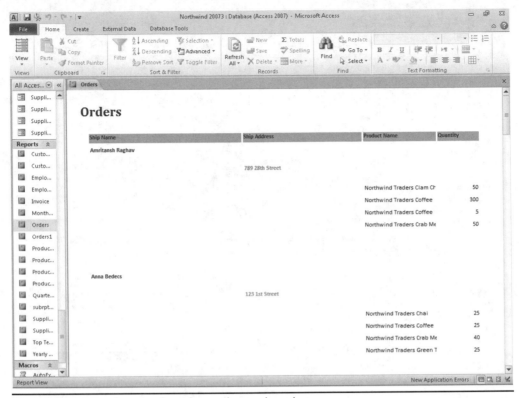

Figure 9-8 *A simple report based on orders and products*

Keeping Your Report Tidy

The wizard has produced for you a pristine looking report, but users will often later make requests that extra fields be added or existing fields be relocated. As a result, your tidy report can start looking rather messy and suddenly things do not quite line up correctly.

You will also find that it is quite difficult when dragging and sizing controls on the form to get the alignment and size uniform. Because of this, frequently you end up with two text boxes, one of which is slightly taller than the other.

Although this is very much cosmetic, users tend to home in on this kind of thing and expect all the controls to be nicely aligned and uniformly sized!

Fortunately, Microsoft provided some tools to help you with this.

View the form in Design View. Select all the controls you want to set to a uniform size and alignment by dragging a box across them with your mouse. Check that only the controls that you want to resize are selected. They will all be shown with a colored outline and handles.

Click the Arrange tab in the ribbon. In the Control Alignment group on the ribbon, you have icons to allow you to align all your controls to left, right, top, or bottom. For example, if we have several text boxes that are displayed in a vertical row, but do not line up vertically with each other, clicking the Left icon will line them all up on the control that is furthest left within the selection.

This sorts out the alignment, but you may then have a situation where some are different widths or heights compared to others. In the same ribbon used for alignment, you have a Size group containing icons for To Tallest, To Widest, To Shortest, and To Narrowest. Click this and all the controls in the selection will be set to the same height or width according to the icon you clicked.

The Position group of the ribbon allows you to set the gaps between controls using the Equal Horizontal and Equal Vertical icons.

Controls can be easily moved in minute increments in any direction by selecting the control and holding down the CTRL key. If you then press any of the arrow keys while the CTRL key is held down, your control will slowly move in the desired direction.

I have found this a really handy feature in Access for tidying up a report and making it look more professional to the users.

You can also change the background color of the report and individual controls by setting the Back Color property. If you are changing the background color of the report, you need to click each section of the report (Report Header, Page Header, Section Header, Detail, and so on) to change the background color. If you click the button with the three dots on it, in the Background Color property you will see a palette of colors to choose from.

You can also add a picture to the background of the report. The Picture property will allow you to upload a picture, which then becomes embedded in that form. This could be a picture associated with that form or a company logo. However, remember that pictures take up memory and too many can make your database unwieldy.

The picture property is on the overall report object itself, instead of the individual sections (as in background color). You need to set the Picture Tiling property to Yes to make the picture repeat down the length of the report. This feature can be very useful for adding a company logo, although there is a danger of it detracting from the information on the report.

If you need other text on the report, use a label control and change the Caption property to your text. As in all the controls, you can change the font, color, point size, and so on to suit your needs.

You can set the Close Button property to No in order to stop the user using the Close button to exit your report. Bear in mind that you will need to provide them with another means of exiting if you do this.

You can also use the Min Max Buttons property to stop the user from changing the size of the report, and do the same thing with the Control Box property.

Using Formulas on Your Report

A feature of reports is that you can include formulas to provide totals and other user information.

View the Orders report that you created in the previous section in Design mode. Right-click the horizontal gray bar for "Ship Name Header" and click Sorting and Grouping. Your screen should now look like Figure 9-9 with a sorting and grouping pane at the bottom of the design window for your report.

Click More and an orange submenu will display. Click the Footer Section drop-down (the last item on the submenu) and change this to "with a footer section."

Close the Sorting and Grouping section. Notice there is an extra section in your report called "Ship Name Footer." This footer is displayed every time the Ship Name changes.

Drag a text box onto your new footer section. Line it up with the Quantity box in the Detail section. Display the properties sheet for this text box and enter **=Sum([quantity])** into the Control source property. Set the corresponding label to read "Total."

Drag another text box onto your new header section but align it to the left-hand side of the report. Make the size of the box fairly wide. On the properties sheet set the control source to: **="Summary for " & "'Ship Name' = " & " " & [Ship Name] & " (" & Count(*) & " " & IIf(Count(*)=1,"detail record","detail records") & ")"**

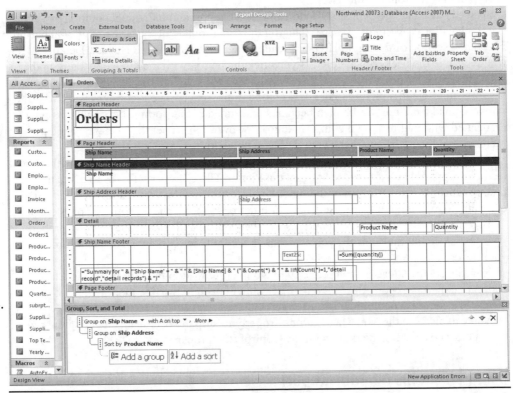

Figure 9-9   *The Report Design window with sorting and grouping shown*

This expression concatenates text and field names and functions to produce a single text statement for use on the report. For example, [Ship Name] is a field name within the Record Source, and the function Count(*) will provide the number of records in the section. The IIf function is used to differentiate between "detail record" for one record and "detail records" for several.

Delete the corresponding label since it is not needed in this case.

View your report in Report View mode. It should now look like Figure 9-10.

Your text boxes with formulas in them now display details for each Ship Name in the report.

You have probably noticed it is quite a time-consuming job adding in new sections of the report and adding in formulas. This is why it is a very good idea to let the Report Wizard do the initial hard work in creating your report, and then afterward you can customize it.

Using a Custom Ribbon on the Report

When you design a report, it always looks like you are stuck with the standard Access ribbon when it is displayed, but this is far from the case. See Chapter 11 on how to design custom

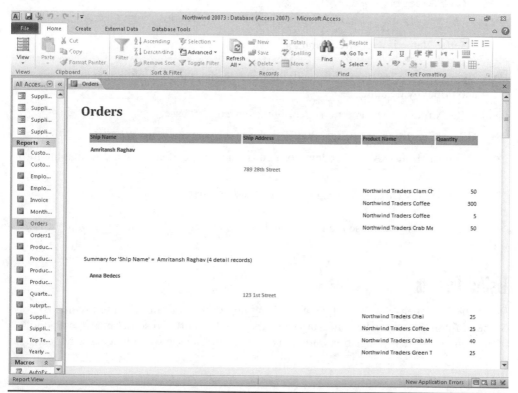

Figure 9-10   *Utilizing formulas with your report*

ribbons for particular reports. Once you have your ribbon designed, you simply use the Ribbon Name property on the report to integrate it into your report.

You can even remove the ribbon totally on a form using this methodology

Using VBA on Forms

VBA is not so common on reports as on forms due to the fact that the form is a means for the user to view and print data. There is not normally user interaction once the report has been displayed except for the user taking action to print out a hard copy.

However, reports also have their own modules and there is a whole event-driven structure both for the report and the controls on it. As you have already seen, reports and controls have a rich collection of properties, which allows an enormous amount of manipulation, letting you change what the user sees according to certain circumstances.

Opening Your Report in VBA

To load a report, use the OpenReport method of the DoCmd object (see Chapter 16 for more information on this object).

```
DoCmd.OpenReport _
(ReportName,View,FilterName,WhereCondition,WindowMode,OpenArgs)
```

The ReportName is a required parameter, but the others are optional:

▶ **View**   An acView constant specifying the view that the form will open in. This is acNormal by default.

▶ **FilterName**   The name of a query in the current database.

▶ **WhereCondition**   An SQL WHERE clause without the word WHERE.

▶ **WindowMode**   An acWindowMode constant that specifies the window that the form opens in.

▶ **OpenArgs**   This sets the report's OpenArgs property.

You can also use the Close method of the DoCmd object to close the report when it is finished.

Using Events

When the user opens your report, they are firing off events that can be put to use in VBA. Some of these events can be confusing when they are fired off and sometimes it is a good idea to put a simple message box into each event so you can see when it actually happens.

You can view the events by right-clicking the report in Design mode and then clicking Build Event in the pop-up. Click Code Builder and this will take you into the module for that report.

In the drop-down at the top-left corner of the module pane (that usually reads ReportHeader or ReportDetail), select Report. In the drop-down in the right-hand corner of the module pane, you will be able to access all the events.

The following are the main events you are likely to use:

Activate

The Activate event happens when the user activates the report by putting the focus on it. It is not the same as the Open or Load event, since the report may already be displayed but does not have the focus.

Click

The Click event is fired off when the user clicks the mouse somewhere on the report. Do not forget that controls also have their own on-click events, so you need to guard against where the user is clicking.

Close

The close event happens when the report is closed, either by the user clicking the Close button, or through your own code. You may use this event to open another form by using:

```
Private Sub Report_Close()
DoCmd.OpenReport ("MyReport")
End Sub
```

Current

The Current event occurs when the user clicks a new row within the report. From its name, it is easy to confuse it with the Load event because this means that you are selecting a new record on the form instead of actually loading the form.

Load

The Load event occurs when the report is opened and its data is displayed.

Open

The Open event differs from the Load event in that the Open event does not occur until the report query has been run. At this point, your report has data on it and your code can interact with it, whereas when a Load event occurs, the controls have not been populated.

Print

A Print event is fired off when a report is printed out. This can be used to keep a log of who printed the report out and when.

Timer

The Timer is a useful event if you want to run a procedure at a fixed time interval, such as re-querying the report so the data is not stale due to the actions of other users:

```
Private Sub Report_Timer()
Me.Requery

End Sub
```

You need to set the Timer Interval in the report properties sheet. It is set to 0 by default (which means it never runs). It is measured in milliseconds and the maximum value is 65536, which equates to about a minute. Do not set this to a very low figure (below 1000) since your timed procedure will then be constantly running and no one will be able to use the report.

Common Dialog Control

Using API calls (see Chapter 20 for more information), you can access the standard Microsoft dialogs for opening files, saving files, printing, and selecting colors. All the dialogs for these purposes that you see in standard Microsoft applications are yours for the taking to use within your own programs.

By using particular API calls, you can choose what dialog to display and be able to set various parameters to alter the appearance of the dialog to suit the purpose of your program. Even better, you can then retrieve the parameters that the user has selected and have your code act on them accordingly. For example, if the user selects a file to open, you can easily find out the file and pathname, and write the code accordingly.

An important point is that these are only dialogs to provide a common interface to the user. You must still write the code to handle the selections or events that the user chooses; it does not happen automatically. For example, if you display the Save dialog, and the user types a filename and presses OK, nothing will happen unless you have written the code to collect the filename chosen and the code to save the data to that filename.

Microsoft provides an important helping hand here so you do not have to reinvent the wheel to provide common user interface components. However, you still have to do some of the work in selecting the options that will be available on the dialogs and interpreting what to do with the user's selection.

In all the following examples, you will need to create a form with a button to call the various procedures. You do this by selecting Create in the Access menu and then clicking the Form Design Icon in the Forms group of the ribbon. Click Design in the Access menu and drag a command button from the Controls group of the ribbon onto your form. Dismiss the wizard dialog by clicking Cancel. It is assumed in all the following examples that this button object is called Command0.

The Open File Dialog

The first thing you need to do is enter the module for the form you have created by right-clicking the form, selecting Build Event from the pop-up menu, and then choosing Code Builder. This will take you into the VBE window for that form.

Enter the following code into the module in the definitions section at the top:

```
Private Declare Function GetOpenFileName Lib "comdlg32.dll" Alias _
        "GetOpenFileNameA" (pOpenfilename As OPENFILENAME) As Long

  Private Type OPENFILENAME
        lStructSize As Long
        hwndOwner As Long
        hInstance As Long
        lpstrFilter As String
        lpstrCustomFilter As String
        nMaxCustFilter As Long
        nFilterIndex As Long
        lpstrFile As String
        nMaxFile As Long
        lpstrFileTitle As String
        nMaxFileTitle As Long
        lpstrInitialDir As String
        lpstrTitle As String
        flags As Long
        nFileOffset As Integer
        nFileExtension As Integer
        lpstrDefExt As String
        lCustData As Long
        lpfnHook As Long
        lpTemplateName As String
End Type
```

The purpose of this is to declare the API function called GetOpenFileName and to create a new data type called OPENFILENAME. The data type is used to hold variables to manipulate the Open File control.

You then need to create a subroutine to use the API call to display the Open Form dialog and to return the selection the user has made. Add the following code to your module:

```
Private Sub ShowFileDialog()
    Dim MyFile As OPENFILENAME
    Dim ReturnValue As Long
    Dim strFilter As String
    MyFile.lStructSize = Len(MyFile)
    MyFile.hwndOwner = Me.hwnd
```

```
        strFilter = "Text Files (*.txt)" & Chr(0) & "*.TXT" & Chr(0)
        MyFile.lpstrFilter = strFilter
        MyFile.nFilterIndex = 1
        MyFile.lpstrFile = String(257, 0)
        MyFile.nMaxFile = Len(MyFile.lpstrFile) - 1
        MyFile.lpstrFileTitle = MyFile.lpstrFile
        MyFile.nMaxFileTitle = MyFile.nMaxFile
        MyFile.lpstrInitialDir = "C:\"
        MyFile.lpstrTitle = "Select a File"
        MyFile.flags = 0
        ReturnValue = GetOpenFileName(MyFile)
        If ReturnValue = 0 Then
            MsgBox "Cancel Button was pressed"
        Else
            MsgBox MyFile.lpstrFile
        End If
End Sub
```

This procedure sets up a variable called MyFile based on the data type OPENFILENAME and variables to hold the return value from the API call and a string value to hold the filter for the file selection. The MyFile object is then populated with the parameters needed to display the file dialog such as flags, initial directory, and title. The dialog box is then called by using the function GetOpenFileName based on the variable of MyFile. This populates the variable ReturnValue, which holds True or False depending on whether a file was selected. If the file was selected, the variable MyFile.lpstrfile returns the name.

Notice that the handle property (hwnd) of your form is used to populate Myfile.hwndOwner. This is why the API call has to work from a form or report.

You can also change the filter to the needs of your application very easily. Currently, this sets it to text files only, but this can be changed to other options. This is so that when the dialog opens you can restrict it to certain types of files such as text. This is important if you are using the dialog to allow the user to select a file for importing into your database.

This procedure also supplies the starting folder and provides a title for the dialog. Finally, the API call is made, placing a value into the variable ReturnValue. If this value is zero, then the user pressed the Cancel button, but if it had a value, then a file was selected that is held in MyFile.lpstrFile.

You then call this subroutine from your command button. This assumes you have added the following code to a module and that the command button you are using is called Command0:

```
Private Sub Command0_Click()
ShowFileDialog
End Sub
```

Bear in mind that the dialog only selects the file for you. You will need to write further code to open and process the file.

The Save File As Dialog

The Save File As dialog works in almost exactly same way as the preceding Open dialog example, but the title (MyFile.lpstrTitle) needs to be changed to a different string, such as "Select a file to Save to."

The parameters are set in exactly the same way as the Open File example mentioned earlier and the user will be prompted to browse to a file or to enter in a new file name. The file name selected is captured in the variable MyFile.lpstrfile in the same way, and you can then write code to save the data to that file name.

The Color Dialog

The Color dialog allows the user to select a color from a palette or create and select a custom color, as shown in Figure 10-1.

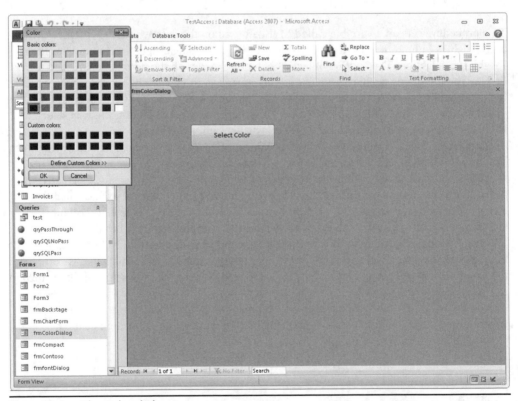

Figure 10-1 *The Color dialog*

The first thing you need to do is enter the module for the form you have created by right-clicking the form, selecting Build Event from the pop-up menu, and then choosing Code Builder. This will take you into the VBE window for that form.

Enter the following code into the module:

```
Private Declare Function ChooseColor _
    Lib "comdlg32.dll" Alias "ChooseColorA" _
    (pChoosecolor As COLORSTRUC) As Long


Private Type COLORSTRUC
    lStructSize As Long
    hwnd As Long
    hInstance As Long
    rgbResult As Long
    lpCustColors As String
    Flags As Long
    lCustData As Long
    lpfnHook As Long
    lpTemplateName As String
End Type
```

This code creates the declaration for the API call ChooseColor and creates a data type called COLORSTRUC to hold the parameters to display the Color dialog.

You then need to add code to create a procedure to display the Color dialog and to return the color selected:

```
Private Sub ShowColorDialog()
    Dim x As Long, CSel As COLORSTRUC, CustColor(16) As Long

    CSel.lStructSize = Len(CSel)
    CSel.hwnd = Me.hwnd
    CSel.Flags = &H80
    CSel.lpCustColors = String$(16 * 4, 0)
    x = ChooseColor(CSel)
    If x = 0 Then
      MsgBox "The user pressed Cancel"
    Else

        MsgBox CSel.rgbResult
    End If

End Sub
```

Notice that the handle property (hwnd) of your form is used to populate CSel.hwnd. This is why the API call has to work from a form or report.

The API call is made, returning a value into the variable x. If the return value is zero, then the user canceled the operation, but if there is a return value, then the selected color value can be found in CSel.rgbresult.

By calling ShowColorDialog from anywhere within your form code, you can make the Color dialog appear and allow the user to select a color.

Notice that the color is returned as an RGB value. You can use this for any color property on the form, such as:

```
Me.Detail.BackColor = 47456
```

This will set the BackColor property to the choice that the user made in your dialog.

The Print Dialog

The Print dialog is remarkably easy to display and has the added advantage that you do not need to write any code to do the printing!

```
DoCmd.RunCommand acCmdPrintSelection
```

This simple command will display the standard Print dialog and allow the user to select what will be printed and choose a printer. It can be run from anywhere in your code.

Unfortunately, the RunCommand method cannot be used for all dialogs, which is why the File Open, Save File As, and Color dialogs have been created using API calls. Also, using API calls, you can obtain information on the user's selection, which you cannot do from the RunCommand method.

Working with
the Ribbon

In Office 2007, an important change happened with the user interface. The ribbon style menu structure superseded the previous menu structure. This probably had the greatest impact on the user, since it defines how the user navigates through the Office menu structure for each application.

If you use Access 2010/2007 already, then you will have come across the ribbon since you access all the menu functions in a totally different and sometimes confusing way. Fortunately, the VBA Editor window has maintained the same menu structure we all know and love, so you can still use your accumulated knowledge here.

A number of Access VBA developers are producing Access add-ins that emulate the Access classical menu. After reading this book, you may want to try your luck at doing the same.

The ribbon opens up a whole new way of programming the user interface. With Access 2003 and previous editions, you could create a menu structure for a form by using a macro (non-VBA type). This is still there for purposes of backward-compatibility, but your menu now appears in a menu option called Add Ins, while the rest of the ribbon structure remains as is.

The ribbon has meant learning a completely new way of creating a custom user interface. In Access, it is slightly more difficult than the other Office components, such as Excel and Word, because Access does not use the XML format for saving files.

You can customize the ribbon in Access 2010 by using the backstage view on the File tab of the Access menu, but from a programming point of view it is better to work directly with the XML source.

The ribbon is defined using XML. Because you cannot insert this straight into an XML file for Access, you need to create a system table called USysRibbons. This table can hold the definition for many menus and ribbons so they can be used on different forms and reports and also as the default ribbon when the database is opened.

When the Access file is opened and you have a USysRibbons table set up, Access reads in the XML code for the ribbon specified and applies your custom structure. You can specify the name of a default ribbon for the whole database by clicking the File tab, clicking Options in the left-hand pane, and then selecting Current Database in the left-hand pane of the pop-up window. In the Ribbon and Toolbar options, you will see a drop-down for Ribbon Name. This will show all the ribbon names you have included in your USysRibbons table.

The custom structure can be manipulated at runtime using VBA code, and you can also make use of the predefined structure of the ribbon.

For a first-time user, it looks frightening, but fortunately Microsoft has provided a tool to help you and make life easy. You can also find help at the official MSDN web site at http://msdn.microsoft.com/en-gb/office/aa905530.aspx.

This contains a very useful download file of all the control IDs in the Office ribbon, and since there are over 1,700 of them, it is very useful for reference purposes. You can also access a number of technical articles on this page.

Creating a Ribbon Customization

To create a custom ribbon, you must first create a system table called USysRibbons within an open database. To do this, click Create on the Access menu bar and then click the Table Design icon in the Tables group of the ribbon.

You need to create two fields in the new table. The first is called RibbonName and is a text field to hold the name you give to your custom ribbon. The second field is called RibbonXML and this needs to be set to a memo field. Your table design window should now look like Figure 11-1.

Save the table with the name of USysRibbons. You do not need a primary key on this table. You will not see it appear in the navigation pane on the left-hand side of the Access window unless you enable the view of system tables. To do this, right-click the bar at the very top of the navigation pane and select Navigation Options. In the Display Options section of the pop-up window, check the box for Show System Objects. Click OK and your new table will appear.

Open USysRibbons for data entry by double-clicking it. In the field RibbonName, enter a name for your custom ribbon such as MyRibbon. In the RibbonXML field, you need to enter the XML code for the ribbon. The following sample XML can be used to remove the ribbon completely. The File tab will still be visible because this is part of the Backstage view, not the ribbon. The Backstage view allows you to open and close databases, set the Access default options, and provide information about the current database.

```
<customUI xmlns="http://schemas.microsoft.com/office/2006/01/customui">
<ribbon startFromScratch="true">
</ribbon>
</customUI>
```

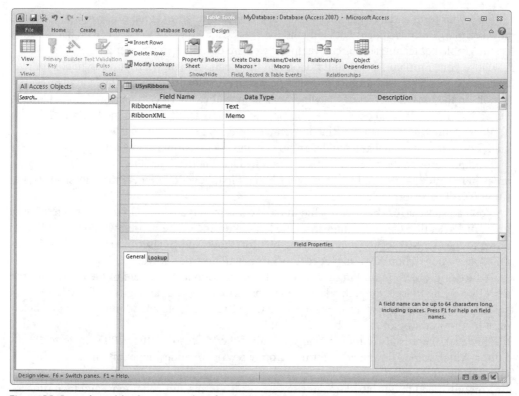

Figure 11-1   *The table design window for the USysRibbons table*

The URL used in the preceding code could possibly change in the future, but this is highly unlikely. It is a standard URL used in sample ribbons on the Microsoft web site and is built into the Microsoft Custom UI Editor (see "Using The Custom UI Editor" later in this chapter).

You have now entered a definition for a custom ribbon. Close the table and Exit the database completely. Reload your database so that Access will now pick up this new system table. This is a system table and will not show in the Navigation pane unless you set it to show system tables using Navigation Options. To do this, right-click All Access Objects at the top of the Navigation pane and select Navigation Options from the pop-up menu. Check the box for System Objects and click OK.

Create a new form by clicking Create in the Access menu and then click the Blank Form icon in the Forms group of the ribbon.

Change the form view to Design View by clicking the View drop-down in the Views group of the ribbon. Right-click the form and select Properties. On the drop-down (Selection Type) at the top of the property windows, select Form. Scroll down to the Ribbon Name property and enter the value "MyRibbon" (or whatever you called your ribbon) in this property. This should be visible in the drop-down for this property.

Save your form and then click the Form view icon in the Views group of the ribbon. You will now see that your form opens with only the file (backstage) option visible. The Navigation pane is still visible but techniques to remove this as well are described in Chapter 24.

Close your form and the default ribbon and the menu will reappear. You can make your custom ribbon the default ribbon for your Access application by clicking the Windows Start button (in the top-left corner of the window) and then clicking Access Options. Click Current Database in the left-hand pane of the pop-up window and scroll down to the Ribbon and Toolbar Options section. In the Ribbon Name drop-down, select your custom ribbon and click OK. Close the database and then reopen it and your custom ribbon will appear.

Working through the preceding process, you will have noticed that there are a few problem areas in this method of building your own ribbon. First, how do you get error messages if the ribbon XML is incorrect?

You can show errors by clicking file in the Access menu, clicking Options in the left-hand pane, and selecting Client Settings from the left-hand pane of the pop-up window. Scroll down to the General section and check the box for Show Add-in User Interface Errors. Click OK. Once your ribbon XML is loaded, any errors will now be shown.

A further problem is working with the XML in the RibbonXML field of the table. This is a bit like trying to look through a keyhole at what will become a large piece of XML. One solution is to design a new form bound to the USysRibbons table and to put a large text box on it to allow editing of the RibbonXML field.

However, there is also a tool to help you, called the Microsoft Office 2007 Custom UI Editor, which can be downloaded for free from www.openxmldeveloper.org/articles/CustomUIeditor.aspx.

You only need to download it, agree to Microsoft's terms and conditions, and then run the installer. If you work in a corporate environment, you will need permission from your employer to download this. (I have worked in companies where you can be dismissed for downloading applications from the Internet.)

Strictly speaking, this tool is really for use with XML files from Excel or Word, but you can develop your XML code in here, using all the error checking and call back facilities and then copy and paste the XML into the RibbonXML field of your USysRibbons table.

By the way, there is no limit to the number of custom ribbons you can create within the USysRibbons table.

Using the Custom UI Editor

After you have installed the Custom UI Editor, click the Windows Start button and click All Programs. You will see a new program called Custom UI Editor for Microsoft Office. Click this and you will see the opening screen as shown in Figure 11-2.

The interface is very simple and allows you to edit the ribbon on all Office 2010 documents. However, we are only interested in Access.

An advantage of the editor is that it has built-in error checking for your XML. Simply click the red tick icon in the editor toolbar (four icons from the left) and your XML will be validated, with error messages displayed as to where the problems are.

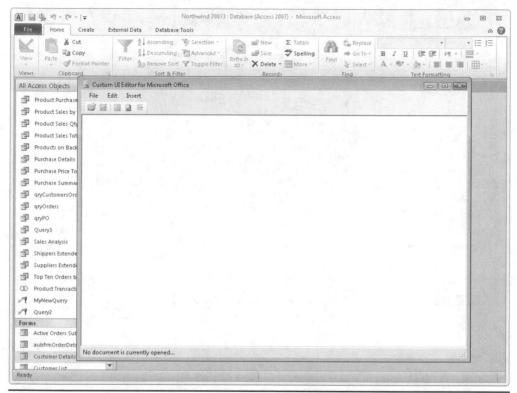

Figure 11-2 *The opening screen of the Custom UI Editor for Microsoft Office*

Microsoft has very helpfully provided a sample ribbon customization for Excel in this application. To make this work, you must first load in a standard Excel 2007/2010 XML file by using File | Open from the menu. Next, click Insert | Sample XML | Excel – A Custom Tab. Why are we using Excel? Because there is no sample XML for Access, and as it happens the Excel sample also works quite well in Access! The XML code shown in the Excel example will help familiarize you with how to construct a ribbon before you start experimenting on your own.

Your screen will now look like Figure 11-3. You can see a whole load of XML code, which will provide a customization for the ribbon. A change you will need to make is in the fourth row of the code. TabHome needs to be changed to TabHomeAccess in the InsertAfterMso parameter. You also need to change GroupFont to GroupFontAccess in the sixth row.

Copy and paste the XML into the RibbonXML field in your USysRibbons table. One of the annoying things about this table is that changes do not take place until the database has been closed and reopened, so you must now do this.

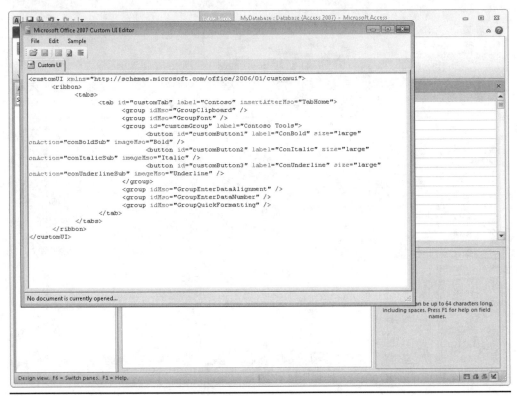

Figure 11-3 *The XML screen for a custom ribbon*

When you open the form where you referenced the ribbon name property to this record, you will see that an extra entry now appears on the menu called Contoso. Your screen should look like Figure 11-4. If you click this, you will see a ribbon with three groups in it.

The first and second groups that you see are exact copies of existing ribbon groups. The Copy group is exactly the same as if you had clicked Home on the menu and then looked at the group Copy. Similarly, the new Font group is exactly as shown when you click Home on the menu and see the Font group. This part shows how you can leverage existing ribbon functionality to build a custom ribbon.

The third group in your new ribbon is a custom group, and this shows the real power of the ribbon. By looking at the XML, you can see that three buttons have been created: **ConBold**, **ConItalic**, and **ConUnderline**.

If you try clicking any of these buttons, you will receive an error message stating Access cannot run the macro. This is a piece of code defined by the **onAction** parameter, and at the moment this does not exist.

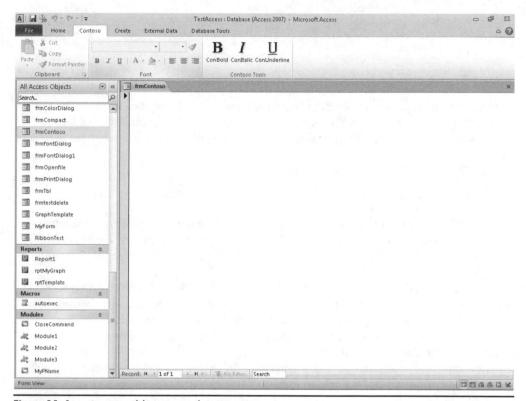

Figure 11-4   *Custom ribbon control Contoso*

Take some time to look through this sample piece of XML and see how it is constructed. The code is shown here:

```
<customUI xmlns="http://schemas.microsoft.com/office/2006/01/customui">
    <ribbon>
        <tabs>
            <tab id="customTab" label="Contoso" insertAfterMso="TabHomeAccess">
                    <group idMso="GroupClipboard" />
                    <group idMso="GroupFontAccess" />
                    <group id="customGroup" label="Contoso Tools">
                        <button id="customButton1" label="ConBold"
size="large" onAction="conBoldSub" imageMso="Bold" />
                        <button id="customButton2" label="ConItalic"
size="large" onAction="conItalicSub" imageMso="Italic" />
                        <button id="customButton3" label="ConUnderline"
size="large" onAction="conUnderlineSub" imageMso="Underline" />
                    </group>
                    <group idMso="GroupEnterDataAlignment" />
                    <group idMso="GroupEnterDataNumber" />
```

```
                    <group idMso="GroupQuickFormatting" />
           </tab>
        </tabs>
     </ribbon>
</customUI>
```

One of the most important points to bear in mind is that XML is case-sensitive and you need to follow the exact case when putting together your own XML; otherwise, it will not work. Whereas in VBA this all gets taken care of via the editor, it is very important to get it right here.

The XML starts off with a root element:

```
<customUI xmlns="http://schemas.microsoft.com/office/2006/01/customui">
```

Elements are then defined for <ribbon> and <tabs>. The tabs are effectively the menu items on the menu bar in Access. There is then a tab definition for the new menu item called Contoso. This line provides it with an internal ID, the name as it will appear on the menu bar, and where it will be positioned on the menu bar.

The next lines add in the ribbon groups for **clipboard** and **font**. The third group added in is a custom one with a custom internal ID and a label to define it. Buttons are then added in as child elements, providing custom internal IDs, labels, sizes, and images to use. You can see how all these parameters work by comparing what you see in the **ribbon** group on the Access screen to the actual XML.

The custom group also has a closing element to finish it off: </group>. This defines that the definition of the custom group has finished.

Curiously, three other groups are also defined after this, but their names do not exist in the ribbon model, so they have been ignored.

The XML is then finished off with closing tags for tab, tabs, ribbon, and Custom UI.

Creating Code for Your Custom Buttons

As already mentioned, the buttons in the ribbon custom group only produce an error message because they have no code to run. You need to create code that utilizes the **OnAction** parameter from the custom ribbon control that was created.

To make your callback code work, you will need to add a reference in VBA to the Microsoft Office 12.0 Object Library. To do this, click Tools | References in the VBE menu and scroll down the list of libraries to Microsoft Office 12.0 Object Library. Tick the check box for this and click OK.

Usefully, the Custom UI Editor assists you in doing this. This is one of the big advantages of using it instead of trying to work directly with the USysRibbons table. If you look at the toolbar displayed, the icon on the far right has a label of "Generate Callbacks" if you hover your mouse over this. Click this and you will see skeleton code for all three custom buttons within the XML. Open the VBA Editor window in Access and insert a module by clicking Insert | Module. Make sure you insert it in the workbook that has the custom ribbon; otherwise, it will not work.

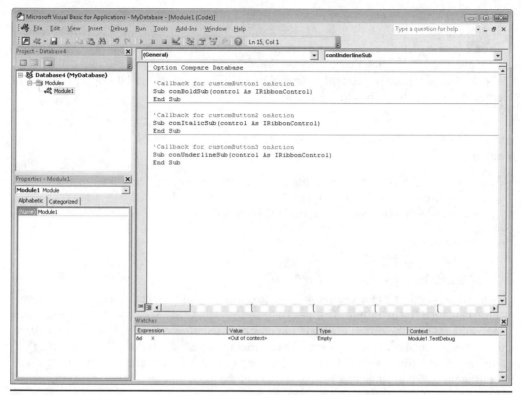

Figure 11-5   *The VBA Editor window showing the skeleton callback code*

Copy the skeleton code from the Custom UI Editor window by selecting all of it and pressing CTRL+C. Select the module on the VBA Editor window and press CTRL+V to paste it into your code. Your screen should now look like Figure 11-5.

If you go back to your Access form, select your custom ribbon group and click one of the buttons, you will now find that no error message appears. Nothing actually happens, but just copying in the skeleton code has provided code for the **OnAction** parameter and has suppressed the error message.

You now need to add some code into the callback code to make the buttons do something. You can create the code for the first button as follows:

```
'Callback for customButton1 onAction

Sub conBoldSub(control As IRibbonControl)
Screen.ActiveControl.FontBold = True
End Sub
```

This simply sets the active control on your form (the control with the focus) to bold. Pretty simple stuff, but by using your imagination you can go a lot further on this.

The preceding example only provides code that will take a specific action when the ribbon button is clicked.

You can also include code that will pass back a return value for the purposes of the title of the group, which then allows us to alter the title of the ribbon group programmatically.

To do this, you need to paste the field RibbonXML into the Custom UI Editor. The element for group should be altered to read

```
<group id="customGroup" getLabel="MyLabel">
This originally read:
<group id="customGroup" label="Contoso Tools">
```

Instead of specifying a static label for the group, you are now going to alter this dynamically using the subroutine MyLabel.

In the module for this spreadsheet, insert the following code:

```
Sub MyLabel(control As IRibbonControl, ReturnValue As Variant)
ReturnValue = "My new title"
End Sub
```

The code is similar to the **OnAction** code that was created, but there is now an additional parameter called **ReturnValue**. This passes back a string called "My new title", which is used as the title for the ribbon group. If you now click Contoso, you will find that the custom group title has changed to the new text. The restriction on using this code is that it is only called when your form is loaded in. This gives opportunities for the title to be changed according to a certain parameter such as the day of the week, but once it has changed, it cannot be called again without reloading the form.

Images

You can use all the images available in the add-in Office207IconsGallery on the MSDN web site to customize your ribbon buttons. The best way to access this add-in is to go to msdn .microsoft.com and then search for Office2007IconsGallery. This will take you straight to the page to download this add-in.

For example, if you want to use a smiley face, use the parameter imageMso="HappyFace" instead of imageMso="Bold".

How Can You Use VBA Code with the Ribbon

From a VBA programming angle, the big question is how can you use VBA code dynamically with the ribbon? The answer to this, unfortunately, is that ways are fairly limited.

Using VBA, you can find out if a particular ribbon control is enabled, is visible, or has been clicked. You can get the control's label, screentip, or supertip (screentip and supertip are the same thing), and you can display the control's image. You can execute a particular control.

As you have already seen, you can add code to a control and you can change the title of a ribbon group, but this can only take place when the Access file is loaded in.

Access 2010 has over 1,700 ribbon controls, and each has a name. Use this name to identify the control in the collection when you are working with it.

A simple example of code to access a ribbon control is as follows:

```
MsgBox Application.CommandBars.GetEnabledMso("FileSave")
```

This code can be run from any module in your application and does not have to be on a form or report. Use a standard VBA message box that you used back in Chapter 1. This should return **True** in that the FileSave control is enabled. Note that these names are case-sensitive and if you put in "filesave," this will produce an error.

The next question is, how do you get the name of a particular control with so many available? To do this, you need to place your cursor on the ribbon bar of the Access window and right-click. Take the option Customize Quick Action Toolbar or press C. You will see a form displayed as shown in Figure 11-6.

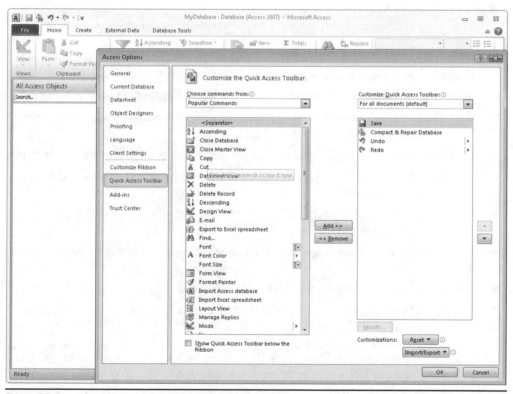

Figure 11-6   *The Customize Quick Action Toolbar screen*

By selecting the drop-down Choose Commands From in the top-left corner of the form, you can select control lists in any of the menu tabs or any of the other groups available. You can even see the custom tab called Contoso that you created earlier.

If you select one of these options, you will then see all the controls and groups associated with it. If you hover your cursor over any of the controls, you will see its name in brackets at the end of the tooltip string.

One important rule is that the list shows both groups and controls within those groups. The controls have icons; the groups do not. If you try to use this code on a group name, you will get an error. For example, GroupFont is a group (there is no icon next to it), so the statement

```
MsgBox Application.CommandBars.GetEnabledMso("GroupFontAccess")
```

will give an error. However, if you substitute "FontSize" for "GroupFontAccess" the code will run correctly.

As already stated, you can see the custom ribbon group you created earlier called Contoso. If you hover your cursor over your custom controls, you will see that they all have names, but the sad thing is that they all have the same name (CustomControl) and you cannot access them by using this code.

You can use the following methods in conjunction with the existing controls within Access:

▶ **ExecuteMso**   Runs the control as if the user had clicked it.

▶ **GetEnabledMso**   Returns True or False according to whether the control is enabled.

▶ **GetImageMso**   Returns the control image into a variable defined as IPictureDisplay. You also need to define width and height.

▶ **GetLabelMso**   Returns the label for that control, which is often the same as the name.

▶ **GetPressedMso**   Applies to a check box and toggle buttons and returns true if the control has been pressed.

▶ **GetScreentipMso**   Returns the string for the screentip of that control. This is often the same as the name and the label.

▶ **GetSupertipMso**   Returns the super screentip for the control and is usually more descriptive.

▶ **ReleaseFocus**   Releases the focus on the command bar object.

▶ **GetVisibleMso**   Returns True or False for a given ID of an Mso (Microsoft Office control).

You can also use the parameters defined in the callback code to access user actions, such as if the user checked a check box or entered some text into an edit box. You will see examples of this further on in this chapter.

More on the Ribbon

Using the custom UI Editor, try adding the following code to the Ribbon XML that you constructed earlier. This should be added in after </group> and before </tabs>:

```
<group id="Group1" label="My Control">
<checkBox id="Checkbox1"
label="Checkbox sample"
onAction="MyCheckbox"
/>
```

Your example file in the Custom UI Editor should now look like this:

```
<customUI xmlns="http://schemas.microsoft.com/office/2006/01/customui">
     <ribbon>
          <tabs>
               <tab id="customTab" label="Contoso"
insertAfterMso="TabHomeAccess">
                    <group idMso="GroupClipboard" />
                    <group idMso="GroupFontAccess" />
                    <group id="customGroup" getLabel="MyLabel">
                         <button id="customButton1" label="ConBold"
size="large"     onAction="conBoldSub" imageMso="HappyFace" />
                         <button id="customButton2" label="ConItalic"
size="large" onAction="conItalicSub" imageMso="Italic" />
                         <button id="customButton3" label="ConUnderline"
size="large" onAction="conUnderlineSub" imageMso="Underline" />
                    </group>
                    <group idMso="GroupEnterDataAlignment" />
                    <group idMso="GroupEnterDataNumber" />
                    <group idMso="GroupQuickFormatting" />


                    <group id="Group1" label="My Control">
                    <checkBox id="Checkbox1"
                    label="Checkbox sample"
                    onAction="MyCheckbox"
                    />
                    </group>
               </tab>
          </tabs>
     </ribbon>
</customUI>
```

Note that you can have only one **Custom UI** root within the XML file. If you try a second root for this, you will get errors and the ribbon XML will not work.

The purpose of this extra XML is to create a sample check box in a custom ribbon control on the Home tab of the user interface. It uses four callbacks, but these have not yet been defined. If you open the Home tab, you will get error messages that the procedure **MyCheckbox** does not exist.

You have now defined a check box with a callback called **MyCheckbox**. Copy and paste your XML into the RibbonXML field of the USysRibbons. Exit the database and then reload it. Open the form where you have set your new ribbon and click Contoso on the menu bar. Your screen will now look like Figure 11-7, with your new ribbon control My Control at the end of the ribbon containing a check box.

You can use the Generate Callbacks icon to help generate the code for the callback. This helps you with the parameters passed across. For example, with a check box there is a parameter called "pressed."

Copy the callback for Checkbox1 and paste it into the module you created earlier in the VBA Editor. Save the file and close it down. When you next load the file, no error messages will appear since the callback is now defined.

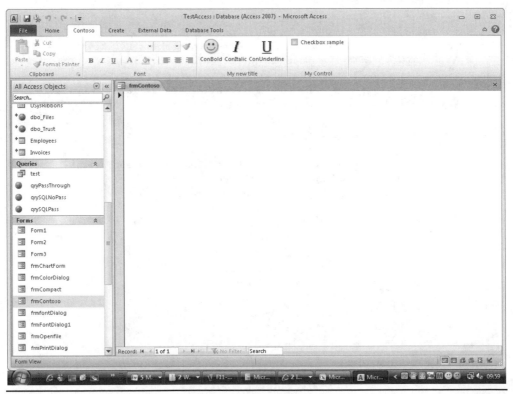

Figure 11-7   *Access screen showing new ribbon control*

You can now enter code for when the user ticks the check box or unticks it:

```
Sub MyCheckbox(control As IRibbonControl, pressed As Boolean)
MsgBox pressed
End Sub
```

When the user activates the check box, you will get a message box displaying "True," which becomes "False" when the box is deactivated. You can insert appropriate code here to deal with the check box being checked or unchecked by the user.

You can also use your ribbon control to capture user input by including an edit box in your ribbon control.

To do this, add the following XML below your check box XML code:

```
<editBox id="Editbox1"
label="Editbox sample"
onChange="MyChange"/>
```

Note that in the case of the edit box, there is no **onAction** event. Instead, there is an **onChange** event. This different event can be confusing to the first-time user, but one of the ways of checking is to click the Generate Callbacks button. If you enter **onAction** instead of **onChange**, you will get an error message.

Your overall XML should now look like this:

```
<customUI xmlns="http://schemas.microsoft.com/office/2006/01/customui">
    <ribbon>
          <tabs>
               <tab id="customTab" label="Contoso"
insertAfterMso="TabHomeAccess">
                    <group idMso="GroupClipboard" />
                    <group idMso="GroupFontAccess" />
                    <group id="customGroup" getLabel="MyLabel">
                         <button id="customButton1" label="ConBold"
size="large"      onAction="conBoldSub" imageMso="HappyFace" />
                         <button id="customButton2" label="ConItalic"
size="large" onAction="conItalicSub" imageMso="Italic" />
                         <button id="customButton3" label="ConUnderline"
size="large" onAction="conUnderlineSub" imageMso="Underline" />
                    </group>
                    <group idMso="GroupEnterDataAlignment" />
                    <group idMso="GroupEnterDataNumber" />
                    <group idMso="GroupQuickFormatting" />

               <group id="customGroup1" label="My Control">
               <checkBox id="Checkbox1"
               label="Checkbox sample"
               onAction="MyCheckbox"
               />
```

```
<editBox id="Editbox1"
label="Editbox sample"
onChange="MyChange"
/>


            </group>
         </tab>
      </tabs>
   </ribbon>
</customUI>
```

Copy and paste your XML code into the Ribbon XML field of USysRibbons table. Exit the database and then reload it. If you now click the Home menu item, you will see that your custom ribbon control, My Control, now has a text entry box as well as your original check box. If you type something into the text box and press ENTER, you will get an error message because the callback to MyChange has not yet been defined.

Again, to create the callback, click the callback icon in the Custom UI Editor and copy and paste the code for Editbox1 **onChange**. This is a very useful feature because it gives you the correct passing parameters within the **callback** subroutine. The checkbox control had a parameter called **pressed** that was a Boolean (True or False), whereas the text box has a **text** parameter to hold the value that the user typed in.

Your callback code should now look like this:

```
Sub MyChange(control As IRibbonControl, text As String)
MsgBox text
End Sub
```

This simply provides a message box to show what has been typed in. Go back to the spreadsheet and click Home on the menu bar. Enter some text into your new text box on the My Control ribbon control and press ENTER. Your text will then be displayed in a message box on screen.

Suppose you want to include something more complicated in your ribbon control such as a combo box (a drop-down control). This can also be accomplished in a fairly straightforward manner.

In the Custom UI Editor, add in the following XML below your edit box XML:

```
<comboBox
id="MyCombo"label="My Combo"
onChange ="OnChange"
getItemCount ="GetItemCount"
getItemLabel ="GetItemLabel"
/>
```

Your overall XML should now look like this:

```
<customUI xmlns="http://schemas.microsoft.com/office/2006/01/customui">
     <ribbon>
          <tabs>
               <tab id="customTab" label="Contoso"
insertAfterMso="TabHomeAccess">
                    <group idMso="GroupClipboard" />
                    <group idMso="GroupFontAccess" />
                    <group id="customGroup" getLabel="MyLabel">
                         <button id="customButton1" label="ConBold"
size="large"      onAction="conBoldSub" imageMso="HappyFace" />
                         <button id="customButton2" label="ConItalic"
size="large" onAction="conItalicSub" imageMso="Italic" />
                         <button id="customButton3" label="ConUnderline"
size="large" onAction="conUnderlineSub" imageMso="Underline" />
                    </group>
                    <group idMso="GroupEnterDataAlignment" />
                    <group idMso="GroupEnterDataNumber" />
                    <group idMso="GroupQuickFormatting" />

                    <group id="customGroup1" label="My Control">
                    <checkBox id="Checkbox1"
                    label="Checkbox sample"
                    onAction="MyCheckbox"
                    />
                    <editBox id="Editbox1"
                    label="Editbox sample"
                    onChange="MyChange"
                    />
                    <comboBox
                    id="MyCombo"
                    label="My Combo"
                    onChange ="OnChange"
                    getItemCount ="GetItemCount"
                    getItemLabel ="GetItemLabel"
                    />
                    </group>
               </tab>
          </tabs>
     </ribbon>
</customUI>
```

As with the edit box, there is an **onChange** event, but there are also a **getItemCount** event and a **getItemLabel** event to define the combo box.

As before, copy and paste the XML into the Ribbon XML field of the USysRibbons table. Exit the database and reload it. If you click Home in the menu bar and look at your custom ribbon control, this now has a drop-down, but it is not populated.

In the Custom UI Editor, use the Create Callbacks icon to copy across the three callbacks for **OnChange**, **GetItemCount**, and **GetItemLabel**.

Paste these into your VBA module. You need to also define an array to hold the values for the drop-down. Do this by putting the following statement in the declarations area of the module:

```
Dim ComboArray(3)
```

This will set up an array with four elements beginning at index 0.

You then need to add in the following code for your callbacks:

```
Sub GetItemCount(control As IRibbonControl, ByRef returnedVal)
returnedVal = 4
End Sub


Sub GetItemLabel(control As IRibbonControl, index As Integer, ByRef returnedVal)
ComboArray(0) = "Option1"
ComboArray(1) = "Option2"
ComboArray(2) = "Option3"
ComboArray(3) = "Option4"

returnedVal = ComboArray(index)

End Sub


Sub OnChange(control As IRibbonControl, text As String)
MsgBox text

End Sub
```

Looking at these in turn, **GetItemCount** returns the number of items in the combo box list, which is 4.

GetItemLabel is more complicated. This populates the four-element array that you set up with option labels and then returns the array referenced by the index parameter (which is based on the number of items declared in **GetItemCount**).

Finally, **OnChange** displays the selected text when the user chooses an item from the combo box list.

Once you have put all this code into your module, you must then save the file and close the database. The reason for this is that **GetItemCount** and **GetItemLabel** are only called when the file is loaded into Access. This means you can only declare your combo list at this point and it cannot be changed dynamically during the operation of the spreadsheet. This is something of a drawback.

When you load your file, click Home in the menu bar and click the combo box in your custom control. You will see your four options listed (see Figure 11-8). Click one of those options and the text will appear in a message box on the spreadsheet screen.

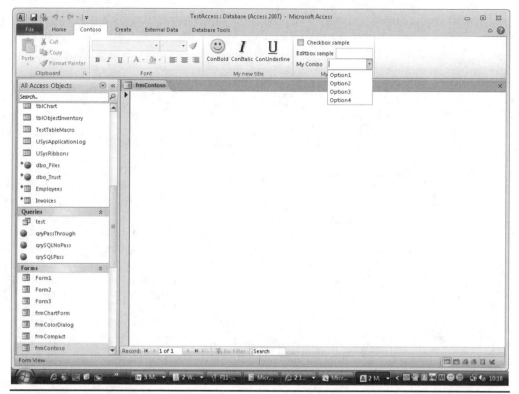

Figure 11-8   *An Access ribbon showing a custom drop-down control*

In conjunction with the button control, these provide simple ways for your ribbon control to interact with the user, and for you to provide code to deal with that interaction.

Manipulating the ribbon is very complicated in Access 2010 but it is very rewarding to see the results.

SQL Queries

S QL queries do not form part of the VBA language but it is very important to understand how they work and what they can do.

The object of this chapter is to show you the queries you can use with VBA and how you can use them.

In a relational database, it is very unusual to open a single table and view meaningful information from it. This is because all the tables store different bits of information and only by joining these tables together can you see a proper view of the data. For example, one table might provide customer names and addresses and another table will show all the orders that have been placed by those customers. In order to extract all the orders for each customer, a query needs to be put together joining the customer and the order tables using a common key field (usually a numerical ID).

SQL queries are the life blood of any Access application in presenting data to the user and for manipulating data. They can be used in various ways through VBA.

Some of the examples in this chapter use the Access sample database Northwind to illustrate the data. To open this database, load Access but do not select a database. In the pane in the center of the window (Available Templates), click Sample templates. This will display the icon for Northwind, among others. Click this and click the Create button on the right-hand side of the window while holding down the SHIFT key (so the database does not autorun).

When this has loaded, you will need to expand out the Navigation pane on the left-hand side of the window to see the database objects. Do this by dragging the right-hand border of the Navigation pane across the window to the right.

Using the Query Design Window

Queries can be easily constructed in Access by using the Query Design window. This provides a GUI that allows the user to easily build a query on several tables. To use the Query Design window, click Create in the Access menu and then click the Query Design icon in the Macros & Code group of the ribbon. You will then see the window shown in Figure 12-1.

In the pop-up window called Show Table, click the tables and queries you want to use and then click the Add button. Click the Close button when complete. You can return to this window to add more tables or queries by right-clicking in the Query Design window and clicking Show Table.

Select the Customers and the Orders tables only.

The tables you have selected will be shown graphically in the Query Design window, listing all the fields available in each table. You can drag the tables around the window to reposition them for easy viewing.

Access will also try to link the tables together for you, although this does not always work. Do not rely on Access to do this for you since it can be wrong sometimes.

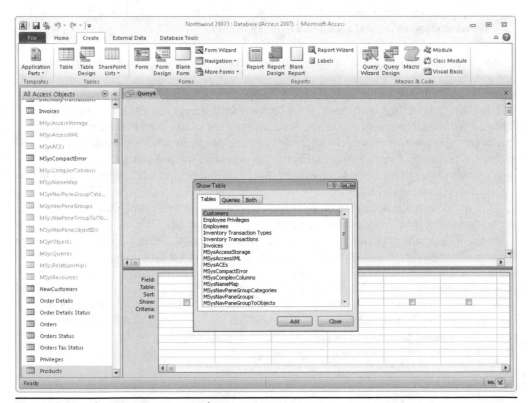

Figure 12-1   *The Query Design window on opening*

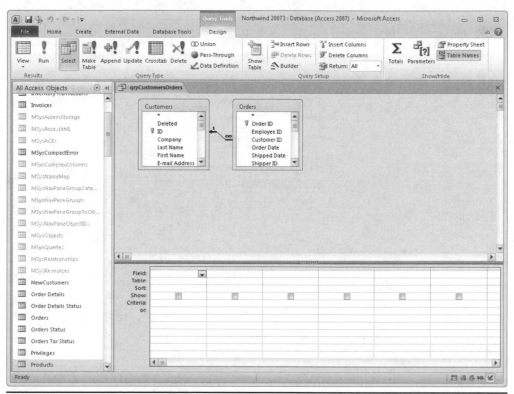

Figure 12-2   *The Query Design window showing the Customers and Orders tables*

In the example shown in Figure 12-2, the Customers and the Orders tables have been selected.

Notice that Access automatically makes a join between the ID field in the Customers table and the Customer ID field in the Orders table. This is correct in joining the two tables.

Access has been doing a bit of thinking for us, which can be annoying sometimes, and has surmised that there is a one-to-many relationship between customers and orders. In other words, one customer can have many orders, and this is illustrated graphically by the 1 and 00 symbols on the join line.

If you want to join using other fields, you can right-click the join line and select Delete. You can then select a field for joining in one table and drag it to the field you wish to join to in the other table. This will create a new join line on the GUI.

You can have more than one join connecting two tables and have many different tables within one query, although this does affect the query performance. The result is a "spider's web" that can be quite difficult to debug should there be anything wrong with it.

Because of this, Access has decided that this should be a right join so all orders are shown regardless of whether there is a corresponding customer. This is illustrated graphically by the small arrow on the left end of the join line.

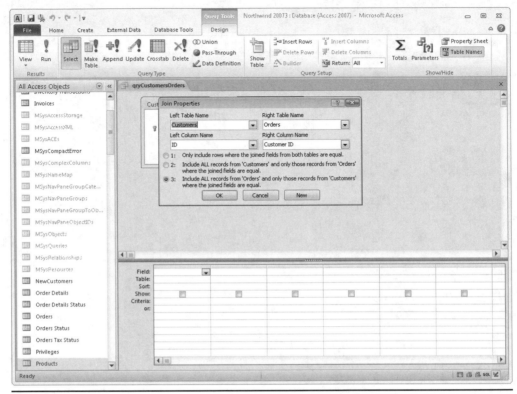

Figure 12-3 *The Join Properties window in the Query Design window*

Place your cursor anywhere on the join line, right-click, and then select Join Properties. A window like that in Figure 12-3 will appear.

This provides options in which you can make a straight join (where the joined fields are equal) or a left or right join where all the records are retrieved from one of the tables (but only the records from the other table where the joined fields are equal). In this particular case, where a right join has been made all orders will be shown, matching to customers where possible.

For the query to work, you need to add some fields into the results section of the window. You can either double-click the field name or drag it down to the Field row of the results area. You can also use the drop-downs for Field and Table in the results area.

Add in the fields Company, Order Date, and Ship Name in this way. You can also enter criteria in the Criteria row. For example, under Order Date, enter >#01/01/2006#. Your Query Design window should now look like Figure 12-4.

Notice that your date criterion has a hash sign (#) at the start and end to designate it as a date. It is entered according to the locale that Windows is set to, so in North America you would use the mm/dd/yyyy format, otherwise the dd/mm/yyyy format.

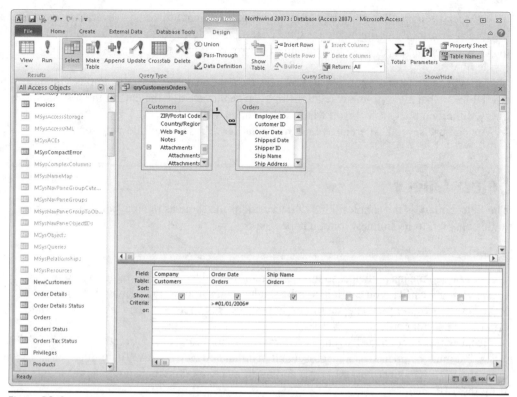

Figure 12-4   *A Query Design window with fields and criteria added*

One interesting point about the treatment of dates is that in the actual SQL query behind this GUI, the date is always changed to the mm/dd/yyyy format if it is in the dd/mm/yyyy format (regardless of the locale settings). It is important to realize this when putting together SQL for use inside of VBA.

Click the Run icon or the View | Datasheet icon in the results group of the ribbon and you will see all the records returned.

Click the drop-down from the View icon in the Results group of the ribbon and Select SQL View. This will display the SQL statement for the query you have constructed:

```
SELECT Customers.Company, Orders.[Order Date], Orders.[Ship Name]
FROM Customers RIGHT JOIN Orders ON Customers.ID = Orders.[Customer ID]
WHERE (((Orders.[Order Date])>#1/1/2006#));
```

Save this query with the name of **MyQuery**.

The SQL statement is what you will incorporate into your VBA code. If you have a good knowledge of SQL, you can write it out in the SQL window without bothering with the GUI front end, although it is easy to make mistakes doing this. The GUI front end will still reflect your SQL.

If a query you are going to use in VBA is complicated, encompassing several tables, it is a good idea to work it out first using the Query Design window. This allows you to see if your query will work and provides more meaningful error messages than if you were running it inside of VBA.

You will find that more complicated queries are not updatable. If, for example, you have two tables with a many-to-many relationship, you cannot change the data in the resultant query, either via the Query Result window or through VBA.

You can use several different types of query, as described in the following sections.

Select Query

The Select query is the simplest kind of query and is the same as the one constructed earlier in this chapter. In its simplest form, it appears as:

```
Select * from MyTable
```

The star (*) means all fields, so this query returns all the data in the table MyTable.

As you saw earlier, you can join to other tables using straight joins (inner joins) or left/right joins (outer joins) dependent on how you wish to see your data. You can also add in criteria and sorting orders.

Because this query actually returns records, it cannot be executed directly from within VBA, but must be opened as a recordset and manipulated using VBA. To do this, you must enter the VBE window (press ALT+F11) and insert a new module by using Insert | Module from the VBE menu.

Enter the following code:

```
Sub TestQuery()
Dim ReSet As Recordset

Set ReSet = CurrentDb.OpenRecordset("MyQuery")

Do Until ReSet.EOF
    MsgBox ReSet!Company
    ReSet.MoveNext
Loop

End Sub
```

The code assumes that you saved your query as instructed in the earlier section of this chapter as MyQuery.

This code creates a recordset object called ReSet and sets it to point at the query that you created earlier. It then uses a Do Until . . . Loop to iterate through the records and displays the Company field as a message box. Note that the exclamation mark (!) is used in the statement to display the company name instead of a dot or period (.).

Also, it is important to put the **MoveNext** statement in, otherwise your code will never finish and will just stay on the first record. The **MoveNext** statement is easily forgotten when concentrating on other aspects of the code.

You can use the VBA code to perform updates, although it is more efficient to do this through an Update query:

```
Sub TestQuery()
Dim ReSet As Recordset

Set ReSet = CurrentDb.OpenRecordset("MyQuery")

Do Until ReSet.EOF
    If ReSet![Ship Name] = "Karen Toh" Then
        ReSet.Edit
        ReSet![Ship Name] = "Unknown"
        ReSet.Update

    End If

    ReSet.MoveNext
Loop

End Sub
```

The code works the same as before except that we test to see if the Ship Name field shows Karen Toh. Notice that the field Ship Name has a space in the name so it has to be enclosed in square brackets ([]) to show VBA where it starts and finishes.

If the name is Karen Toh, then the record is put into Edit mode and the field is changed to Unknown. The record is then updated.

Similarly, a new field can also be added in this way:

```
Sub TestQuery()
Dim ReSet As Recordset

Set ReSet = CurrentDb.OpenRecordset("MyQuery")

ReSet.AddNew
ReSet!Company = "Richard"
ReSet![Order Date] = "01-Aug-2006"
ReSet![Ship Name] = "Richard Shepherd"
ReSet.Update


End Sub
```

This again works as before, but the **AddNew** method is used to insert a new record. The fields within the recordset are provided with values. Notice that the square brackets are used where there is a space in the field name and that the date is provided in a format that will fit any locale.

The recordset is then updated and the new record is added.

For this to work, it has to adhere to any rules for the tables within the query such as required fields, otherwise it will fail with an error.

If you are using a query on a form, then all the methodology to select, browse records, update, and add new records is already provided (see Chapter 9). However, there are often cases where you need customization of this kind.

Union Query

The Union query is a variation on the Select query. In this case, you wish to combine the results of several select queries. It must be written in SQL within the SQL window and you cannot use the Query Design GUI for this.

In its simplest form it is:

```
Select * from MyTable1 union select * from MyTable2
```

This combines the two select statements from MyTable1 and MyTable2, which seems fairly simple. You can also use select statements from other queries here as well. However, certain points should be kept in mind here.

For this query to work, the data in the first select statement must be identical in structure to the data in the second select statement. This means that each select statement must return the same number of columns and each individual column must have the same data type in both select statements.

Also, the union statement removes duplicate records that it finds, so if there is an identical record in MyTable1 and MyTable2, it will only appear once in the results. If you want to see all the duplicates, then use Union All:

```
Select * from MyTable1 union all select * from MyTable2
```

A Union query can be very useful to combine two data sources where numeric data is related to one common field but needs to be shown as individual columns. You can require the numeric data to be shown for two particular dates, where the dates are column headings.

For example, you may have two tables of data, each with a common reference field called MyRef. One table (MyTable1) has numeric data in with column headings for Monday and Tuesday, and the other (MyTable2) has numeric data with column headings for Wednesday and Thursday. You want to combine this into a query where each reference represents a single record with the data for Monday to Thursday showing in separate columns.

You can initially use a Union query as follows:

```
Select MyRef,Monday,Tuesday,0 as Wednesday,0 as Thursday from MyTable1
Union
Select MyRef,0 as Monday,0 as Tuesday, Wednesday, Thursday from MyTable2
```

Notice that zero values have been inserted into each select statement so the number of columns in each select statement is the same. All the select statements have a column for Monday, Tuesday, Wednesday, and Thursday, and although some of these carry the value of zero, when they are combined they create a set of fields that are the same.

When this query is run it will combine the results from the two tables, but you will see two records for each reference, one with the Monday and Tuesday figures and one with the Wednesday and Thursday figures.

The next task is to make these appear as one row in the result. You can do this by nesting your original query and using a Group By clause:

```
Select MyRef,sum(Monday),sum(Tuesday),sum(Wednesday),sum(Thursday) from (
Select MyRef,Monday,Tuesday,0 as Wednesday,0 as Thursday from MyTable1
Union
Select MyRef,0 as Monday,0 as Tuesday, Wednesday, Thursday from MyTable2
) group by MyRef
```

This can start looking quite messy when the query statements are more complicated, but the use of the Sum function and the Group By clause makes each reference generate only one row in the result.

To make things easier, you can use your Union query as a subquery and then use this as the source for the Group By query.

```
Select MyRef,sum(Monday),sum(Tuesday),sum(Wednesday),sum(Thursday) from
MyUnionQuery  group by MyRef
```

The Delete Query

The Delete query simply deletes records from a table. It can either delete all of them or use a criterion. Because it does not return records, it is run as a command:

In its simplest form it appears this way:

```
Delete * from MyTable
```

This clears out all records from MyTable. You can also use one or more criteria:

```
Delete * from MyTable where CustomerName="Richard"
```

This assumes that MyTable has a field called CutomerName. This will delete all records where the CustomerName field is equal to Richard.

You can use the Query Design window to build a Delete query. It is the same as the earlier Select query, but you must click the Delete query icon in the Query Type group of the ribbon. It is a good idea to look at the results in a data sheet view (by clicking the View icon in the Results group of the ribbon) before you run the query. This will show you what will be deleted without actually enacting the query. If anything is wrong at this point, you have not damaged the database.

To run this from within VBA, you can use the DoCmd object (see Chapter 16 for more information on this object):

```
Sub DeleteQuery()

DoCmd.SetWarnings False

DoCmd.OpenQuery "MyDeleteQuery"

DoCmd.SetWarnings True

End Sub
```

Notice that the DoCmd object has been used to switch the warning messages off and then switch them back on afterward. This is because by running a Delete query the warning message will normally be displayed to tell you that you are about to delete records. If you are running this as part of a VBA procedure, you will not want this message appearing and halting the execution of your code.

Do not forget to set the warnings back again. If you do not, you will receive no warnings at any point within your Access database. If, for example, you decide to edit a query and then close it, you will no longer get the warning message "Do you want to save this?" It will default to "Save," which could be disastrous if you have made changes that no longer work!

You can also run this by using the Execute method. You can either call the query or the actual SQL:

```
CurrentDb.Execute "delete * from MyTable"
```

Do not forget that when deleting records memory is not released until the database is compacted. If you do not do this, it will keep growing until you reach the 2Gb limit where it will be corrupted.

Make Table Query

The Make Table query creates a new table based on the query. If a table already exists with the same name, it will be overwritten, but you will see warning messages about this. Because it does not return records, it is run as a command:

In its simplest form, it appears as:

```
SELECT * INTO MyNewTable
FROM MyTable;
```

This creates a copy of MyTable, calling it MyNewTable. You can also use criteria:

```
SELECT * INTO MyNewTable
FROM MyTable
where CustomerName="Richard"
```

This assumes that MyTable has a field called CutomerName. This will create a new table called MyNewTable, which only contains records when the CustomerName field is equal to Richard.

You can use the Query Design window to build a Make Table query. It is the same as the earlier Select query, but you must click the Make Table query icon in the Query Type group of the ribbon.

To run this from within VBA, use the DoCmd object (see Chapter 16 for more information on this object):

```
Sub MakeTableQuery()

DoCmd.SetWarnings False

DoCmd.OpenQuery "MyMakeTableQuery"

DoCmd.SetWarnings True

End Sub
```

Notice that the DoCmd object has been used to switch the warning messages off and then switch them back on afterward. This is because by running a Make Table query the warning message will normally be displayed to tell you that you are about to delete records. If you are running this as part of a VBA procedure, you will not want this message appearing and halting the execution of your code.

Again, do not forget to set the warnings back as they were. If you do not, you will receive no warnings at any point within your Access database. If, for example, you decide to edit a query, and then close it, you will no longer get the warning message "Do you want to save this?" It will default to "Save," which could be disastrous if you have made changes that no longer work!

You can also run this by using the Execute method. This can be done by either calling the query or the actual SQL:

```
CurrentDb.Execute "SELECT * INTO MyNewTable FROM MyTable;"
```

Append Query

The Append query appends records based on the query into another table. The data you are appending must conform to the rules of the new table. Filed data types must correspond and required fields must be provided, otherwise errors will occur.

When this type of query goes wrong, it is one of the hardest to debug in terms of trying to find out why certain records are not acceptable to the new table. Error records turn up in a new error records table, but even then it can be quite difficult to locate what is causing the problem, especially if there are many fields.

I have found that if problems occur, it is worth splitting the Append query into several small sections using criteria so as to narrow down which section has failed. Narrowing down the failed section further usually reveals what the problem is.

Because it does not return records, it is run as a command. In its simplest form, it is:

```
INSERT INTO NewCustomers
SELECT *
FROM MyTable;
```

This appends all the data in the MyTable table into one called NewCustomers. It does not delete records, so every time it is run the NewCustomers table will keep growing.

You can also use the following criteria:

```
INSERT INTO NewCustomers
SELECT *
FROM MyTable where CustomerName="Richard"
```

This assumes that MyTable has a field called CutomerName. This will add new records into the NewCustomers table from the MyTable table where the CustomerName field is equal to Richard.

You can also specify which fields you want to append into the new table:

```
INSERT INTO NewCustomers ( Company, CustomerName )
SELECT Company, CustomerName
FROM MyTable
```

This assumes that MyTable has fields called CutomerName and Company and that the NewCustomers table has the same. The field names can be different in the destination table, but this must be reflected in the SQL query. Also, it is essential that the data types are the same in each field in each table. They can also be in a different order in the destination table, but again they must be specified in the SQL query so they are in identical order to the insert and select part of the statement.

You can now see that this type of query can become very complicated and can easily go wrong!

You can use the Query Design window to build a Make Table query. It is the same as the earlier Select query, but you must click the Append query icon in the Query Type group of the ribbon.

It is a good idea to look at the results in a data sheet view (by clicking the View icon in the Results group of the ribbon) before you run the query. This will show you what will be appended without actually enacting the query. If anything is wrong at this point, you have not damaged the database.

To run this from within VBA, you can use the DoCmd object (see Chapter 16 for more information on this object):

```
Sub MakeTableQuery()

DoCmd.SetWarnings False

DoCmd.OpenQuery "MyAppendQuery"

DoCmd.SetWarnings True

End Sub
```

Notice that the DoCmd object has been used to switch the warning messages off and then switch them back on afterwards. This is because by running an Append query the warning message will normally be displayed to tell you that you are about to delete records. If you are running this as part of a VBA procedure, you will not want this message appearing and halting the execution of your code.

As stated earlier, do not forget to set the warnings back again. If you do not, you will receive no warnings at any point within your Access database. If, for example, you decide to edit a query and then close it, you will no longer get the warning message "Do you want to save this?" It will default to "Save," which could be disastrous if you have made changes that no longer work!

You can also run this by using the **Execute** method. This can be done by either calling the query or the actual SQL:

```
CurrentDb.Execute " INSERT INTO NewCustomers SELECT * FROM MyTable
```

If your query string is particularly long and complicated, you may find it easier to run it over several rows of code. The problem is that you cannot use the continuation character within a string.

To get around this, use a string variable to concatenate your query together:

```
Src = " INSERT INTO NewCustomers "
Src = Src & "SELECT * FROM MyTable"
CurrentDb.Execute Src
```

If you need to use quotes for a string criterion within your query string, use single quote marks instead of double (this will not cause the error of double quote marks).

Update Query

The Update query updates records based on the query to a specified value. The data you are updating must conform to the rules of the table. Null values cannot be updated into required fields and data types must correspond, otherwise errors will occur.

Because it does not return records, it is run as a command. In its simplest form, it appears as:

```
UPDATE MyTable SET CustomerName = "Richard"
```

This updates the table MyTable and changes the value of the field CustomerName to Richard throughout the table. Normally in this query you would use a criterion:

```
UPDATE MyTable SET CustomerName = "Richard"
WHERE (((CustomerName)="Shepherd"))
```

This assumes that MyTable has a field called CustomerName. This will change the CustomerName field to Richard where the CustomerName field has a value of Shepherd.

You can also update multiple fields using multiple criteria:

```
UPDATE MyTable SET CustomerName = "Richard", Company = "MGH"
WHERE (((CustomerName)="Shepherd") AND ((Company)="RBS"))
```

This assumes that MyTable has fields called CustomerName and Company. The query will set the CustomerName field to Richard and the Company field to MGH where the CustomerName has an existing value of Shepherd and the Company field has an existing value of RBS.

You can use the Query Design window to build an Update Table query. It is the same as the earlier Select query, but you must click the Append query icon in the Query Type group of the ribbon.

It is a good idea to look at the results in a data sheet view (by clicking the View icon in the Results group of the ribbon) before you run the query. This will show you what will be updated without actually enacting the query. If anything is wrong at this point you have not damaged the database.

To run this from within VBA, you can use the DoCmd object (see Chapter 16 for more information on this object):

```
Sub MakeTableQuery()

DoCmd.SetWarnings False

DoCmd.OpenQuery "MyUpdateQuery"

DoCmd.SetWarnings True

End Sub
```

Notice that the DoCmd object has been used to switch the warning messages off and then switch them back on afterward. This is because by running an Update query the warning message will normally be displayed to tell you that you are about to delete records. If you are running this as part of a VBA procedure, you will not want this message appearing and halting the execution of your code.

As said previously, do not forget to set the warnings back again. If you do not, you will receive no warnings at any point within your Access database. If, for example, you decide to edit a query and then close it, you will no longer get the warning message "Do you want to save this?" It will default to "Save," which could be disastrous if you have made changes that no longer work!

You can also run this by using the Execute method. This can be done by either calling the query or the actual SQL:

```
CurrentDb.Execute " UPDATE MyTable SET CustomerName = 'Richard'"
```

If your query string is particularly long and complicated, you may find it easier to run it over several rows of code. The problem is that you cannot use the continuation character within a string.

To get around this, use a string variable to concatenate your query together:

```
Src = " UPDATE MyTable SET CustomerName = 'Richard' "
Src = Src & "WHERE (((CustomerName)='Shepherd'))"

CurrentDb.Execute Src
```

If you need to use quotes for a string criteria within your query string, use single quote marks instead of double (this will not cause the error of double quote marks).

Pass Through Query

The Pass Through query is a special query for interaction with external databases. It is discussed in Chapter 19.

Using Custom Functions within Queries

When you create a query, you often come across a situation where you need to do something to a field, but there is no easy way of doing it in SQL.

To get around this, you can write a function in VBA and then incorporate it into your SQL query.

An example (which I have come across in the commercial world) might be that in your query, if a particular field value is all in uppercase, then another value field must be zero, otherwise it has its numeric value showing.

Though this is rather strange stuff, you would have huge problems doing this in a SQL query in Access. The solution for that was to write a function that checked a string to see if it was all in uppercase:

```
Function CheckUpperCase(Target As String) As Boolean
Dim Flag As Integer
For n = 1 To Len(Target)
```

```
        If Asc(Mid(Target, n, 1)) >= 97 Then
            CheckUpperCase = False
            Exit Function

        End If


Next n
CheckUpperCase = True
End Function
```

This was then incorporated into a Select query:

SELECT iif(CheckUpperCase(Company),0,ValueField) AS Rslt

FROM MyTable

The iif statement was used to interpret the Boolean return value and display zero or the field value accordingly. This example assumes that MyTable had fields called Company and ValueField in it.

This was one of these situations that when it was discussed at a meeting sounded totally impossible, but by careful use of VBA a solution was provided.

If you use a custom function within a SQL query, close the VBE window when you run it. If you do not do this, the VBE window will be refreshed as the SQL query is running. This adds a large overhead, and if the query is returning many records, it will take longer to run.

Table Macros

A new feature of Access 2010 is the ability to create table macros. These perform a similar function to triggers in databases such as Oracle and SQL Server. For example, suppose that when a record is updated in a specific table, you wish to create another record in a further table. This created record may not relate to the first record but may just be an item held for memorandum purposes.

When you create a trigger on a heavy duty database, it will perform an update, delete, or insert function on a specified table on the database. It is fired by an event happening on the original table itself.

Access 2010 now gives you this functionality, but it is somewhat restrictive. The logical way to have designed this would have been to allocate each table a VBA module with events such as update, delete, and insert, similar to forms and reports. The developer would then be able to attach VBA code to the event and would have the full flexibility to create the code that they wanted.

Instead, the table macros use a pseudo-macro development screen, which greatly restricts what the developer can achieve. However, it is a big step forward for Access and opens up interesting possibilities.

Creating a Table Macro

Create a sample table in your current database that contains two numeric fields. To do this, click Create on the Access menu and then click the Table Design icon in the tables group of the ribbon. Create two numeric fields (Number1 and Number2). Your Table Design window should now look like Figure 13-1.

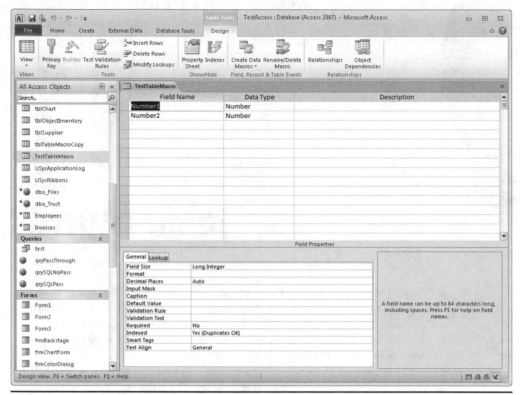

Figure 13-1   *Designing a sample table for a Table Macro*

Save your table with the name **tblTestTableMacro**. Do not worry about defining a primary key. This is not required for this example. Click Design in the Access menu and then click Create Data Macros in the Field, Record, and Table Events group of the ribbon. Click After Insert.click on the drop-down on the action screen and select Edit Record. You will see a window like Figure 13-2.

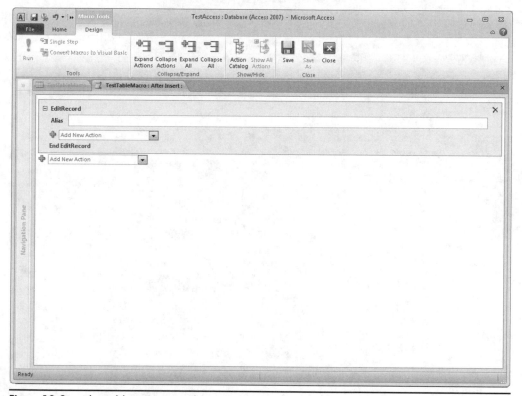

Figure 13-2   *The Table Macro window*

In the first "Add New Action" drop-down that appears, select SetField. Your design window will look like Figure 13-3.

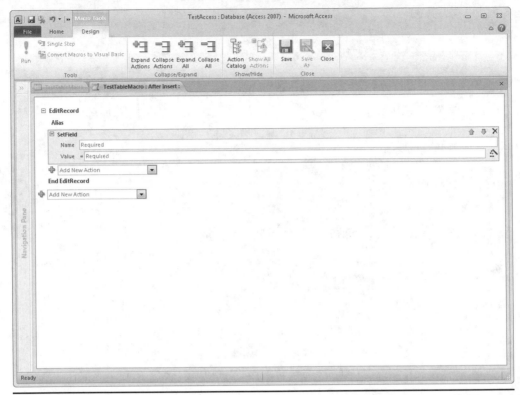

Figure 13-3   *Adding a new action*

After selecting Set Field, you will see a design window for your particular action to set a field value. Enter the name of the field as **Number2** and the value as **3*[Number1]**. Your design window will now look like Figure 13-4.

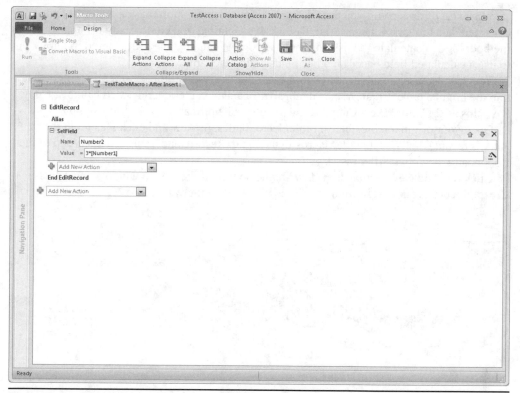

Figure 13-4   *The design window after a new action has been added*

If you need to edit your action, simply click the Set Field text in the action. This will bring you back to the design section.

Save the table by clicking the Save icon and then close the table macro window.

Open the table in View Mode by clicking the View icon in the Views group of the ribbon and entering a new value into the Number1 field. You will find that the Number2 field is automatically populated with three times the value of Number1. Even if you enter a value into the Number2 field first, it will still be overwritten by the table macro.

What sort of uses could you put this to within your application? If you had a table that collected data to work out something like a risk weighting, you could easily use this methodology to calculate the risk weight based on the data that the user entered. It allows you to use a calculated field based on other fields within the table.

You can also use the table macros to create records in other tables as the user enters data into the original table. Create a second table with a single numeric field called Number2Copy. Save this as **tblTableMacroCopy**. You will not need a primary key for this example.

Open your original table, tblTestTableMacro, in design view and click Design in the Access menu. Click Create DataMacros in the Field, Record, and Table Events group of the ribbon, and then click After Insert.

Click the Add New Action drop-down at the bottom of the design window and select Create Record. Your design window will now look like Figure 13-5.

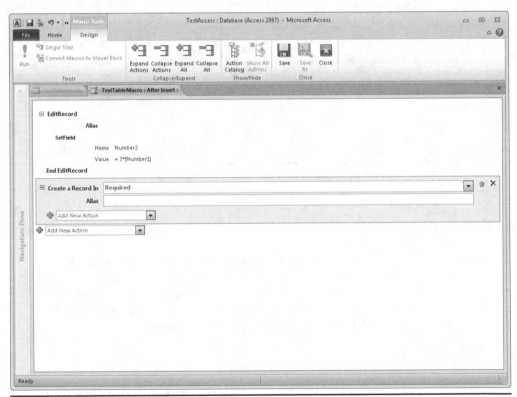

Figure 13-5 *The Create Record action*

Use the Create Record In option to select your second table (tblTableMacroCopy). Click the Add New Action field within the gray box for this action and select SetField.

Enter the field name as **Number2Copy** (the single numeric field that you included in your new table), and the value as **[tblTestTableMacro].[Number2]**.

Your design window will now look like Figure 13-6.

Save the macro and the table using the save icons, close the Data Macro window and then open your original table (tblTestTableMacro) in View mode. Add a new record by populating the Number1 field. You will see that the Number2 field is still calculated, but if you also open your second table (tblTableMacroCopy), you now have a new record in it based on the record you entered in the first table.

This is a demonstration of the possibilities of the table macros. It is a shame you cannot use VBA here and instead must use the pseudo-macro language, but it still provides a new dimension to your application.

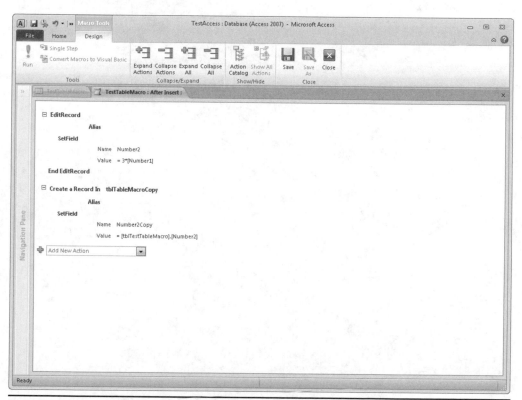

Figure 13-6   *Design window with Create Record action added*

Object Models

In this part, you will learn all about the various object models used in Access and how to use these within your code. These object models are at the heart of VBA programming for Access. They empower you to do anything in code that you can do from the Access menu, and as you will discover in the practical examples later in the book, let you do plenty more that cannot be done from the Access ribbon!

You will also learn how to use Access object models to interact with other Microsoft applications. For example, you will learn how to send custom e-mails through Microsoft Outlook and create a custom Excel spreadsheet.

CHAPTER 4

The Access Object Models

The Access object models are at the heart of using VBA in Access. They distinguish programming in Access from programming in other VBA applications by providing additional commands to manipulate tables, queries, forms, and reports and by providing all the functionality that the user would normally obtain from the menu structure of Access. For example, the object model in Microsoft Excel contains commands and objects specifically relating to workbooks and worksheets, giving you the means to manipulate ranges and cells. In Access, several object models are used and the whole application is oriented toward a structure of tables, queries, forms, and reports.

The object model is written around this structure. Access is effectively a three-tier application: the client services tier, the object model, and the data services layer. The usual Access interface that you view is the client services tier and is the layer that normally communicates with the user.

Underneath this sits the various object models. The important ones are Access, DAO (Data Access Objects), and ADO (ActiveX Data Objects). Each time you do something in your database, you are issuing commands through one of these object models. For example, if you create a new query, the underlying code uses the **QueryDefs** collection and the **QueryDef** object in the DAO object model to hold the details of your query.

Similarly, you can use the **CurrentDb** object to obtain the file name (and path) of the database:

```
MsgBox CurrentDb.Name
```

The **CurrentDb** object is part of the Access object.

Using the object models and a programming language such as Visual Basic, it's not difficult to develop your own Access front end with exactly the same functionality as the Microsoft Access front end. Every menu command and function key on the Microsoft Access l front end is represented within the object models. This is not to say that these are the exact objects that Access uses itself, but Microsoft has empowered you with all the objects and methods for you to do anything in code that can be done from the Access menu, and as you will find out in the practical examples later in this book, a whole lot more besides.

Strangely enough, if you decided to write your own front end, there would be relatively little code to write because all the functionality is contained in the object model. Below the object models sits the data services layer, which holds the data in the tables and is modified by commands from the object models.

The object models contain a large number of objects—for example, **CurrentDb**, **TablesDef**, **QueryDef**, **Forms**, and **Reports**. These objects are discrete entities that offer various pieces of data analysis functionality. Most important, they can be controlled from your code.

When programming in Access using VBA, you use standard VBA commands and functions such as For..Next, If..Then..Else, and MsgBox, but you use the object model to communicate with the Access application by manipulating the properties and methods of the various objects at your disposal, such as the **TableDef** object or the **QueryDef** object.

An object is a programming structure encapsulating both data and functionality that is defined and allocated as a single unit and for which the only public access is through the programming structure's interfaces.

An object is a part of the Access program. The objects are arranged in a hierarchy. For example, at the top of the Access object model is the **Application** object, which is Access itself. For example, under the **Application** object is the **CurrentDb** object, and within the **CurrentDb** object are **TableDef** objects. Within each **TableDef** object are **Field** objects, and so on.

Each object can contain settings, called properties, and actions that can be performed on the object, called methods. For example, if you want to view or edit the SQL for a specific query, you can look at the SQL property of a particular query within the **QueryDefs** collection. An example might be

```
MsgBox CurrentDb.QueryDefs("MyQuery").SQL
```

You can also write to some of the properties (if they are not read-only). In this way, you can change a query definition:

```
CurrentDb.QueryDefs("MyQuery").SQL = "select * from MyTable"
```

Properties and Methods Explained

All objects in the object models have properties or methods or both. Some have very few; others have many, depending on the complexity of the object. A *property* is a scalar attribute that defines various parameters of an object. An example is the **Visible** property of an open form, which can be **True (−1)** or **False (0)** and dictates whether the form is visible to the user or hidden. This is done here using built-in constants for True or False (numeric values are in parentheses).

The **Forms** object has a **Count** property that defines how many forms are open in the Access application. The properties hold the parameters that define the object. Properties are very much dependent on the objects they are part of, and their values can be text or numeric.

Methods are ways of executing actions based on a particular object. They provide a shortcut to doing something on a particular object. For example, you may want to delete a field from a table on-the-fly. To do this, use the **Delete** method on the fields collection based on that particular **TableDef** object. Similarly, the **TransferSpreadsheet** method in the **DoCmd** object transfers data between your database and a spreadsheet. The hard work has been done for you, and all you have to do is call these methods from your code.

Take your computer, for example. It is an object and you can define properties and methods for it. A property is a measurable aspect of an object, so for your computer you could have the following properties:

Property	Value
Make	Compaq
Year	2009
RAM	8GB
Hard Disk	320GB
Processor	Intel

Note that these are not all numeric. It is easy to get the idea that a property is always something directly measurable, such as the height of an object, and is therefore always numeric. However, properties may also be text, Boolean (True or False), graphic (in the case of pictures or icons), or enumerated from a specific list relating to that property. They can be any data type.

Methods are words that represent actions that can be performed by the object. For your computer, these could be

► Cold boot

► Warm boot

► Shut down

► Set up

Transferring this theory to an Access database and using the CurrentProject object as the example, you have properties such as:

Property	Description
Path	The path to the Access file
FullName	The full name with path of the workbook
AccessConnection	The connection string for this Access database—this can be used to make a connection from another Access database (see Chapter 19)
Name	The file name of the Access database

Of course, many other properties exist, but this gives you an idea of what some properties look like.

Examples of object methods on the **CurrentDb** object include the following:

Method	Description
CreateQueryDef	Creates a new query based on tables within the database
CreateTableDef	Creates a new table in the database
Execute	Executes a SQL statement on the database—an extremely useful method
NewPassword	Changes the password for the database or sets a new one if there is no previous password

Properties can be either read-only or read/write. Read-only means you can access the property's value (setting) but not change it. Read/write means you can both access and change a property's value. This can have an important effect on your program because you may find your code writing to properties that can only be read.

To preserve the integrity of the other property's object model, it may be important to keep the property read-only.

For example, the **Count** property of any collection of objects is always read-only. Altering the **Count** of **TableDefs** within a **TableDefs** collection could lead to very unpredictable results. For instance, there might be ten tables within the database. If you could change it to five tables, you would lose tables because they would be deleted!

Methods are effectively like subroutines or shortcuts to actions that you can call from your code to perform certain actions, such as setting a password on the database or opening a recordset based on a table. To try writing the code to set a password would be impossible because you do not know the finer points of the encryption system used for the password and where it is stored in the Access file structure. Without VBA, you'd need to know the intricacies of C and have the source code to set the password. However, Microsoft did all the hard work for us. They know the answers to all these questions, so all you need is one line of code calling the **NewPassword** method. With methods, you usually pass parameters as well—for example, the **NewPassword** method has to be given parameters for the old password and the new password.

Some parameters are optional when calling a method. They are indicated as being optional by being shown in square brackets ([ ]).

Manipulating Properties

If a property is read/write, it can be manipulated. This means you can substitute other values into it to provide different effects, depending on the object and the property. For example, you may want to use code to alter the SQL in a query. You can do this by writing your new SQL to the **SQL** property in the **QueryDef** object for that query.

Properties are generally manipulated by using code at runtime, when your program is executing. However, some properties are available at design time and can be changed using the Properties window within VBE. Design time is when you are viewing the code window and designing and making changes to your code.

To see an example of this, open or create a new report (the example assumes this has been saved with the name MyReport). While in Design View, open the Property Sheet by pressing ALT+ENTER (assuming that you do not already have the property sheet open) and scroll down to the property **Caption**. This will allow you to enter a text string that will appear in the control bar at the top of your report. However, you can change these properties using code, in response to user actions.

An example of the syntax for reading properties is shown here:

```
MsgBox Reports("MyReport").Caption
```

Bear in mind that the report has to be open for it to be in the **Reports** collection.

All collections have indexes that define individual objects within the collection. The title **"MyReport"** shown in parentheses defines that it is MyReport within the **Reports** collection that the code is referring to. There could be several reports loaded at once, and this is how VBA distinguishes between them.

Some objects are grouped together into other objects, or collections. For example, Access can have many forms or reports open at once. Each individual form or report is an object. All currently open Reports in the Access application are grouped together into the Reports object or collection. Accessing an individual item or member in a collection involves either specifying its numeric position in the collection or accessing its name (if it has one). The preceding code example accesses the report named **MyReport** in the **Reports** collection and displays the caption property.

Note that a dot is used as a separator between the object and the property. This is a bit like using a backslash (\) when defining pathnames for files. You can have more than one dot separator because objects can have sub-objects and properties can have subproperties. For example, a **TableDef** is a collection of **TableDefs** (table definitions), so one of the properties of the **TableDef** object is a **Fields** collection. If you want to refer to one field out of the collection, it would look like this:

```
MsgBox CurrentDb.TableDefs("MyTable").Fields(0).Name
```

This will display Name of the first field in the table MyTable. This demonstrates how the property is part of the overall picture of the object that is the Table. This can also be used to display other field properties such as Type and Size.

You can also change properties if they are not read-only. For example, you can change the name of a field by using the following code:

```
CurrentDb.TableDefs("MyTable").Fields(1).Name = "NewTest"
```

This will change the name of the second field in the table (the Fields index starts at zero) to NewTest. This is an example of needing to know what you are doing when writing to properties so that you can preserve the integrity of your application. The danger is that if you change the name of field names from within VBA code, it will almost certainly have a direct effect on queries, forms, and reports that use that table.

Just because the field name has changed does not mean Access automatically changes every object that is dependent on that table. So you would need to write extensive code to ensure that all the relevant changes are made throughout the database.

Calling Methods

As explained earlier, methods effectively are subroutines based on objects that take certain actions, sometimes dependent on parameters passed to them. The method is effectively a shortcut to an action, but you may need to specify parameters to define to VBA exactly what it is you want to do.

An example is using the **TransferSpreadsheet** method in the **DoCmd** object (see Chapter 16 for more information). You have to pass parameters, such as the TransferType, TableName, and FileName so VBA knows what it is required to transfer. For example, in the following code,

```
DoCmd.TransferSpreadsheet acExport, , "MyTable", "C:\temp\MyTable"
```

C:\temp\MyTable defines the location of the file to be exported to; this is a mandatory parameter for this method. The argument acExport defines that you are exporting data, and MyTable is the source for the data. Other optional parameters can be passed, too, such as a spreadsheet type if required and Has Field Names. Optional parameters are shown in the tip text for the method with square brackets around them, such as [HasFieldNames]. The tip text appears as you type in the VBA statement. This tip text box has a yellow background and shows all available parameters.

Sometimes it is unnecessary for a method to have arguments, such as when you use the **DoCmd** object to close a form or report. If the code is being run from the form or report itself, you do not need to specify the object type or the name of the object, since they are already there by default.

```
DoCmd.Close
```

This will close the form or report it is being run from, as if the user had clicked the "x" at the top-right corner of the window.

When we used the example earlier to transfer data to a spreadsheet, the second argument for the spreadsheet type was left blank because it will default to the current version of Excel installed on your machine.

```
DoCmd.TransferSpreadsheet acExport, , "MyTable", "C:\temp\MyTable"
```

This is called passing by order because the parameters are being passed in the order in which they are defined in the function, separated by commas.

When you enter the opening parenthesis, a list of parameters will appear, highlighted in bold as you enter each one. You have to stick to the order shown. If this is a function that assigns the result to a variable, you do not need to include the parentheses. You will get an error in some cases if you include them.

Some methods, such as **TransferSpreadsheet**, have a large number of parameters, and many of them are optional. Optional parameters are shown with square brackets ([ ]). Passing by order becomes more complicated with optional parameters because you may be using a function that has ten possible parameters even if you want to use only two of them. Consider the following example for importing data from a spreadsheet. This example assumes you already have a current spreadsheet file called MyTable on the root directory of the C drive.

```
DoCmd.TransferSpreadsheet acImport, , "MyTable1", "C:\MyTable", ,"A1:G10"
```

Notice that four parameters are being passed to open the file, although at least two parameters are not being used, as shown by the Null values between the commas. This is because these are optional parameters and do not have to be given a value. For example, a spreadsheet type has not been given because the default is the current version of Excel installed. Also, no HasFieldNames argument has been provided because the default is False.

The split between mandatory and optional parameters depends on what the method is doing and how the code in the Excel Object Library has been written. Optional parameters are always shown with square brackets ([ ]) around them.

It looks confusing, and anyone reading the code will not be able to immediately interpret what is going on and what the parameters mean. If you are looking at a VBA application that has been written by someone else, it may take more time to interpret what is going on than if the passing by name method was used. Code should always be easy for another person to understand in case they have to perform maintenance on it. If you have written a professional application for commercial use and you are suddenly unavailable to maintain it, someone else needs to be able to look at your work and quickly understand your code.

Passing by name is another way of passing parameters that makes it less confusing and shows the names of the parameters being passed. Passing by name enables you to selectively pass arguments without having to specify Null values for arguments you don't want to use. It also makes it easier to understand what is being passed to the method. If you pass by name, the preceding example can be rewritten as follows. As before, this example assumes you already have a spreadsheet file called MyTable on the root directory of the C drive.

```
DoCmd.TransferSpreadsheet TransferType:=acImport,TableName:="MyTable", _
FileName:="C:\MyTable",Range:="A1:G10"
```

You can define each parameter by naming the parameter and following it with a colon and an equal sign (:=). When passing by name, you can pass the parameters in any order, unlike passing by order, which strictly defines the order passed.

Collections Explained

In object-oriented programs, it is important to understand the concept of collections. *Collections* are objects that contain a group of the same objects. An example is the **TableDefs** collection, which contains all the table objects for a given database. All the TableDefs are like objects because they have the same properties and methods. An object such as a **Query** has different properties and methods and so cannot be part of the **TableDefs** collection, but it would fit into the **QueryDefs** collection.

In Access, all objects are either singular objects referenced by name or objects in a collection referenced by index or name. Collections also have their own properties and methods apart from the objects that they hold. For example, collections always hold a **Count** property that represents the number of objects within the collection, and they sometimes have an **Add** method to add a new object into the collection.

These objects also have their own properties and methods and can also contain further collections of objects. An example is the **TableDefs** collection, which contains a collection of **TableDef** objects (table definitions), representing all tables in Access. As you have already learned, it has a **Count** property to index the number of **TableDefs**, and it has an **Append** method to create a new **TableDef**. Each **TableDef** within the collection has properties such as **DateCreated** and methods such as **CreateField** or **CreateIndex**. However, there is also a collection of Fields within each **TableDef** that then has its own properties, methods, and collections.

In Access, you can have a collection of Fields inside a **TableDef** called the **Fields** collection, and each Field inside this collection will have an index number and a name to identify it. The index number is a reference for an object within that collection, commencing at 0.

The same thing is true of the **TableDefs** collection, which defines all the tables within the Access database. There is a collection of table definitions called the **TableDefs** collection, and each **TableDef** object inside will be enumerated with an index number and a name to identify it. Other collection objects are available, such as **QueryDefs**, **Forms**, and **Reports**, but the **TableDef** and **TableDefs** collections make good examples on how to use collections.

Collections can be cycled or iterated through. *Cycling* is the best term to describe what happens in a For Each..Next loop. For Each..Next loops are covered in Chapter 4. You use the following syntax: For Each Object within Collection, Next. This cycles through each object within the collection, giving you the chance to examine or manipulate the properties of it or to use a method by calling it, for example

```
CurrentDb.TableDefs("MyTable").CreateField("NewField")
```

Try putting the code shown in the following listing in a VBA module. If you do not already have a module displayed, use Insert | Module from the VBE menu. Your screen should look like Figure 14-1.

Press F5 to run it and you will see each table's name displayed, as shown in Figure 14-2.

```
Sub ShowName()
Dim w As TableDef
For Each w In CurrentDb.TableDefs
     MsgBox w.Name
Next w
End Sub
```

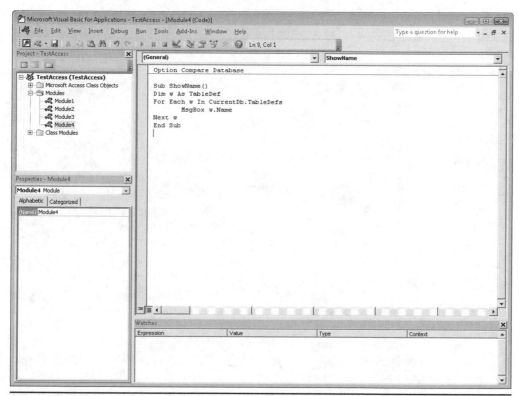

Figure 14-1   *Message box displaying names of Table Definitions*

Initially, this code sets up a variable **w** to represent a **TableDef** object. This represents the current table definition being cycled through. The code then cycles through the **TableDefs** collection using a For Each..Next loop. The code takes each table definition in turn, gets the name property, and displays it in a message box onscreen, as shown in Figure 14-1. Your code sheet should look like Figure 14-2.

The **Dim** statement is short for *Dimension*; it creates a space in memory for a variable. In this case, it creates space for a standard table definition. You can run this routine without the **Dim** line, but it does have advantages because it will give you automatic assistance with properties and methods. When you type the **Dim w As** statement, a list box appears when you get to the **TableDef** part. When you type in **MsgBox w.name**, a list box will appear after you type **w** that shows all the properties and methods you can use. This is extremely helpful when programming because it allows you to immediately see what your options are for the next piece of code.

The structure of the object models is extremely complicated, and you should not expect to remember every object, collection, property, and method within it. If you do not use the automatic list boxes that appear as you type object code in, you will be constantly referring to

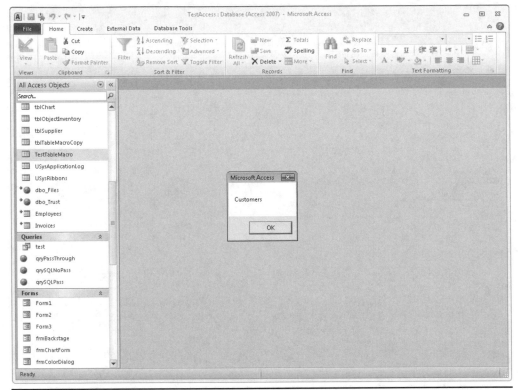

Figure 14-2   *Displaying names of all Table Definitions within the Table Definitions collection*

the Object Browser for this information because it can be difficult to know what command to use next. It is also easy to make mistakes that cause your code to produce errors when you run it.

Using the Object Browser

The Object Browser is a useful tool for looking at the properties, methods, and constants of an object—in this case, the Access and DAO (Data Access Objects) **Application** object. To access the Object Browser, select View | Object Browser from the VBE menu or press F2. Use the pull-down that says <All Libraries> to find the Object Library you require, and click it. This will show all the classes of, for example, the Access object and the properties and methods. It will also show the relationships and hierarchy of the objects themselves. Figure 14-3 shows how it looks onscreen.

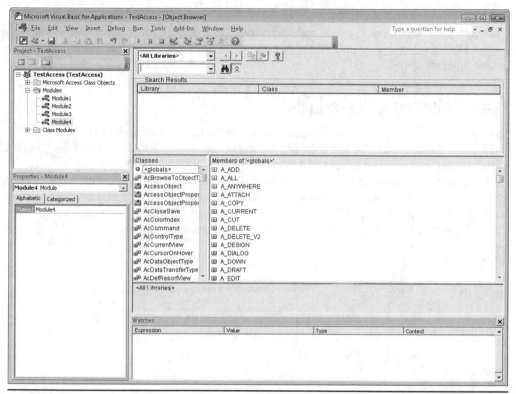

Figure 14-3   *The Access object model in the Object Browser*

By default, the Object Browser references two separate object models. This is Access and DAO. The Access object model references the application itself, using collections such as Forms and Reports, and the DAO object model is pointed at the use of the data itself and uses objects such as TableDefs and QueryDefs.

You can search on specific strings by entering your search string into the box underneath the pull-down showing <All Libraries> and then clicking the binoculars symbol or pressing ENTER. For example, you may want to know which parts of the DAO object model deals with QueryDefs. Simply type **QueryDef** into the Search box, click the binoculars symbol, and you will see all references containing the word *QueryDef*. This is far easier than investigating each hierarchical structure, which could take some time.

You can click a class (which is an object) to see all the properties, methods, and collections underneath it. If you have searched on the word *QueryDef*, click the Class QueryDefs (which is the actual collection of all queries) and examine the methods and properties available in the Members box to the right of the class. Methods have a green icon, and properties have a gray icon with a hand holding it.

Clicking a property will show whether a property is read-only or if you can write to it. It will also show the object that owns it. The pane at the bottom of the Object Browser will show the property type and if it is read-only. Clicking a method displays the syntax for parameters and which ones are optional and mandatory. The window at the bottom of the Object Browser displays the full syntax of the method, with optional properties shown in square brackets ([ ]).

Communicating with the Tables

One of the main uses of VBA in Access is to communicate with tables and to manipulate the data within them. To do this, you must use the **Recordset** object, which is part of the DAO object model (and can also be part of ADO).

The following example is based on the employees table of the Northwind sample database. You can load this database by loading Access and then clicking Sample in the center navigation pane (Available Templates). This will display an icon to load the Northwind database.

Insert the following code into a module within the Northwind database:

```
 Sub ViewData()
Dim RecSet As Recordset
Set RecSet = CurrentDb.OpenRecordset("Employees")

Do Until RecSet.EOF

    MsgBox RecSet![Last Name]
    MsgBox RecSet![First Name]
    RecSet.MoveNext

Loop
RecSet.Close
Set RecSet = Nothing
End Sub
```

This code first creates a **Recordset** object called RecSet by using the **Dim** statement. The **Recordset** object is then set to point to the table Employees by using the **OpenRecordset** method of the **CurrentDbobject**. You could also use a query name instead of a table name, or you could use an SQL select statement here.

One of the problems with using an SQL statement is that you need to make sure it works, otherwise you will get an unexpected error message.

Using a Do Until … Loop statement with the condition set to EOF (End Of File), the recordset is iterated through and message boxes will display the Last Name and First Name of each employee.

A **MoveNext** statement moves to the next record so the EOF marker is eventually reached. This is a very important statement because if it is not included, the code remains on the same record and goes nowhere. This is very easy to miss when you are concentrating on the code to read the fields, leaving you running a procedure that can never end.

Notice the statements to get the field data. An exclamation mark (!) is used instead of a dot (.) because the field names are not actually part of the Recordset object model and this must be distinguished.

Also, because Last Name and First Name contain spaces, the field names need to be enclosed in square brackets ([ ]), otherwise an error will occur.

This is a simple means to iterate through a recordset and show the data in each field. However, using VBA you are more than likely going to want to manipulate the data or add a new record.

To change the data, a similar methodology can be used, but we need to use the **Edit** and **Update** methods:

```
Sub EditData()
Dim RecSet As Recordset
Set RecSet = CurrentDb.OpenRecordset("Employees")

Do Until RecSet.EOF

    If RecSet![First Name] = "Nancy" Then
        RecSet.Edit
        RecSet![Company] = "Northwind"
        RecSet.Update

    End If

    RecSet.MoveNext

Loop
RecSet.Close
Set RecSet = Nothing
End Sub
```

This uses the same **Recordset** object as before, but there is now an **If** statement that checks whether the First Name is Nancy. If this is true, then the recordset is put into Edit mode and the Company field for that record is changed to Northwind. The record is then updated in the database.

If you run this code, you will see that the Company field in the Employees table for any employee with the first name of Nancy is changed to Northwind.

Any changes you make to data must adhere to the rules of the table. You cannot place text into a numeric field and you cannot put a null value into a required field. Also, the table must not already be open in design mode.

You can also add new records to the table:

```
Sub AddData()
Dim RecSet As Recordset
Set RecSet = CurrentDb.OpenRecordset("Employees")
```

```
RecSet.AddNew
RecSet!Company = "MyCompany"
RecSet![Last Name] = "Shepherd"
RecSet![First Name] = "Richard"
RecSet.Update
RecSet.Close
Set RecSet = Nothing

End Sub
```

Again, a **Recordset** object is created, but this time we do not need to iterate through it. The **AddNew** method is used and the fields for the new record are populated with data. Not all are required fields, so for the purposes of this example only three are populated. The recordset is then updated and the record is added to the table. Note that you do not need to do anything with the ID field since this is an autonumber field and is updated automatically.

You have probably noticed by now how much code references the "tree" of objects. For example, you can start with the **Application** object, reference the CurrentDb underneath it, then reference a **TableDef** within the **TablesDefs** collection, and finally reference a Field.

The **Application** object is the root, the **CurrentDb** and **TableDef** objects are the branches, and the **Field** object is the leaves. This can become somewhat laborious if you're working with many lines of code and you have to keep writing out this enormous reference to identify a particular value. As a shortcut, you can refer to the TablesDef name, for example:

```
MsgBox CurrentDb.TableDefs("Employees").Fields.Count
```

This will work, but fortunately, there is a way to cut down the amount of referencing and keep the integrity of the code by using the **Dim** statement to create a **TableDef** object in memory.

Using Transactions

One of the problems with processing data through VBA is that an unexpected error may be encountered, perhaps due to the data type being incompatible. There could also be a power outage that might stop your program. When this happens, some records will have been processed, but not all of them.

The question is how far your code has processed records. At this point, the data's integrity has been compromised—with some records having been processed, and others still waiting—and you have no idea where the break happened.

If you are running a large process, it is a good idea to use a Transaction. This allows your code to amend the recordset, but it does not actually get written back to the table until a **Commit** statement is made. The **Commit** statement is the final VBA statement, so if for any reason, your procedure fails part way through, the table remains as it was before.

The code is similar to previous examples:

```
Sub EditData()
Dim RecSet As Recordset, WrkSp as Workspace
Set RecSet = CurrentDb.OpenRecordset("Employees")
```

```
Set WrkSp = DBEngine.Workspaces(0)
WrkSp.BeginTrans
Do Until RecSet.EOF

    If RecSet![First Name] = "Nancy" Then
        RecSet.Edit
        RecSet![Company] = "Northwind"
        RecSet.Update

    End If

    RecSet.MoveNext

Loop
If MsgBox("Save all changes?", vbQuestion + vbYesNo) = vbYes Then
  WrkSp.CommitTrans
Else
  WrkSp.Rollback
End If
RecSet.Close
WrkSp.close
Set RecSet = Nothing
Set WrkSp = Nothing
End Sub
```

In this example, there is a new **Workspace** object called WrkSp. This is set to the current workspace. Before your code is run to edit the recordset, a **BeginTrans** statement is used. This defines the beginning of the transaction and ensures that nothing can happen to the data until a **CommitTrans** statement is issued.

When the code has iterated through the recordset, a message box is displayed to ask to save all changes. If the user selects Yes, then a **CommitTrans** statement is made, which saves all the changes to the table. If the user chooses No, then a **Rollback** statement is made which erases all the changes.

Creating an Object in Memory

You can use this methodology to deal with any objects, but this example works with TableDefs and Fields.

When you create a **TableDef** object in memory, you define a variable to represent that table by dimensioning a variable with the **Dim** statement. You can call your variable anything you want as long as it has not already been used in your code and is not a reserved word (see Chapter 2).

The advantage of creating a **TableDef** object is that it can be set to represent a particular table with a **Set** statement. After that, you can use that variable to reference that table, and the automatic list boxes showing the underlying properties, methods, and collections will still work with it. You can work without the **Set** statement, but it means working without the automatic list boxes and providing a full hierarchy in every line of code. This example works with the Northwind database Employees table:

```
Dim Db As Database
Dim MyTable As TableDef, MyField As Field

Set Db = CurrentDb

Set MyTable = Db.TableDefs("Employees")

Set MyField = MyTable.Fields("Company")

MsgBox MyField.Size
```

The **Dim** statements create three variables: **Db** as Database, **MyTable** as TableDef, and **MyField** as Field. The first **Set** statement sets **Db** to point to the CurrentDb. Why can you not use the **CurrentDb** object directly here instead of going through an intermediate object? This is because the way in which the DAO object model is set up does not allow you to use the **TableDefs** collection directly on the CurrentDb object.

The second **Set** statement sets **MyTable** to point at the **Employees** table within the **TableDefs** collection of database, and the third **Set** statement sets **MyField** to point to the field "Company" within the Employees table.

Now you can use **MyField** as the field object for "**Company**" and display the size property of the field. This has the added advantage that all the list boxes of properties and methods will automatically appear as you write your code to show the options available for that particular object. Type **MyField** and then a dot in the procedure, and the list box will appear next to your code. You need only click the item required in the list box to complete your code.

Hierarchy

Within the object models is a hierarchy of objects. It is important to understand how this hierarchy works because of the implications in referring to objects. In most organizations there exists a hierarchy of jobs, for example. In the armed forces, you have generals of varying grades at the top of the hierarchy, with four-star generals at the very top. The structure then cascades down to colonels, majors, captains, and lieutenants. Orders are sent down from the top via the command structure. The object models work in a very similar way.

Consider the **Application** object as the four-star general in charge; a structure that radiates out from the general. The **CurrentDb** collection object could be considered a colonel, with the **TableDefs** collection object below it a major. Field objects would be the captain level.

The hierarchy is very important for issuing commands, and the order in which they are issued must go down the hierarchy. For example, a major cannot give an order to a general or a colonel. The major must accept orders from generals and colonels, but the major can give orders to captains and lieutenants. In the same way in the Excel object model, a **Field** object does not have properties and methods (commands) that apply to the **TableDef** object or the **CurrentDb** object. You cannot use a **Field** object and then issue a command to create a field to the **TableDef** object. This will create an error message because the **Field** sits within the **TableDef** object, not the other way around.

```
Fields("Company").TableDefs("Employees").CreateField
```

Just as a major cannot give a general an order to advance and attack, this will not work because the **TableDefs** object is at a higher level than the **Fields** object in the hierarchy. It breaks all the rules of the hierarchy.

There is one way around this: if the general happens to be the major's father! The general would listen to his son and then give the order, even though the suggestion comes from lower down the tree. VBA can work the same way by using the **Parent** property. This gives access to the methods of the **Parent** object.

Open the Northwind sample database. To do this, open Access and then click Sample in the left-hand Navigation pane and click the Northwind icon that appears.

Open the form "Order Subform for Order Details" in Design View. You will find this in the Forms section of the Navigation pane. In the module for this form, add the following code to the Form Current event:

```
MsgBox Me.Parent.Name
```

Save the form and close it. Open the form Order Details and a message box will appear giving the name of the parent form, which is Order Details. When you open the parent form, you also open your subform, which then fires the Form Current event. Your code picks up the name property from the parent object and displays it.

The highest object in the Access object hierarchy is called **Application** (this represents Access itself). The Access object deals with forms, reports, the current database, the **DoCmd** object, and various functions.

The DAO (Data Access Object), as its name implies, deals with accessing and manipulating the data in the database, creating tables and queries and record sets.

If you are using external databases and tables, you can also use the ADO (Active Data Objects) model. This is explained further in Chapter 19 on working with external databases.

The structure of the object model is discussed in more detail in Chapter 15. To know the structure of the object model well, you need to examine the Object Browser (press F2 on the code sheet to access it) and experiment on a module with the various objects.

CHAPTER 5

The Main Objects

I n the preceding chapter, we looked at the object models in terms of how they work, the hierarchy, and passing parameters. In this chapter, we'll look in more detail at the main collections and objects that you will be using within your code to communicate with the application and the database.

The objects discussed are **Application**, **Me**, **CurrentDb**, and **Recordset**.

Application Object

The **Application** object is at the highest point in the hierarchy of the object model and represents the whole Access application. It contains all the objects for the active Access application including DAOs (Data Access Objects). It also contains several useful functions for returning data from tables and queries, similar to the filters you would use.

You can also use it to quit the Access application and close down completely. The Application object is the default object and does not have to be specified within the syntax of the statement. For example, the following statement can be used to get the name of the first printer in the Printers collection:

```
Printers(0).DeviceName
```

Main Properties, Methods, and Collections

This section details the main properties, methods, and collections you will use within the Application object.

CurrentDb

CurrentDb is a top-level DAO (Data Access Objects) object. It allows you to create recordsets and use your VBA code to interact with them. Because it is one of the main objects, it is dealt with in more detail in this chapter.

CurrentProject

The **CurrentProject** object represents the actual Access project and contains the details of all forms, reports, macros, and modules.

These are included in the following collections:

> AllForms
> AllReports
> AllMacros
> AllModules

These collections are very useful since they will provide details of all the forms and reports within the project, not just the ones that are actually loaded at that point in time. For example, there is also a Forms collection under the Application object, but this only refers to forms that are open, which can be restrictive.

You can refer to an AllForms collection as follows:

```
MsgBox CurrentProject.AllForms("MyForm").DateCreated
```

This will display the date and time that the form MyForm was created. Chapter 32 (Create an Objects Inventory) shows how to use these collections further.

A very useful property of the **CurrentProject** object is the Path property. This can be used to supply the path that the database was loaded in from:

```
MsgBox CurrentProject.Path
```

When you distribute an Access application, users may load it from completely different pathnames, depending on how their network drives are mapped. You may wish to interact with other files within your Access folder, such as importing or exporting to text or Excel files.

When the user loads your application you do not know exactly what the path is back to the folder where the application was loaded from, but the Path property will tell you.

This is very useful also if the application is moved from one server to another, such as from a test environment to a live environment. If you hardcoded the pathnames, you would need to make changes within the code and this can easily lead to errors. Using the Path property gets around this.

DAvg

This method **DAvg** allows you to extract the average value for a numeric field from a specified table. An example is:

```
MsgBox DAvg("MyField", "MyTable")
```

MyField must be a numeric value. The method will return the average of all the MyField values within the table. You can use an optional criterion as follows:

```
MsgBox DAvg("MyField", "MyTable","MyName='Richard'")
```

Notice that single quotes are used within the string parameter to denote that the MyName criterion is a string.

DCount

This method allows DCount lets you extract the number of records from a specified table. An example is:

```
MsgBox DCount("MyField", "MyTable")
```

You can use an optional criterion as follows:

```
MsgBox DCount("MyField", "MyTable","MyName='Richard'")
```

Notice that single quotes are used within the string parameter to denote that the MyName criterion is a string.

DbEngine

DbEngine is a top-level DAO(Data Access Object) object. You can use this object to work with transactions.

One of the problems with processing data through VBA is that an unexpected error may be encountered, perhaps due to the data type being incompatible. A power outage could also stop your program. When this happens, some records will have been processed, but not all of them.

The question is how far your code has processed records. At this point, the data integrity has been compromised with some records having been processed, but others are still waiting, and you have no idea where the break happened.

If you are running a large process, it is a good idea to use a Transaction. This allows your code to amend the recordset, but it does not actually get written back to the table until a **Commit** statement is made. The **Commit** statement is the final VBA statement, so if for any reason your procedure fails part way through, the table remains as it was before.

The code is similar to previous examples:

```
Sub EditData()
Dim RecSet As Recordset, WrkSp as Workspace
Set RecSet = CurrentDb.OpenRecordset("Employees")
Set WrkSp = DBEngine.Workspaces(0)
WrkSp.BeginTrans
Do Until RecSet.EOF
```

```
        If RecSet![First Name] = "Nancy" Then
            RecSet.Edit
            RecSet![Company] = "Northwind"
            RecSet.Update

        End If

        RecSet.MoveNext

Loop
If MsgBox("Save all changes?", vbQuestion + vbYesNo) = vbYes Then
   WrkSp.CommitTrans
Else
   WrkSp.Rollback
End If
RecSet.Close
WrkSp.close
Set RecSet = Nothing
Set WrkSp = Nothing
End Sub
```

In this example, there is a new **Workspace** object called WrkSp. This is set to the current workspace. Before your code is run to edit the recordset, a **BeginTrans** statement is used. This defines the beginning of the transaction and ensures that nothing can happen to the data until a **CommitTrans** statement is issued.

When the code has iterated through the recordset, a message box is displayed to ask to save all changes. If the user selects Yes, a **CommitTrans** statement is made, which saves all the changes to the table. If the user chooses No, then a **Rollback** statement is made that erases all the changes.

DFirst

This method **DFirst** lets you extract a field value in the first record found in a table. An example is:

```
MsgBox DFirst("MyField", "MyTable")
```

This will return the value of MyField for the first record in the table MyTable. You can use an optional criterion as follows:

```
MsgBox DFirst("MyField", "MyTable", "MyValue>6")
```

DLast

This method **DLast** allows you to extract a field value in the last record found in a table. An example is:

```
MsgBox DLast("MyField", "MyTable")
```

This will return the value of MyField for the last record in the table MyTable. You can use an optional criterion as follows:

```
MsgBox DLast("MyField", "MyTable", "MyValue<=10")
```

DLookup

The **DLookup** method allows you to extract a field value found in a table using a criteria string. An example is:

```
MsgBox DLookup("MyField", "MyTable", "MyValue=5")
```

This will return the value of MyField in the table MyTable where MyValue is equal to 5. The criteria parameter is optional, but if this is not entered, the method will work in the same way as **DFirst**.

This will only return one value. If there are several records within the criteria, only the value for the first one will be returned.

DMax

The method **DMax** allows you to locate the maximum field value in the first record found in a table. An example is:

```
MsgBox DMax("MyField", "MyTable")
```

This will return the maximum value of MyField in the table MyTable. MyField can be any data type. You can use an optional criterion as follows:

```
MsgBox DMax("MyField", "MyTable", "MyValue>6")
```

DMin

The method **DMin** allows you to locate the minimum field value in the first record found in a table. An example is:

```
MsgBox DMin("MyField", "MyTable")
```

This will return the minimum value of MyField in the table MyTable. MyField can be any data type. You can use an optional criterion as follows:

```
MsgBox DMin("MyField", "MyTable", "MyValue>6")
```

DoCmd

DoCmd is a very important object for Access VBA programmers as it emulates all the macro commands available in the macro window. It is discussed in detail in Chapter 16.

DSum

The method **DSum** lets you sum field values for a given field within a table. An example is:

```
MsgBox DSum("MyField", "MyTable")
```

This will return the sum of all MyField values in the table MyTable. MyField must be a numeric data type. You can use an optional criterion as follows:

```
MsgBox DSum("MyField", "MyTable", "MyName='Richard'")
```

Notice that single quotes are used within the string parameter to denote that the MyName criterion is a string.

DVar/DVarP

The methods **DVar** and **DVarP** let you estimate the variance of field values for a given field within a table. An example is:

```
MsgBox DVar("MyField", "MyTable")
```

This will return the variance of all MyField values in the table MyTable. MyField must be a numeric data type. You can use an optional criterion as follows:

```
MsgBox DVar("MyField", "MyTable", "MyName='Richard'")
```

Notice that single quotes are used within the string parameter to denote that the MyName criterion is a string.

The **DVar** method is used to estimate the variance across a population sample, and the **DVarP** method is used to estimate the variance across a population.

Forms

The **Forms** collection represents all the forms in the application that are open and loaded. It allows considerable scope for manipulation using properties and methods. You can also change the properties, and by using the controls collection within a form object you have access to the properties and methods of an individual control, which provides a very powerful means of on-the-fly manipulation.

You can iterate through the **Forms** collection using the following code:

```
For Each frm In Forms
    MsgBox frm.Name
 Next frm
```

This will display the name of each form loaded, but notice that it does not include forms that are not loaded.

You can address controls on a form by using the Controls collection:

```
MsgBox Forms("MyForm").Controls("label0").Caption
```

This will display the caption of the control called label0. You can also use this to change the caption of the label control.

Printer

Printer will allow you access to the default printer properties. You can view the name of the default printer using the following code:

```
MsgBox Printer.DeviceName
```

Printers

Printers is a collection of all the printers available to the application and contains all the properties for each printer. You can iterate through the collection with the following code:

```
Dim Prt As Printer
For Each Prt In Printers

    MsgBox Prt.DeviceName
Next Prt
```

This will display all the names of the print devices available and will mirror the printer drop-down in the standard Print dialog in Microsoft Office.

Quit

As the name **Quit** implies, this will quit the application. It is quite dangerous to use because you will be given no warnings, and nothing outstanding will be saved off. You can also use DoCmd.Quit, which does provide warnings.

References

The **References** collection contains all the references to external object libraries that are used within VBA. You can iterate through the collection with the following code:

```
Dim Reff As Reference
For Each Reff In References
    MsgBox Reff.Name

Next Reff
```

Reports

The **Reports** collection is very similar to the Forms collection discussed earlier. It only contains reports that are open and loaded, but it does give you access to the properties of controls on the report. You can iterate through the **Reports** collection as follows:

```
Dim Rep As Report
For Each Rep In Reports

    MsgBox Rep.Name

Next Rep
```

This will display the name of each report loaded, but notice that it does not include reports that are not loaded.

You can address controls on a report by using the **Controls** collection:

```
MsgBox Forms("MyForm").Controls("label0").Caption
```

This will display the caption of the control called label0. You can also use this to change the caption of the label control.

Screen

The **Screen** object provides properties for the screen of the application. You can use it to find out what the active form or report is:

```
MsgBox Screen.ActiveReport.Name
```

You can also use it to change the MousePointer icon. This code changes the MousePointer icon to an hourglass or busy icon:

```
Screen.MousePointer = 11
```

This code changes it back to the default:

```
Screen.MousePointer = 0
```

You could use Docmd.Hourglass to do this, but you can use a range of values here for different icons.

SysCmd

One of the most useful functions of the **SysCmd** object is to display a progress bar or meter similar to the one you see when a query is running. It is very simple to do. First, you initialize the meter:

```
SysCmd acSysCmdInitMeter, "Making Progress...", 100
```

This statement provides a label to describe the progress bar and sets an upper limit of 100 for the value. This can be set to any value.

Next, you create a statement to update the meter:

```
SysCmd acSysCmdUpdateMeter, 10
```

This gives a value of 10 to show how far the meter has moved. In this case, the upper limit is 100, so this will fill in 10 percent of the progress bar.

Finally, when your process has finished, you need to remove the meter:

```
SysCmd acSysCmdRemoveMeter
```

This is very useful when you have a long process running that may embody several large queries. You can provide the user with an indication of how far the process has run instead of them seeing the progress bar for each individual query.

Version

Version will tell you the version of Access that is being run. This is useful to know when the user loads your application because the application may load correctly and begin running, but you may have made use of features peculiar to a later version of Access. You can then display a warning message or even force the user to quit the application.

```
If Application.Version <> "12.0" Then
    MsgBox "You need a later version of Access to run this
application", vbCritical
    Quit
End If
```

Me Object

The **Me** object is a special object that applies to forms and reports. Since it represents the active form or report, it can only be used on modules for forms or reports and not on inserted modules.

You can also use the forms or reports collection instead:

```
Forms("MyForm")
```

However, when writing code on a form or report module, it is easier to use the **Me** object.

Main Properties, Methods, and Collections

This section details the main properties, methods, and collections you will use within the **Me** object.

ActiveControl

ActiveControl represents the active control on the form or report. You cannot reference it on the Form Load or Form Activate events, because at that point there is not an active control.

```
Private Sub Detail_Click()
    MsgBox Me.ActiveControl.Name

End Sub
```

This will return the name of the control that has the focus.

If the control is a list box or drop-down, you can use the object to get the item selected. This code tests whether the first item in the list has been selected. It returns True (-1) if it has been selected, and False(0) if it is not selected.

```
MsgBox Me.ActiveControl.Selected(0)
```

AllowAdditions

On a form, you can set the **AllowAdditions** property to allow or deny users from adding new records to the underlying data source:

```
Me.AllowAdditions = True
```

This code allows users to add new records on the active form.

AllowDeletions

On a form, you can set the **AllowDeletions** property to allow or deny users from deleting records in the underlying data source:

```
Me.AllowDeletions = False
```

This code prevents users from deleting records on the active form.

AllowEdits

On a form, you can set the **AllowEdits** property to allow or deny users the right to edit records in the underlying data source:

```
Me.AllowEdits = True
```

This code allows users to edit records on the active form.

AllowFilters

On a form or report, you can set the **AllowFilters** property to allow users to allow filters or deny them from using filters:

```
Me.AllowFilters = True
```

This code allows users to use filters.

Caption

You can use the **Caption** property to set the caption on the form or report:

```
Me.Caption = "MyCaption"
```

Dirty

The property **Dirty** can be used on a form to determine if any changes have been made to the data on the form:

```
MsgBox Me.Dirty
```

This returns True if a change has been made and False if no change has been made. The form must be bound to a table or query for this to work.

Filter

The **Filter** property returns the filter that is being used on the form:

```
MsgBox Me.Filter
```

It can also be used to set the filter on the form:

```
Me.Filter = "MyField>4"
```

Hwnd

Hwnd returns the handle for the window of the form or report. It is useful if using API calls within the module for the form or report since some API calls require this as a parameter. See Chapter 20 for more information on API calls.

```
MsgBox Me.Hwnd
```

Picture

The **Picture** property allows you to manipulate the background picture on the form or report:

```
Me.Picture = "C:\Users\Richard\Pictures\MyPicture.jpg"
```

Once loaded, the picture becomes part of the form or report and does not rely on the path.

Printer

You can access, and in some cases change, the properties for the printer device for the form or report. The following code will provide the printer name for the active form or report.

```
MsgBox Me.Printer.DeviceName
```

RecordSource

The **RecordSource** property will provide the record source that is bound to the form or report, such as a table or query.

```
MsgBox Me.RecordSource
```

Refresh

The **Refresh** method updates the underlying records of a form immediately so as to enact any changes the user has made.

```
Me.Refresh
```

Repaint

The **Repaint** method is used to complete any pending screen updates and recalculations on a form. Sometimes if there is a long-running process on the form, the form can be left half-drawn on the screen, which looks untidy to the user. Doing a **Repaint** before the process is run tidies the form up.

```
Me.Repaint
```

Requery

The **Requery** method re-queries the form and updates all the controls accordingly. In a multiuser environment, another user could have changed data in a table that affects the form that the current user is viewing. The current user will be viewing stale data unless a Requery takes place.

```
Me.Requery
```

RibbonName

RibbonName holds the name of the ribbon specific to that form or report. If it is empty, then the default ribbon is displayed. Chapter 11 discusses how to create custom ribbons in Access.

```
Me.RibbonName = "MyNewRibbon"
```

ScrollBars

The **Scrollbars** property dictates how the form will show scroll bars. It takes the following values:

Value	Setting
0	No scroll bars
1	Horizontal only
2	Vertical only
3	Both

```
Me.ScrollBars = 2
```

This code will put a vertical scroll bar on the form.

SetFocus

This method sets the focus on the form or report. The focus may have been on a control on the form or report or on another form or report.

```
Me,SetFocus
```

Undo

The **Undo** method allows you to give the user an option not to save their changes. If the code is placed in the **Form_BeforeUpdate** event (see Chapter 9 for more information on forms), then you can use a message box to ask the user for a confirmation to save. If the user answers No, then the code uses the Undo method and all changes on the form are undone.

```
Me.Undo
```

Visible

You can use the Visible property to hide the form or report without closing it when it is not in use. The settings are True (visible) and False (not visible).

```
Me.Visible = False
```

This code will hide the form.

CurrentDb Object

The **CurrentDb** object represents the current databases in terms of tables, queries, and recordsets. It is used in VBA for communicating with the tables and queries.

Main Properties, Methods, and Collections

This section details the main properties, methods, and collections you will use within the **CurrentDb** object.

CreateQueryDef

The **CreateQueryDef** method creates a new query based on a name and a SQL text string:

```
CurrentDb.CreateQueryDef "NewQuery", "select * from MyTable"
```

This will create a new query called NewQuery, which will have the SQL "select * from MyTable."

CreateTableDef

The **CreateTableDef** method is used to create a new table definition. However, unlike the **CreateQueryDef** method, it needs further code to create the field definitions and to append the new table definition to the database:

```
Sub CreateTable()
Dim MyTable As TableDef

Set MyTable = CurrentDb.CreateTableDef("NewTable")

MyTable.Fields.Append MyTable.CreateField("LastName", dbText, 100)

CurrentDb.TableDefs.Append MyTable

End Sub
```

This code initially creates a **TableDef** object using the **Dim** statement. It then uses the **CreateTableDef** method to create a new table called NewTable.

The **CreateField** method is then used to create new fields for the table, in this case creating a field called LastName with a text type and size of 100 characters. This is appended to the new table definition.

Finally, the new table definition is appended to the **TableDefs** collection in the current database.

Execute

Execute is a very useful method for executing a SQL statement. It must be a statement that does not return records such as a delete, update, create table, or insert query.

```
CurrentDb.Execute ("delete * from newTable")
```

No warning messages are shown when the **Execute** statement is run, so there is no need to turn them off beforehand and reset them afterwards.

Name

The **Name** property will provide the path and filename of the current database.

```
MsgBox CurrentDb.Name
```

If you only need the path without the filename, use the **Path** property of the current project.

OpenRecordset

The **OpenRecordset** method creates a **Recordset** object and is used as a precursor to manipulating the recordset in terms of deleting, adding, and editing records.

```
Dim RecSet As Recordset
Set RecSet = CurrentDb.OpenRecordset("MyTable")
```

This code creates a **Recordset** object based on the table MyTable. The parameter MyTable can also be a query name or a SQL string that returns records.

Additional optional parameters can also be used:

▶   **Type**   A **RecordsetTypeEnum** constant that indicates the type of recordset to open such as dynaset or snapshot. A dynaset is read-write whereas a snapshot is read-only.

▶   **Options**   A **RecordsetOptionEnum** constant that specifies characteristics of the new recordset, such as Append Only or Read Only.

▶   **LockEdit**   A **LockTypeEnum** constant that determines locking for the recordset such as Optimistic or Pessimistic.

The **Recordset** object is discussed in more detail in the next section of this chapter.

QueryDefs

The **QueryDefs** collection represents all the query definitions within the database. You can iterate through this collection to see the names of all the queries and the underlying SQL:

```
Dim Qd As QueryDef
For Each Qd In CurrentDb.QueryDefs

    MsgBox Qd.Name & " " & Qd.SQL

Next Qd
```

You can use this collection to change the SQL of a given query.

TableDefs

The **TableDefs** collection represents all the table definitions within the database. You can iterate through this collection to see the names of all queries and the underlying fields:

```
Dim Td As TableDef
For Each Td In CurrentDb.TableDefs

    MsgBox Td.Name & " " & Td.Fields.Count

Next Td
```

This code will show the names of all the tables in the database and the number of fields in each.

Recordset Object

The **Recordset** object represents open recordsets based on tables or queries. It is used for performing deletes, edits, and updates on records. It is usually used in conjunction with the CurrentDb.OpenRecordset method:

```
Dim RecSet As Recordset
Set RecSet = CurrentDb.OpenRecordset("MyTable")
Do Until RecSet.EOF
    MsgBox RecSet![MyField]
    RecSet.MoveNext
Loop
```

This code is a simple example of how to iterate through a recordset based on the table MyTable, showing the value of MyField for each record.

All the following examples use the variable RecSet to define the **Recordset** object.

Main Properties, Methods, and Collections

This section details the main properties, methods, and collections you will use within the **Recordset** object.

AddNew

The **Addnew** method is used to add new records to the **Recordset** object. It has the effect of creating a new blank record, which is then populated via the fields with data. The **Update** method is then used to write the data to the table.

```
RecSet.AddNew
RecSet![MyField1] = "MyData1"
RecSet![MyField2] = "MyData2"
RecSet.Update
```

Bear in mind that the data you enter into each field must satisfy the rules for that field. For example, you cannot put text into a numeric field, and you must enter data for a required field, otherwise an error message will be generated.

BOF

The **BOF** property returns True or False as to whether the recordset is at the Beginning Of File (BOF). If it is true, then it is at the first record.

```
MsgBox RecSet.BOF
```

Close

The **Close** method closes the recordset and releases the underlying table:

```
RecSet.Close
```

It is important to do this at the end of your code because otherwise the underlying table will show it as being still in use. This will mean that you will be unable to make any structural changes to the table.

It is also a good idea to set the **Recordset** object to Nothing to release the memory. Some Recordset objects can be very large and can become memory-hungry if not fully erased.

```
Set RecSet = Nothing
```

Delete

The **Delete** method deletes the current record in the recordset:

```
RecSet.Delete
```

Unlike **AddNew**, you do not need to use the **Update** method after the delete.

Edit

The **Edit** method is used to edit records in the **Recordset** object. It allows changes to be made to data in specified fields. The **Update** method is then used to write the data to the table.

```
RecSet.Edit
RecSet![MyField1] = "MyNewData1"
RecSet![MyField2] = "MyNewData2"
RecSet.Update
```

Bear in mind that the data you enter into each field must satisfy the rules for that field. For example, you cannot put text into a numeric field, and you must enter data for a required field, otherwise an error message will be generated.

EOF

The **EOF** property returns True or False as to whether the recordset is at the End Of File (EOF). If it is true, then it is at the last record.

```
MsgBox RecSet.EOF
```

Fields

Fields is a collection representing all the fields within the **Recordset** object. It is useful if you need to obtain details on the field before any updating takes place.

```
With RecSet.Fields(0)
   MsgBox .Name
   MsgBox .Type
   MsgBox .Value
   MsgBox .Size
 End With
```

This code provides details of the first field in the record. Notice the index starts at 0.

FindFirst

The **FindFirst** method uses a specified criterion to find the first instance of a record within the recordset. The recordset must be opened as a snapshot or dynaset (which is updatable) for the method to work:

```
Dim RecSet As Recordset
Set RecSet = CurrentDb.OpenRecordset("MyTable", dbOpenDynaset)
RecSet.FindFirst ("MyField='Data'")
MsgBox RecSet!MyField
RecSet.close
Set RecSet=Nothing
```

This code will move to the first record where the field MyField contains the value Data.

FindLast

The **FindLast** method uses a specified criterion to find the last instance of a record within the recordset. The recordset must be opened as a snapshot or dynaset (which is updatable) for the method to work:

```
Dim RecSet As Recordset
Set RecSet = CurrentDb.OpenRecordset("MyTable", dbOpenDynaset)
RecSet.FindLast ("MyField='Data'")
MsgBox RecSet!MyField
RecSet.close
Set RecSet=Nothing
```

This code will move to the last record where the field MyField contains the value Data.

FindNext

The **FindNext** method uses a specified criterion to find the next instance of a record within the recordset. The recordset must be opened as a snapshot or dynaset (which is updatable) for the method to work:

```
Dim RecSet As Recordset
Set RecSet = CurrentDb.OpenRecordset("MyTable", dbOpenDynaset)
RecSet.FindNext ("MyField='Data'")
MsgBox RecSet!MyField
RecSet.close
Set RecSet=Nothing
```

This code will move to the next record where the field MyField contains the value Data. If the recordset is still at the first record, this will return the same results as a **FindFirst** method.

FindPrevious

The **FindPrevious** method uses a specified criterion to find the previous instance of a record within the recordset. The recordset must be opened as a snapshot or dynaset (which is updatable) for the method to work:

```
Dim RecSet As Recordset
Set RecSet = CurrentDb.OpenRecordset("MyTable", dbOpenDynaset)
RecSet.FindPrevious ("MyField='Data'")
MsgBox RecSet!MyField
RecSet.close
Set RecSet=Nothing
```

This code will move to the previous record where the field MyField contains the value Data. If the recordset is at the last record, this will return the same results as a **FindLast** method.

MoveFirst

The **MoveFirst** method selects the first record in the recordset.

```
RecSet.MoveFirst
```

MoveLast

The **MoveLast** method selects the last record in the recordset.

```
RecSet.MoveLast
```

MoveNext

The **MoveNext** method selects the next record in the recordset.

```
RecSet.MoveNext
```

This method is essential when iterating through a recordset. It is very easy to forget to include it in your code.

MovePrevious

The **MovePrevious** method selects the previous record in the recordset.

```
RecSet.MovePrevious
```

NoMatch

The NoMatch property is used after doing a Find such as FindFirst. It returns True if a match was found from the criteria, and False if not. It can then be used with an **If** statement to take appropriate action.

```
RecSet.FindFirst ("MyField='Data'")
MsgBox RecSet.NoMatch
```

RecordCount

The **RecordCount** property returns the number of records within the recordset. It is useful to test a query or table to find out if there is any data in it by using the following:

```
MsgBox RecSet.RecordCount
```

Requery

The **Requery** method re-queries the recordset. In a multiuser environment, other users may have made changes to the underlying table while your code is running, making the data in the recordset stale.

Update

The **Update** method is used to update the underlying table after an AddNew or Edit has taken place within the recordset. If no update is done, then changes will be lost.

The DoCmd Object

The **DoCmd** objcct is a special object model in Access VBA. It is fairly simple in structure but contains a number of methods that are very useful to an Access developer. It is almost impossible to write a complex Access application and not use **DoCmd** somewhere.

The methods encompass all the actions available to the developer when using macro sheets as opposed to VBA modules, so you effectively have all the macro functions built into VBA.

Some of the methods are now obsolete and no longer work in the latest versions of Access, but are still included for backward compatibility so that it will not produce an error message and stop your code from running. The problem of course is that it will not do what it was intended to do.

The **DoCmd** methods are simple to use within VBA. An example would be:

```
DoCmd.Quit
```

This will exit the database completely.

DoCmd Methods

This section shows the main methods of the **DoCmd** object that you will use within a VBA application.

Beep

Beep sounds a chime on the user's computer, provided that they have not muted the speakers! The syntax is:

```
DoCmd.Beep
```

This provides a very easy way of making a sound, although it is very limited in what it can do. If you need more flexibility, see Chapter 20 on API calls. API calls can also be used to play a variety of sounds.

Close

Close is used to close an object, usually a form or report, although other object types can be specified. It has three optional parameters. The syntax is:

```
Docmd.Close (ObjectType,ObjectName,Save)
```

ObjectType is an acObjectType constant representing the type of object to close. Examples are acForm and acReport. The object name is the name of the form or report to be closed, and Save is an acCloseSave constant that specifies whether to save the object or not.

This method is normally run on a form or report module of a "Close" button, so the optional parameters are not required. Although the user may be able to close the form by clicking the X in the top-right corner, you may want your code to have more control over the closing of the form.

CloseDatabase

CloseDatabase is the same as if you had clicked the Microsoft Office button in Access and then clicked the "Close Database" button. It has no parameters.

```
DoCmd.CloseDatabase
```

Hourglass

The **Hourglass** method lets you turn the cursor into an hourglass (or whatever icon is chosen to show a running procedure), or turn it back into the cursor. This is very useful because the hourglass cursor does not always appear when VBA code is running, and users like to have some reassurance that something is happening.

The syntax is:

```
DoCmd.Hourglass True
```

This turns the hourglass mouse pointer on. To turn it off, use:

```
DoCmd.Hourglass False
```

HourglassOn is True or False to denote whether to show the Hourglass.

If you switch the Hourglass on, remember to switch it back to a normal cursor afterwards. Also, I have found that if a piece of code crashes before the cursor is switched back, it will give the user the impression that everything is still running when it is not.

Maximize

Maximize will, just as its name implies, maximize the active window as if the user had clicked the Maximize button on it. It is normally used in the Open or Activate event of forms and reports to ensure that the window fits on the user's screen. Users frequently have different screen resolutions, and what looks good on your development screen can look terrible on a user's screen. Using this when a form or report is opened gets around this problem.

The syntax is:

```
DoCmd.Maximize
```

It has no parameters. Note that if you are not from North America, "Maximize" is spelled with a z, not an s. It is an easy mistake to make, leaving you wondering why you get an error when it runs!

There is also a **Minimize** method, which works in the same way, but minimizes the active window.

OpenForm

The **OpenForm** method will open a form. It is very useful when you have a hierarchy of forms that the user navigates through. The syntax is:

```
DoCmd.OpenForm _
(FormName,View,FilterName,WhereCondition,DataMode,WindowMode,OpenArgs)
```

The FormName is a required parameter, but the others are optional:

▶ **View**   An acFormView constant that specifies the view that the form will open in. This is acNormal by default.

▶ **FilterName**   The name of a query in the current database.

▶ **WhereCondition**   An SQL WHERE clause without the word WHERE.

▶ **DataMode**   An acFormOpenDataMode constant that specifies the data entry mode for the form.

▶ **WindowMode**   An acWindowMode constant that specifies the window that the form opens in.

▶ **OpenArgs**   This sets the form's **OpenArgs** property.

OpenQuery

The **OpenQuery** method will open a query so that the user can scroll through the results. However, it is better to open a form (based on a query) as a datasheet so that the user has all the filtering functionality. The syntax is:

```
DoCmd.OpenQuery(QueryName,View,DataMode)
```

The QueryName is a required parameter, but the others are optional.

▶ **View**   An acFormView constant that specifies the view that the form will open in. This is acNormal by default.

▶ **DataMode**   An acFormOpenDataMode constant that specifies the data entry mode for the form.

Action queries (such as delete, insert, or append) can be run in this way, but you can also use:

```
CurrentDb.Execute "MyQuery"
```

OpenReport

The **OpenReport** method will open a report and is very useful where you have a hierarchy of reports that the user navigates through. The syntax is:

```
DoCmd.OpenReport _ (ReportName,View,FilterName,WhereCondition,WindowMode,OpenArgs)
```

The ReportName is a required parameter, but the others are optional:

▶ **View**   An acFormView constant that specifies the view that the form will open in. This is acNormal by default.

▶ **FilterName**   The name of a query in the current database.

▶ **WhereCondition**   An SQL WHERE clause without the word WHERE.

▶ **WindowMode**   An acWindowMode constant that specifies the window that the form opens in.

▶ **OpenArgs**   This sets the form's **OpenArgs** property.

OpenTable

The **OpenTable** method will open a table so that the user can scroll through the results. However, it is better to open a form (based on a table) as a datasheet so that the user has all the filtering functionality. The syntax is:

```
DoCmd.OpenTable(TableName,View,DataMode)
```

The TableName is a required parameter, but the others are optional:

▶ **View**   An acFormView constant that specifies the view that the form will open in. This is acNormal by default.

▶ **DataMode**   An acFormOpenDataMode constant that specifies the data entry mode for the form.

PrintOut

The **PrintOut** method will print out the active object in the database, which can be a form, a report, or a datasheet. The syntax is:

```
DoCmd.PrintOut(PrintRange,PageFrom,PageTo,PrintQuality,Copies,CollateCopies)
```

The parameters are all optional:

▶ **PrintRange**   An acPrintRange constant specifying the range to print—the default is acPrintAll.

▶ **PageFrom**   The page number to print from. This is required if you use acPages for PrintRange.

▶ **PageTo**   The page number to print to. This is required if you use acPages for PrintRange.

▶ **PrintQuality**   An acPrintQuality constant to specify print quality—the default is acHigh.

▶ **Copies**   The number of copies required. The default is 1.

▶ **CollateCopies**   True (default) or False.

Quit

Quit is used to quit the Access application. The syntax is:

```
DoCmd.Quit(Options)
```

Options is an optional argument and is an acQuitOption constant. The default is acQuitSaveAll. If a user has added a filter to a form, there is a danger that this will be saved, which means when other users open that form the filter will still be there.

RunCommand

RunCommand lets you run certain menu commands. The syntax is:

```
DoCmd.RunCommand(Command)
```

Command is a required parameter and is an acCommand constant. Some of these are no longer available in later versions of Access so it can be a matter of trial and error to find out what still works. As an example, acCmdPrintSelection is still valid.

SetWarnings

The **SetWarnings** method is used to suppress warning messages. For example, if you are running a delete query, you would normally get a warning message that a number of records will be deleted.

If you are running this as part of a VBA procedure, you do not want warning messages pausing your code, and this is the way to turn them off. The syntax is:

```
Docmd.SetWarnings True
```

The WarningsOn argument is set to True to display the system messages, and False to suppress them:

```
Docmd.SetWarnings False
```

If you turn the warnings off, make sure you switch them back on when your code has finished. This method has an effect throughout your Access application. For example, you could be experimenting with a query and find that it does not work correctly. You decide to close it without saving and reload the original query.

If warnings are set to false, there is no warning message when you close the query (asking if you want to save changes). The default is save so your incorrect query is saved, messing up your earlier development work.

TransferSpreadsheet

TransferSpreadsheet gives a simple means to transfer data between an Excel spreadsheet and a table. If exporting to a spreadsheet, then a query can also be used as the source.

The syntax is:

```
DoCmd.TransferSpreadsheet _
(TransferType,SpreadsheetType,TableName,FileName,HasFieldNames,Range,UseOA)
```

The arguments are all optional:

▶ **TransferType**   This is acImport or acExport, depending on whether you are bringing data in from the spreadsheet or pushing it into the spreadsheet from the database.

▶ **SpreadsheetType**   This is an acSpreadsheetType constant so that older versions of Excel are still supported. Surprisingly, Lotus 123 format is also included.

▶ **TableName**   This is the table that data will be imported into or exported from. If you have chosen to export, you can also use a query here.

▶ **FileName**   The full name including the path of the spreadsheet file that you are importing/exporting to.

▶ **HasFieldNames**   True or False to indicate whether the spreadsheet has field names at the top.

The default is False.

▶ **Range**   This only applies to importing and specifies a range of cells to import. This argument must be left blank when exporting.

▶ **UseOA**   This argument is not used.

TransferText

TransferText is a useful command to interface with text files. It is very similar to clicking External Data in the Access menu and then clicking the Text File icon in the Import or Export group of the ribbon.

Before using this command, it is a good idea to import or export the file manually as a "dry run" to see what snags you run up against. If it works correctly, you can save your import or export specification with a particular name and this makes life far easier when using the **TransferText** method.

The syntax is:

```
DoCmd.TransferText _
(TransferType,SpecificationName,TableName,FileName,HasFieldNames, _
HTMLTableName,CodePage)
```

The arguments are all optional:

▶ **TransferType**   This is an acTextTransferType constant and is generally acImportDelim, acImportFixed, acExportDelim, or acExportFixed. The default is acImportDelim. This defines whether the fields are deliminated by a comma(,) or are fixed width, and whether you are importing or exporting to the text file.

▶ **SpecificationName**   This is the name of the specification you saved when you did your "dry run." It contains extra information such as which fields to include, how to treat dates, and what the deliminator character is.

▶ **TableName**   The name of the table to import/export to. If you are exporting, you can also put a query name here.

▶ **FileName**   The full name, including the path of the text file you are importing/exporting to.

▶ **HasFieldNames**   True or False as to whether the first row of import has field names. The default is false.

▶ **HTMLTableName**   A string that is the name of a table or list in an HTML file that you are importing/exporting to. This is only used for HTML files.

▶ **CodePage**   A long value giving the character set of the code page.

Using Access to Interact with Other Office Programs

A ll Microsoft Office applications use VBA as their underlying macro language, and they all have their own object model in the same way that Access has.

Because of this, Access VBA provides an enormous advantage over non-Microsoft programming languages when it comes to driving other Office programs. For example, you can create a Word document from within Access without Word ever appearing on screen. This may sound farfetched, but it is very easy to do. For example, you may design some code to manipulate data in a database. Your user may require the output to end up in a Word document or as part of that document. Access gives you the facility to open an external Word document, enter your data into it, and then save it, without even having any knowledge of how the file structure works in Word.

This can be done by using the **CreateObject** method in VBA. In order to use **CreateObject**, first add a reference in your application to the appropriate Microsoft Office Object Library file—in this case, the Word Object Library. If you have Office installed, this file will already be available and will automatically appear in the References list without your having to browse for its location. If you do not have all of Microsoft Office installed, you may not have this library file available unless it has been installed previously as part of another application.

When you add a reference to an Object Library, it then allows you to create objects for that application and to use the object model of that application, just as if you were programming in VBA inside that application.

You can add a reference by selecting Tools | References from the menus. All available reference files will appear in a dialog. You need to select the Microsoft Word Object Library and check the check box next to it, as shown in Figure 17-1.

Note that the location shown at the bottom of the References window points to an OLB file that is basically the Object Library for Word. The location points to the OLB file in the directory where Microsoft Office was originally installed. Click OK and you will be ready to use Word in VBA.

Here is a sample of code to create a new Word document and to save it to the local hard drive. This code will produce the same results whether Word is loaded or not, but it always looks more spectacular if Word is not running onscreen—making it seem as if you have done something very clever!

```
Sub Test_Word()
Dim oWd As Word.Application, oWdoc As Word.Document
Set oWd = CreateObject("Word.Application")
Set oWdoc = oWd.Documents.Add
oWdoc.Sections(1).Range.Text = "My new Word Document"
```

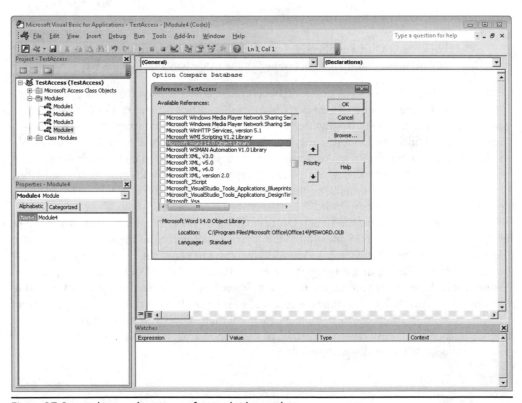

Figure 17-1   *Selecting the Microsoft Word Object Library*

```
oWdoc.SaveAs ("MyTest")
oWdoc.Close
oWd.Quit
Set oWdoc = Nothing
Set oWd = Nothing
End Sub
```

The first line declares the variables for the application and the document objects. Because you have a reference to the Object Library included, you will see the Word objects, methods, and properties appearing in the drop-down lists as you type the code in. If you did not include the reference to the Object Library, VBA will not recognize these object types and the application will fail.

You then use the application variable (**oWd**) to hold the created object for the Word application. Note that in the **CreateObject** parameter the description goes inside quote marks. This description uses the class name for the object and does not appear automatically because it is being entered as a string. You are not offered a list of choices for it. The string "Word.Application" is the class name for the application object within Word, which is why it is used here.

The **oWdoc** variable is now set to hold a new document based on the application variable (**oWd**). This is exactly the same as if you had loaded Word and then clicked the Office Start button and created a new Word document.

The text "My new Word Document" is then added to the first section of the document. This appears on the first section because you loaded the Word document, basically in the same way as if you had opened Word and then opened the file in Word. The cursor automatically defaults to the top of the document when this happens, and exactly the same thing happens in your code, because you are emulating the document being opened.

The document is saved as MyTest to the Documents folder on the local hard drive, and the Word document is then closed. Leaving it open causes reservation problems, which means that your application has exclusive write access to it. If anyone loads this document into Word, they can only load it as read-only because your application has the reservation on it. This can also cause problems when exiting Access. Because this is a virtual application, the document stays in memory if it is not closed (even if Access is shut down) properly, even though Access only had a reference to it. However, this particular instance of Word does not appear on the Windows taskbar because it was created virtually in code. The only way to detect its presence is to look in Task Manager.

If you do not close the virtual object down properly, when Windows shuts down, the virtual Word application will ask if the document needs saving because it still thinks there is an open document. This can be extremely confusing to the user, since they may have no idea that a Word application was open. To avoid this situation, the variables **oWd** and **oWdoc** are set to Nothing, and all memory held by them is released.

Try loading your newly created file into Word and you will see that it works as a perfectly normal Word document, just as if you created it using Microsoft Word.

This is a very simple example of manipulating Word from within Access using VBA. This can be very useful—for example, you could have a standard document with tables that the macro populated from the database data. You can run your macro and the data will be transferred into the document tables.

Recently, I had the task of writing a program to populate an SLA (Service Level Agreement) Report. The SLA Report was a Word document with many tables of data and charts, but the input came from several databases. Using the methods just detailed, I was able to write VBA code that worked through the database, extracted the relevant data, and placed the figures in the correct tables or charts in the Word document. Previously, it had taken someone half a day to do this manually, but the code accomplished it in under five minutes.

```
Sub Test_Word()
Dim oWd As Word.Application, oWdoc As Word.Document
Dim orx As Word.Range, ot As Word.Table
Set oWd = CreateObject("Word.Application")
Set oWdoc = oWd.Documents.Add
Set orx = oWdoc.Range
Set ot = oWdoc.Tables.Add(orx, 4, 5)
ot.Cell(1, 1).Range.Text = "test"
oWdoc.SaveAs ("MyTest")
oWdoc.Close
oWd.Quit
Set oWdoc = Nothing
Set oWd = Nothing
End Sub
```

This example cannot be done from within the Access menu unless you manually copy and paste, which can get laborious if there is a lot of data. This is a good example of the macro language giving the user enormous power to automate tasks within Microsoft Office and enabling you to work outside the menu structure that Microsoft has put in place.

Driving Microsoft Outlook

You can use exactly the same technology to drive Microsoft Outlook and make it send e-mails from your database or capture address book entries. Of course, Access has e-mail features for e-mailing an entire database, but this method lets you supply just a part of the sheet.

In order to use this code, you must have Microsoft Outlook installed on your computer (not Outlook Express or Windows Mail), although Outlook does not need to be actively running for this to work.

Start off by adding a reference to the Object Library file for Outlook. You do this by selecting Tools | References from the Visual Basic Editor menu. Choose the Microsoft Outlook Object Library and then click the check box next to it, as shown in Figure 17-2. Next, enter the following code into a module:

```
Sub Test_Outlook()
Dim oFolder As Outlook.MAPIFolder
Dim oItem As Outlook.MailItem
Dim oOutlook As New Outlook.Application
```

```
Dim MoOutlook As Outlook.NameSpace
Set MoOutlook = oOutlook.GetNamespace("MAPI")
Set oFolder = MoOutlook.GetDefaultFolder(olFolderOutbox)
Set oItem = oFolder.Items.Add(olMailItem)
With oItem
      .Recipients.Add ("richard.shepherd@anywhere.com")
      .Subject = "Test Access Email"
      .Body = "This is a test of an email from Access VBA"
      .Importance = olImportanceHigh
      .Send
End With
Set oItem = Nothing
Set oFolder = Nothing
End Sub
```

When this code is run, you will get a pop-up dialog box warning that e-mail address information is being accessed in Outlook. This is to prevent e-mail viruses, which use exactly the same code as this.

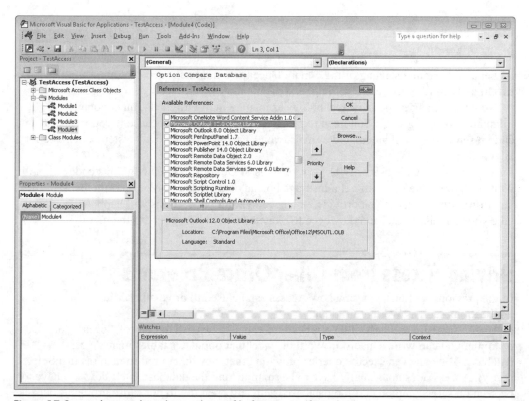

Figure 17-2   *Selecting the Object Library file for Microsoft Outlook*

The first four lines set up variables based on the Microsoft Outlook types. These are for the Outlook application, the NameSpace, the Outlook folder, and the Mail item. The variable **MoOutlook** is set to point to the namespace MAPI. This represents one of the messaging service provider layers that Outlook depends on for data storage. MAPI is the only type of namespace that Outlook supports.

The variable **oFolder** is then set to the default folder for the Outbox for the namespace. This sets up an object that represents the Outbox, into which you can then place your mail item. You do this by setting the variable **oItem** to a new mail item within that folder. This is exactly the same as when you open a new mail item in Microsoft Outlook itself. The code then goes through all the stages it normally does from the front end of Microsoft Outlook to create your e-mail.

The address of the recipient is added. At this point, you can add in your own address as a string to try out the example. If the recipient is internal to your network and is on the Outlook address list, you can simply use the name. The subject is what you would see in the title for the message. The body is the e-mail text itself. Don't forget you can use Chr(13), Chr(10), or vbCrLf to provide carriage returns in a string so you can insert a "Regards" statement at the end.

Importance allows you to set what priority you want the e-mail to have. The Importance constants are shown in a list box as you type this statement in. They are as follows:

```
olImportanceHigh
olImportanceNormal
olImportanceLow
```

Send is the actual sending of the e-mail. Once the e-mail has been sent, the variables **oItem** and **oFolder** are set to Nothing, and the memory is released.

Note that this uses the same technology as many e-mail viruses do, most notably the infamous Love Bug virus. You need to be careful with this code because if you're not, it can end up sending a lot of automated e-mails, which can clog up the mail system and make for angry recipients.

Microsoft has added security to later versions of Outlook, so, although this code will still work very well, the user will get a message box advising that e-mail is about to be sent. In any instructions to users you provide, you need to point out that this will happen when they take your e-mail feature, and they need to okay the e-mail being sent to them.

Driving Access from Other Office Programs

In the previous sections, you saw how Access can be used to drive other Microsoft applications such as Word or Outlook.

By the same token, these other applications can also be used to control Access. For example, you can write a macro in Word or Excel that populates tables in an Access database. You can even execute queries providing that they do not return data (as in a Select query). Access does not actually have to be running, and the database itself does not have to be seen on screen, although if the database is already open it will not cause problems because it is a multiuser application.

The example I am going to use writes to a table within an Access database from inside an Excel workbook. VBA works exactly the same in all Microsoft Office applications, except that the object model is obviously too different from application to application to take the functionality of the application into account.

First, you will need to create a sample table in an Access database for your code to send data to. To do this, click Create in the menu bar and then click the Table Design icon in the Tables group of the ribbon.

Create a single text field called MyText. Data Type must be specified as text. Save the table by giving it the name **TestAccess**. A dialog box will appear requesting a primary key to be defined. For the purposes of this example, a primary key is not required so answer "No."

Load Excel. Once you load Excel, you need to enter the VBA code window. This works exactly the same as in Access: press ALT+F11. The code window has exactly the same functionality as the one you are used to in Access.

When you used a different application from Access, you had to put in a reference to the Object Library file first. We have to do the same thing in Excel by putting in a reference to the Access Object Library in order to tell Word how to find the Access object model. However, because Access uses more than one object library, we need to put a second reference in to DAO (Data Access Objects) as well.

Use Tools | References from the Visual Basic Editor menu as before, but this time select the Microsoft Access Object Library and the Microsoft DAO Object Library and check the boxes next to these libraries, as shown in Figure 17-3. In terms of version numbers for the object libraries, select the highest version number available.

This now gives your code all it needs to manipulate Access. Insert a module by selecting Insert | Module from the Code menu, and then enter the following code. The code assumes that you have a database at "C:\Temp\TestAccess.accdb":

```
Sub Test_Access()

Dim oAApp As Access.Application, oRSet As DAO.Recordset
Set oAApp = CreateObject("Access.Application")
oAApp.OpenCurrentDatabase "C:\Temp\TestAccess.accdb"

Set oRSet = oAApp.CurrentDb.OpenRecordset("MyTable")
oRSet.AddNew
oRSet!MyText = "Test String"
oRSet.Update
oRSet.Close
Set oRSet = Nothing
Set oApp = Nothing
End Sub
```

When this is run, it will open a database called TestAccess in the path C:\Temp\ and will then add a new record to your sample table MyTest.

The code creates an object **oAApp** to hold the Access application object, and an object called **oRSet** to hold the DAO recordset. The variable **oAApp** is set to an Access application

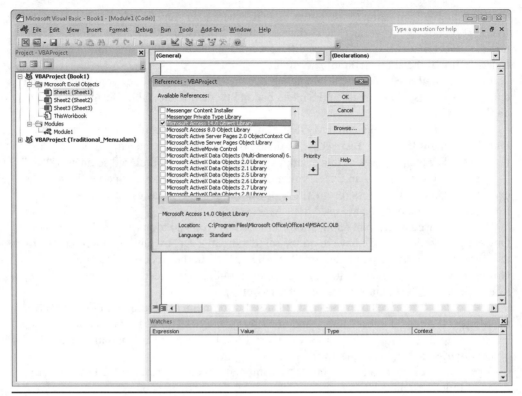

Figure 17-3 *Selecting the Access Library file*

by using the **CreateObject** method. This is exactly the same as if you had opened Access directly and chosen a blank database.

Next, the **oRSet** object is set to point to your sample table "MyTable". This is the same as if you had double-clicked the table name in Access and opened it as a data sheet. A new record is added and the field MyText is set to "Test String". Notice that an exclamation mark is used instead of a dot.

The recordset is then updated and closed and the two objects are set to Nothing to release memory.

As explained previously, it is very important to be sure to properly close and set to Nothing any objects created within VBA code. Otherwise, the memory consumed is left hanging and is unable to be used by other applications later. This can cause problems for users when they exit your application, because an application was not properly terminated and is holding memory that may be needed.

I hope this has given you a taste of the immense power of the VBA language and how you can manipulate other Microsoft applications from within it.

PART

III

Advanced Techniques
in Access VBA

In this part, you'll learn how to create charts and graphs in code, work with external databases, and use API (application programming interface) calls to do things such as play a WAV file and manipulate RibbonX. I'll also discuss class modules and animation. These are powerful topics that will allow you to do some very unusual things with VBA and Access.

Charts and Graphs

From Access 2007 onwards, creating and manipulating charts using VBA has become quite difficult and complicated. There is no **AddChart** method as in Excel VBA and if you create a chart on a report, you will find that the object model for it does not have the usual properties and methods you may be expecting.

Even worse, there is no macro recorder in Access, so you cannot cheat and record the VBA code while you create a chart manually on a report!

To use VBA with charts, you will need to put a reference in your VBA code to the Microsoft Graph 12.0 Object Library. To do this, click Tools | References in the VBE menu and then scroll down to the Microsoft Graph 14.0 Object Library. Your screen should look like Figure 18-1.

Check the box on the reference and click OK.

Next, you need to create a table to hold your chart data. Click Create in the Access menu and then click the Table Design icon in the Tables Group of the ribbon. Create two fields (**aName** as text and **aValue** as a number). Save the table as **tblChart**. Click No on the dialog asking you to create a primary key.

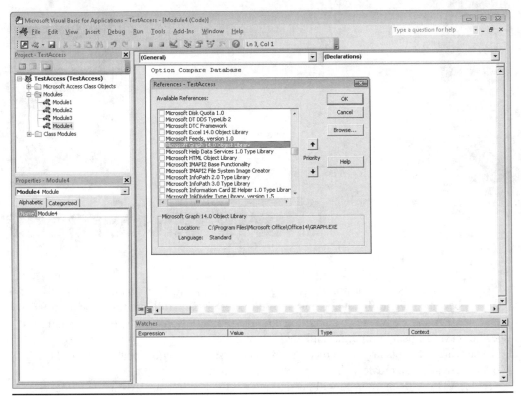

Figure 18-1 *Entering a reference into the Microsoft Graph 12.0 Object Library*

Populate your table with some data. Your table should now look like Figure 18-2.

You now need to create a template graph to be inserted into reports using VBA. Create a new blank report by clicking Create on the Access menu and then clicking the Report Design icon in the Reports Group of the ribbon. Click Design in the Access menu, and in the Controls Group of the ribbon, drag the Chart icon (second row of controls with colored bars) on to your report. Once positioned, drag the cursor to size the Chart control. The graph should be assigned the name Graph0 when you look in the Properties window, but if it is different, then change it to Graph0.

You will then be taken into the Chart Wizard. Select your table tblChart as the source and select both the fields. Select a standard pie chart and then click Finish. The chart object will now appear on your report.

Save the report with the name **rptTemplate**. Although the template has been pre-determined as a pie chart and with a particular table as the source, all these properties can be changed programmatically. However, in order to create a chart to use as a template, some source information must be given.

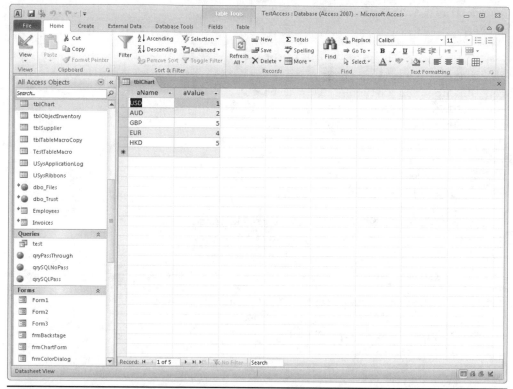

Figure 18-2   *Population of the tblChart Table*

Finally, we get to the interesting bit of the VBA code to create a report, add a chart to it, and manipulate it with VBA. Insert a new module by clicking Insert | Module in the VBE window and adding the following code:

```
Sub CreateGraphOnReport()
Dim rep As Report
Dim ctl As control
Dim ch As Graph.Chart
Dim RepName As String

DoCmd.OpenReport "rptTemplate", acDesign, , , , acHidden
Set rep = CreateReport()

Set ctl = CreateReportControl(rep.Name, acObjectFrame, acDetail)
ctl.OleData = Reports!rptTemplate!Graph0.OleData
DoCmd.Restore
```

```
DoCmd.Close acReport, "rptTemplate"
RepName = rep.Name

rep.OLEUnbound0.RowSource = "tblChart"
rep.OLEUnbound0.RowSourceType = "Table/Query"
rep.OLEUnbound0.ColumnHeads = True
rep.OLEUnbound0.Top = 100
rep.OLEUnbound0.Left = 100

DoCmd.Restore
DoCmd.Save acDefault
DoCmd.Close acDefault

DoCmd.Rename "rptMyGraph", acReport, RepName
DoCmd.OpenReport "rptMyGraph", acViewDesign
DoCmd.Restore


Set ch = Reports("rptMyGraph").OLEUnbound0.Object
ch.HasTitle = True
ch.ChartTitle.Text = "My Chart"
ch.ChartType = xl3DPie

DoCmd.Save acDefault
DoCmd.Close acDefault
DoCmd.OpenReport "rptMyGraph", acViewReport
End Sub
```

This code will create a new report, add a chart to it, save it, and rename it, and then manipulate the parameters of the chart.

The code first sets up objects for the new report and control, as well as for the chart based on the Graph Object library. The report rptTemplate that you created earlier is opened in Design mode and is kept hidden.

The **CreateReport** method is used to create a new report, and then **CreateReportControl** is used to create an object frame in the Detail section of that report. The object frame OLEData is then set to the OLEData from the chart in rptTemplate. This effectively makes it into a Chart control.

The name of the report is stored in a string, since we wish to rename the report and this cannot be done while it is open.

Properties are then set for the OLEObject for RowSource, RowType, Top, and Left. ColumnHeads must be set to True, otherwise the first row of your source table will be left out.

The report is saved and renamed to rptMyGraph and then opened in Design mode. The subsequent code will not work if the report is not in Design mode.

The Chart object created at the start of the code can now be set to the OLEObject on the report. You now have access to all the normal properties and methods you would expect for a chart object, such as changing the type of chart and changing the title.

Note that the **HasTitle** property must be set to True before defining the text for the title of the chart. Also, note that some of the properties must be set for the OLE Object (such as Top and Left) and not for the Chart itself.

Run this code, and your chart should look like Figure 18-3.

Although the code has created the chart on a report, this code can also be used on a form. Also, if you already have a chart control (added using the Chart Wizard) on your report/form and simply want to manipulate it, you can use the following code to create a chart object in VBA:

```
Dim ch As Graph.Chart
Set ch = Me.Graph0.Object
```

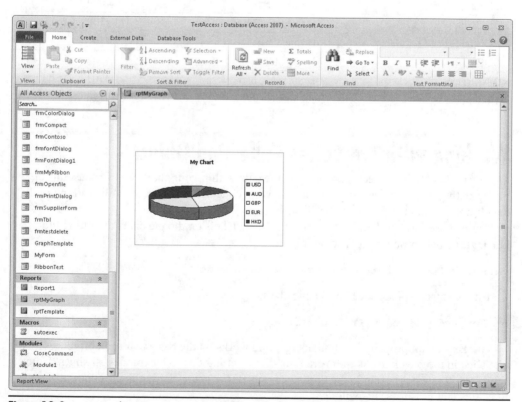

Figure 18-3   *A pie chart on a report created using the VBA example*

In terms of the Chart Type, Excel version 97 and later have built-in parameters to define the various types of charts. These all correspond to the gallery in the Chart Wizard that you see if you insert a chart into a report or form.

Constant	Description	Value
xlArea	Area Chart	1
xlBar	Bar Chart	2
xlColumn	Column Chart	3
xlLine	Line Chart	4
xlPie	Pie Chart	5
xlRadar	Radar Chart	–4151
xlXYScatter	XY Scatter Chart	–4169
xlCombination	Combination Chart	–4111
xl3DArea	3-D Area Chart	–4098
xl3DBar	3-D Bar Chart	–4099
xl3DColumn	3-D Column Chart	–4100
xl3DLine	3-D Line Chart	–4101
xl3DPie	3-D Pie Chart	–4102
xl3DSurface	3-D Surface Chart	–4103
xlDoughnut	Doughnut Chart	–4120

Working with the Series Collection Object

The Series Collection object represents all the data within your chart. It is very useful for manipulating charts in appearance. The following code assumes you are still working with the **ch** object from the previous code listing.

You can use VBA to turn on or turn off the data labels on the pie chart by setting the **HasDataLabels** property to True or False:

```
ch.SeriesCollection(1).HasDataLabels = True
```

You can also explode slices of the pie chart:

```
ch.SeriesCollection(1).Explosion = 8
```

The **Explosion** property is a long integer and works on the basis that each bit represents one slice in the pie chart. As there are four slices, setting this to 8 explodes all slices. If you set it to 4, this would explode the third slice only of the chart. Setting the property to 0 indicates that no slices are exploded.

You can use VBA to manipulate the appearance of labels on your chart.

```
ch.SeriesCollection(1).DataLabels.ShowValue = True
ch.SeriesCollection(1).DataLabels.ShowCategoryName = True
```

The preceding code sets the label on each slice to display both the value and the category name, which is the name declared on the legend of the chart.

You can also change the color of the pie chart segments by using:

```
ch.SeriesCollection(1).Points(1).Interior.Color = QBColor(12)
```

I once had to write some Access reports for foreign exchange trading. One of these had a page for each customer and a pie chart detailing the split in currencies traded. Some customers traded in a whole range of currencies, whereas others only traded in one or two. The problem with using the pie chart was that the segment colors were not consistent for each customer due to the number of currencies being traded.

The customer required each currency to have a specific color segment regardless of which customer it was. This was accomplished by writing code to change the segment color using predefined parameters.

Exporting a Chart as a Picture File

A chart can be easily exported as a GIF, JPEG, or PNG file using the following code. This example assumes you have a chart already defined on a report.

```
Sub OutputChart()
  Dim ch As Graph.Chart
  Set ch = Me.Graph0.Object


  ExportFile = Access.CodeProject.Path & "\" MyChart.gif"

  ch.Export Filename:=ExportFile, FilterName:="GIF"
End Sub
```

Working with External Databases

One powerful feature of Access is that you can easily make connections to external databases and use the tables in the same way you would if they were internal tables within your application.

You can make your code interact with any database as long as the database is ODBC (Open Database Connectivity)-compatible and the appropriate driver is available. ODBC allows applications to access the database in a standard way from many different languages, including VBA. This can be extremely useful if you want to bring data from a database into your application.

For example, you may want to import data from an accounting system into your application. The accounting system doesn't necessarily provide this functionality in the application, but the database has the data you are interested in. If the database has an ODBC driver available, you can bring the data into your application in any shape or form to use as needed.

Databases such as Microsoft Access, Microsoft SQL Server, and Oracle all support ODBC, and provided you have the relevant permissions to the database, you can read data into your database and even write data back if need be. Writing data back should be done with extreme care, however, because you can easily destroy the integrity of a relational database in this way. If you change an ID number in a field that is used for a relationship into another table, then the database may appear to be correct, but its relationship and integrity are totally blown.

The safest way is to only use a read-only ID on the database, and this is probably all that the database owner will grant you.

Because of the flexibility of ODBC, you can use Access as a "junction box" to join up several different databases if required. It does not matter if they use different platforms, so long as they are ODBC-compatible.

For example, you could put links in your Access database to tables on an Oracle database and a SQL Server database. Provided there are key fields that link between the two, such as a customer ID reference or an order number, you can produce data that straddles the two systems.

I have found this very useful for reconciling data held both on SQL Server and Oracle. It would normally be very difficult to create a query on SQL Server that used Oracle tables, but Access and ODBC can provide a solution.

Linking to external databases also makes your Access application smaller because all the data is being held elsewhere. Connecting to other Access databases is a way of getting round the 2GB limit on Access. You use your master database to hold the queries, forms, reports, and VBA code, and the data is stored in another Access database or an external database such as SQL Server.

Using a heavy duty database such as SQL Server or Oracle can also make your application more robust.

Linking to Other Access Databases

Access provides a very easy way to create linked tables to other Access databases. Click External Data on the Access menu and then click Access in the Import group of the ribbon. On the pop-up screen, use the Browse button to locate your database and click the "Link to Data Source by Creating a Linked Table" radio button.

When locating the file in the browser, try and use the actual URL for the server instead of the drive letter. For example, you may have a particular server mapped to J, but another user will have it mapped to H. If you distribute your application to this user, it will not work unless they re-map their drive. Using the URL gets around this ambiguity.

Click the OK button and a pop-up listing all the tables in that database will display. Select the ones you need and click OK.

These will appear as linked tables in the navigation pane. If you double-click the table, you will see the data held in it. You can use these linked tables as if they were part of your database, except that you cannot alter the structure of the table.

ODBC Links and DSNs

Things are more complicated if you wish to link to an external database such as SQL Server or Oracle. To make the connection, you will need four parameters. These are the server name where the database is held, a login ID and password that have been issued to you by the database owner (do not use somebody else's), and the name of the database.

If you do not have access to SQL Server, you can download SQL Server Express free of charge from http://www.microsoft.com/Sqlserver/2005/en/us/express.aspx.

To begin, you must first set up an ODBC link to point to the database you want to work with. This is done by setting up a DSN (Data Source Name). You do this by selecting Control Panel in Windows, then Administrative Tools (Windows XP only), and then Data Sources (ODBC). It also works for Vista and Windows 7.

The ODBC Data Source Administrator dialog will appear, as shown in Figure 19-1.

If you have installed SQL Server or SQL Server Express, the drivers for SQL Server will display.

If you do not already have a data source name (DSN) set up for the database, click Add. This will give you a list of available database drivers, as shown in Figure 19-2. A DSN is exactly what it says: It is a name of an ODBC link to a database that you can use to refer to that ODBC link. A wide variety of these are available and some have titles in different languages, but I am going to demonstrate SQL Server first.

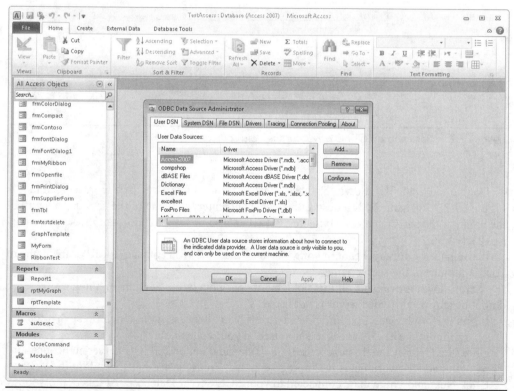

Figure 19-1   *The ODBC Data Source Administrator window*

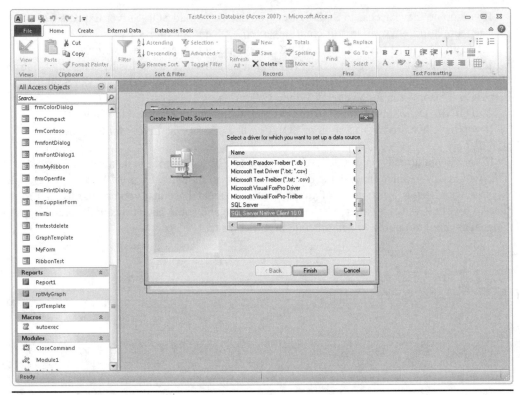

Figure 19-2 *Selecting an ODBC driver for the data source*

Double-click the SQL Server Native Client 10.0 and you will be taken to the screen in Figure 19-3. Give your DSN a descriptive name and enter the name of the server. This will be the name of the server such as MyServer, but it can also be the IP address of the server, such as 123.124.56.24.

If you have SQL Server running on your local machine, you can use [local] or the name of your computer as the server name.

A drop-down is available on this field, but it does not always contain anything useful, so do not be surprised if your server is not listed.

If you prefer, the Description field can be left blank because it only identifies what the DSN is about in the DSN screen; it is not used in your code at all.

Click Next to move to the next screen. Click the radio button for SQL Server authentication. The Login and Password fields will now be enabled. Enter these details. See Figure 19-3.

Click Next and you will be connected to your SQL Server Database. At this point, you may see error messages, usually because your server name is not valid on your network, or because you are using the wrong ID and password. If this happens, check that the server name, ID, and password are all correct and that you are using the proper driver. Check with

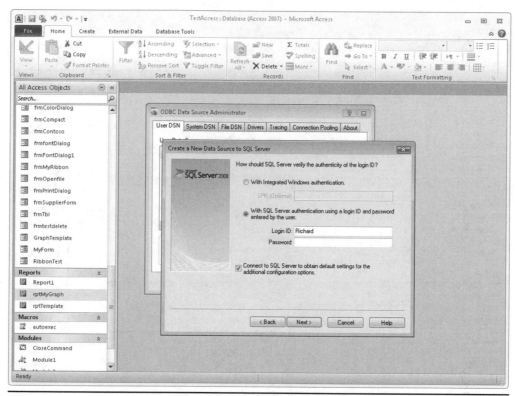

Figure 19-3   *Setting up a DSN*

the owner of the database that your ID and password are set up correctly. If you can get the IP address of the server, try pinging this from the MS-DOS prompt to see if there is a response (use ping <ip address>).

If all has gone well, you will see the next screen, which proves that you now have a connection. At the top of the screen is a check box for "Change the Default Database to." Set this and the drop-down of databases will be enabled.

Use the drop-down to locate the database you need. There may be several databases on the server and your ID may well only work with one of them.

Click Next to move to the next screen and then click Finish. Select Test Data Source on the final screen and you will see a message of success. Click OK and then click OK in the original ODBC Administrator window to close it.

Using a DSN

You now have a valid DSN you can use within Access. On the Access menu, click External Data and then click the ODBC icon in the Import & Link group of the ribbon. You will now see a pop-up, as shown in Figure 19-4.

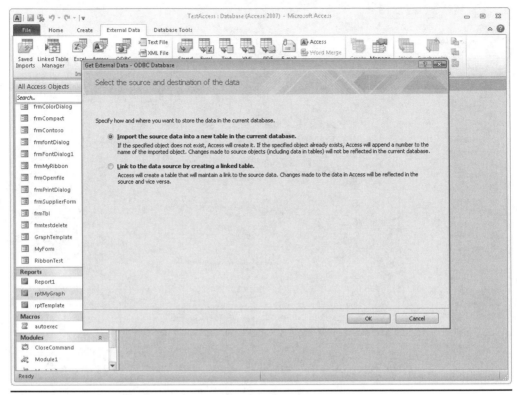

Figure 19-4   *Linking to a DSN*

Select the radio button "Link to the data source by creating a linked table" and then click OK. In the next screen, click the tab for Machine Data Source. Scroll down to select the DSN you just created and click OK

You will then be prompted for a password based on the ID you used when you created the DSN. You may think it is strange putting in the password again when you already used it to create the DSN, but this is extra security to prevent unauthorized access.

Click OK and you will be taken to a screen listing all available tables on that database. There may be a time delay at this point, depending on how many tables your database has. If there are only a few, then the screen will appear instantaneously. However, I have connected to databases that contain thousands of tables and have had to wait several minutes for this screen to appear.

When the Link Tables screen appears, make sure you check the box for "Save Password." If you do not check this, a password prompt will come up when the table is opened.

Select your tables and click OK. On each table, you will need to click "Save Password" on the message box that appears. You may also be asked to specify an index field for particular tables. This is only required if writing data back to the tables and it is usually a unique field within the table. Normally, you would be given read-only access since it is very dangerous to modify data in a relational database if you do not understand the relationships.

You will see your external linked tables appear in the Navigation pane of Access. You can use these tables in the same way as if they were internal tables within your Access applications, with the exception of changing the structure.

Problems Using Linked Tables

A problem can occur when using linked tables if the location of the target database changes. When linking to another Access database, it frequently happens that the target database is moved to another server, in which case your application will cease to function.

You can use Linked Table Manager to sort this out. Click External Data in the Access Menu and then click the Linked Table Manager icon in the Import & Link group of the ribbon. This will display a pop-up window, as shown in Figure 19-5.

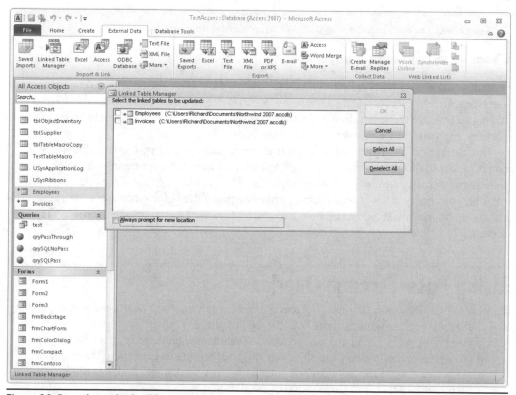

Figure 19-5   *The Linked Table Manager*

Set the check boxes for the tables that you need to re-link and then set the check box at the bottom for "Always prompt for new location." Click OK and you will be prompted to browse to the new target database. The selected tables will then be set to point to this database.

If you use SQL Server or Oracle databases, these very rarely move their location. If they do, you can fix this by going to the ODBC Administrator and editing your DSN to the new server/database name.

Far more likely is the addition of new fields into tables (which you will be expected to incorporate into your application), or even worse, the re-naming of fields. Again a refresh through Linked Table Manager, without the "Always prompt for new location" check box being set, will bring these changes into your linked tables.

Of course, you will have to manually change your queries and code to take account of these table structure changes.

An obvious problem is also the fact that only you have the ODBC DSN set up on your computer. If another user wants to view your application, it will not work until the DSN has been created on the user's computer.

Fortunately, there is an easy way to do this, by adding the following code into your opening form:

```
DBEngine.RegisterDatabase "MyDSN", "SQL Server Native Client 10.0", True, _
"MyServer" _
& vbCr & "Database=MyDatabase"
```

This will create a DSN called MyDSN (or over-write it if it is already there) to connect to a server called MyServer and a database called MyDatabase. You do not need the ID and password because these are already embedded in the linked table, and it would be bad from a security angle to show a password within your code.

One further problem you may encounter is the performance of your queries based on tables linked in this way. If the tables are large or not indexed, your queries may take a long time to run because Access is drawing across the data for each table and then processing it through your query. This can also cause performance problems for other users of the external database and may make you extremely unpopular! However, solutions are shown in the next sections.

Using Pass-Through Queries

Pass-through queries are similar to Access queries except that they run on the server, so that the client end receives nothing more than the data required. They effectively run like a stored procedure on the server and have a huge speed advantage when there is a lot of data.

To put a pass-through query together, you still need a DSN to connect to the database. If you already have your DSN set up, click Create on the Access menu and then click the Query Design icon in the Macros & Code group of the ribbon.

This will call up the Query Design window. Close the Show Table window and click the SQL View icon in the Views group of the ribbon. Click the Pass-Through icon in the Query Type group of the ribbon and then select the Property Sheet icon in the Show/Hide group of the ribbon. This will display the property sheet (see Figure 19-6).

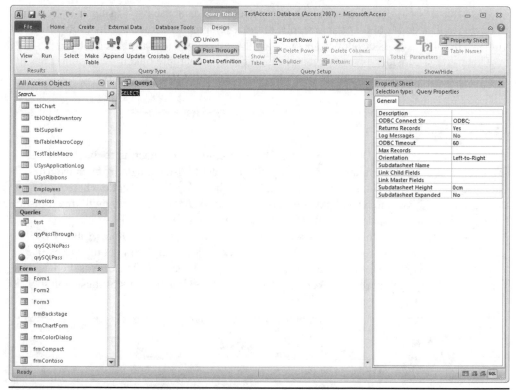

Figure 19-6   *Setting up a pass-through query*

Click the three-dot symbol on the **ODBC Connect Str** property and you can then select a DSN to use. Click the Machine Data Source tab and scroll down to your DSN.

You will then be asked if you want the password included in the connection string, which raises a security issue. If you do not include it, the user will be prompted for the password every time the query is run, which could be annoying. If you include it in the connection string, anyone can see it.

A solution is to include it in the connection string, but to lock down the database so query structures cannot be accessed. See Chapter 24 on how to do this.

A further problem is that you cannot build your query using the Access GUI. You must write your query in SQL and use the same notation that the database platform is expecting. This is because your query will run directly on the database server.

If you are connecting to Oracle or SQL Server, you need to use a percent sign (%) instead of a star (*) for wild card characters and use single quotes instead of double quotes to denote strings. Also, you cannot use IIF. Instead, you must use the notation CASE WHEN.....THEN.....ELSE.....END.

It is often a very good idea to test the query out on the database itself using SQL Server Manager or TOAD (Tool for Oracle Application Development). However, the problem is that you as a humble Access developer may not be allowed anywhere near these tools!

This route is considerably more complicated than using simple linked tables, but it has the huge advantage of speed, which may be very important in your application.

Using ADO

ActiveX Data Objects (ADO) is the Microsoft technology for connecting to databases. ADO is a Component Object Model (COM) that you can direct to use the data from an external database either using a connection string or a DSN. The link tells your code where the database is and gives the ID and password to get into it. ADO provides you with the tools to hook into the database using that ODBC link and to read and write the data.

To use ADO in your code, you must first include a reference to the Object Library by selecting Tools | References from the VBE menu. Scroll down until you get to Microsoft ActiveX Data Objects 6.0 Library and Microsoft ActiveX Data Objects Recordset 6.0 Library, as shown in Figure 19-7. You may have earlier version numbers of these going back

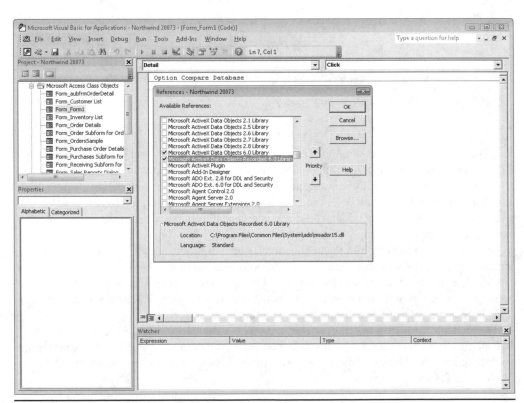

Figure 19-7   *Putting in a reference to ActiveX Data Objects*

to version 2, depending on what version of Windows you are running, but they will still work in the same way. If you do not have Version 6.0, use the latest version you have. Mark both check boxes on the left and click OK.

It is important to have this reference so it gives you full functionality to ADO. It is also good programming practice.

You can now enter the following code into a module. This assumes you are connecting to a SQL Server database, but you can also use other Access databases for the connection string (see the following examples).

```
Sub ADOExtract()
Dim RsADO As ADODB.Recordset, RsAccess As Recordset
Dim Cnct As String,Cnct1 as String, Cnct2 as String

Set Connection = New ADODB.Connection
Cnct1 = "Provider=SQLOLEDB;Driver={SQL Server Native Client 10.0};"
Cnct2="Server=MyServer;Database=MyDatabase;Uid=MyId;Pwd=MyPassword;"
Cnct=Cnct1 & Cnct2
Connection.CommandTimeout = 60
Connection.Open ConnectionString:=Cnct

Set RsAccess = CurrentDb.OpenRecordset("MyDestinationTable")

Set RsADO = New ADODB.Recordset

    With RsADO

        .Open Source:="select * from MySourceTable", _
ActiveConnection:=Connection, CursorType:=adOpenStatic

        Do Until RsADO.EOF
            RsAccess.AddNew
            RsAccess!Field1 = RsADO!Field1
            RsAccess!Field2 = RsADO!Field2
            RsAccess.Update
            RsADO.MoveNext

        Loop

    End With

    Set RsADO = Nothing
    Set RsAccess = Nothing
End Sub
```

This code creates two recordset objects, one as an ADO recordset and the other as a standard Access DAO recordset. It also sets up some string variables to hold the connection string data.

The connection string is created with the parameters for your server, database, ID, and password. A connection timeout is set and the connection is opened to the database.

The DAO recordset is set to point to your destination table.

A new ADO recordset object is created and this is used to open the source table in the SQL Server database using the connection that was created.

The ADO recordset is then iterated through and new records are added into the destination table using the **AddNew** method.

Finally, the objects are set to Nothing to release memory.

The connection string can also use a DSN:

```
OLEDB;DSN=MyDSN;Uid=MyId;Pwd=MyPassword;
```

In addition, the connection string can be used to connect to another Access database:

```
Provider=Microsoft.ACE.OLEDB.12.0;Data Source=C:\myFolder\myAccess2007file.accdb;
```

As with the pass-through query, if you are running the ADO query directly on the external database and you are using SQL Server or Oracle, you need to use a percent sign (%) instead of a star (*) for wild card characters and use single quotes instead of double quotes to denote strings. Also, you cannot use IIF. Instead, you must use the notation CASE WHEN.....THEN.....ELSE.....END.

From this example, you can see how to use ADO to import and manipulate data from another database, but there are some disadvantages.

One is the fact that passwords are included in the connection strings, which raises security issues. You can get around this by locking the database up (see Chapter 24 on how to do this), or you can leave the password out and force the user to enter this. However, this may be unacceptable if you have this running as an overnight job.

The other disadvantage is that this methodology can be a slow means of populating an internal Access table. This works well for small tables of under 100 records, but it is painfully slow in iterating each record where the table size is hundreds of thousands of records. In Excel VBA, there is a **CopyFromRecordset** method, which is extremely useful for this, but nothing like it is provided in the Access Object Model.

To solve this, use the database engine to transfer the data into a temporary table where you can then write code to deal with it:

```
Sub FastTransferofData()
Dim Cnct As String, Ccnt1 as String, Ccnt2 as String
Cnct1 = "ODBC;Provider=MDASQL;Driver={SQL Server};"
```

```
Ccnt2 = "Server=MyServer;Database=MyDatabase;Uid=MyId;Pwd=MyPassword;"
Ccnt = Ccnt1 & Ccnt2
CurrentDb.Execute "insert into DestTble select * from [" & Cnct & "].SrceTble"
End Sub
```

This creates a connection string as before, except that it uses ODBC instead of OLEDB and utilizes a different provider and driver parameters. It then uses a standard SQL Insert query to transfer the records from the external database table (SrceTble) to the Access destination table.

This assumes that the structure of the destination table and the source table are the same.

As shown previously, other connection strings can be used to link to another Access database or to use an existing DSN.

CHAPTER
20

API Calls

Although the Access object model and VBA code are very comprehensive in providing you with methods to do various operations on the database, you may have noticed that there are a number of functions having to do with Windows you still cannot perform. Even Visual Basic itself does not provide the direct means to do some of these.

For example, you cannot find the amount of available space on a disk device. You cannot read the keyboard directly—you can only read incoming keys on a user form, provided that the form or control has the focus. You cannot determine where the mouse position is. Obviously, ways of doing these things exist since Windows Explorer can tell you how much space is on your hard disk and Windows knows which key you pressed. VBA does not have the direct commands to deal with these subjects, but it does allow access to the WIN32 application programming interface (API), which in turn allows you to access a treasure chest of information from Windows directly.

API calls are a very advanced subject and can provide an enormous amount of extra functionality to your programs. It is not the purpose of this book to go too deeply into API calls, however, but I will show you some examples of how they can be used to your advantage.

What Is an API Call?

The API (application programming interface) allows you to access the built-in programming functions from DLL and EXE files, particularly the ones that drive Windows. Other third-party applications also use DLL files for libraries of functions, and if you are lucky, you may even be supplied with documentation on how to work the functions.

The purpose of this chapter is to give you an idea of how you can use API calls within your code. The examples given are not comprehensive, and you can use large numbers of API calls for different functions. Some books are available on API calls if you wish to investigate this topic further.

API calls are normally functions that return a value of some type, although they often take some action at the same time. Certain subroutines also only take action (remember the distinction made in Chapter 3 between a function and a subroutine). To use them, you must first declare the function or subroutine you wish to use; this is the hardest part. The **Declare** statement sets up the description of the function or subroutine statement within the dynamic link library (DLL) file. It describes which DLL will be used, what the name of the function or subroutine is, and what the parameters to be passed are. The declarations are quite complicated, and if any mistake is made, the call will not work and may even crash the system. Before making an API call, make sure your file has been saved, because these calls are not very forgiving when things go wrong. You may find you have to reboot your computer to get things running again, and this will lose any data you have not saved. As I mentioned, API calls are not very forgiving if they go wrong, and pressing CTRL+BREAK to stop them will have no effect whatsoever. For example, simply passing the wrong type of value is enough to cause a crash. However, they are an example of the wonderful versatility of VBA, and when used properly, they can provide functionality not normally available in Access.

Using an API Call

The following are some examples of API calls and how to use them within your VBA code.

Getting Disk Space

For this example, you will use an API call that gets the spare disk space from a disk device.

First of all, you must make the declaration. You do this in the declarations section of a module (at the top of the module page). The syntax for this particular declaration is as follows:

```
Private Declare Function GetDiskFreeSpaceEx Lib "kernel32"  _
Alias "GetDiskFreeSpaceExA" (ByVal lpDirectoryName As  _
String, lpFreeBytesAvailableToCaller As Currency,  _
lpTotalNumberOfBytes As Currency, lpTotalNumberOfFreeBytes  _
As Currency) As Long
```

This is quite a long statement, and it has to be completely accurate to work. If you have access to Visual Basic, all the API declarations are contained in a file called API32.TXT and can easily be copied and pasted into your declarations. Further information can be obtained from the Microsoft Developer Network (MSDN) at msdn.microsoft.com, which is the perfect place to find more advanced information on Access VBA and API calls.

Basically, this statement sets up a reference to the kernel32.dll that resides in the Windows system directory. It specifies the way parameters must be used and what they are called. Its purpose is to put a function into your code that you can use to call this library function from kernel32.dll.

The next step is to put in code to call this function:

```
Sub Test_Api()
Dim x as Double
Dim FreeBytesAvailableToCaller As Currency, TotalNumberOfBytes As _
Currency,  TotalNumberOfFreeBytes As Currency
x = GetDiskFreeSpaceEx("c:\", FreeBytesAvailableToCaller, _
TotalNumberOfBytes, TotalNumberOfFreeBytes)
MsgBox "Total Space " & Format(TotalNumberOfBytes * 10000, "#,##0")
MsgBox "Free Space " & Format(TotalNumberOfFreeBytes * 10000, "#,##0")
End Sub
```

This code sets up variables to hold the values returned by the API call. The actual value returned through the variable calling it (in this case, **x**) is related to errors. It has a value of 1 for success.

The call is then made passing the root directory "C:\" and the variables already defined. It is then a simple case of multiplying the value by 10,000 (this is because of the way in which the API call returns the values) and formatting it to comma format for easy display. A message box (as shown in Figure 20-1) then displays the result.

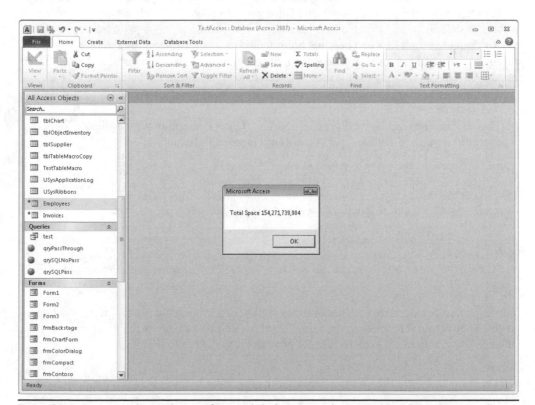

Figure 20-1   *Getting the total space from a disk drive using the GetDiskFreeSpaceEx API call*

You can check the values by going into Windows Explorer (right-click the Windows Start button in the bottom-left corner of the screen and select Explore), selecting the root of C:, right-clicking this, and choosing Properties. A pie chart will appear showing usage of your C: drive, and the values for total space and free space will agree exactly to numbers displayed in the preceding code.

Reading from and Writing to INI Files

API calls can also be used for reading from and writing to INI files. INI files have now been superseded by the Windows Registry in terms of maintaining program parameters and settings, but they are still useful as a simple way of keeping information.

API calls also exist for the Windows Registry, but you need a very good knowledge of what you are doing if you are going to use API calls to alter the Registry. If you make a mistake, you will end up having to reinstall a particular program related to that setting, and at worst you may damage the integrity of Windows and end up having to reinstall Windows.

One of their useful functions is creating INI files for your program. INI files are a means of storing settings for your program, such as control settings that you want to be sticky or the details of user settings for individual applications. Variables and properties in VBA only hold their values while the program is present. Once you close down, all is lost, and everything returns to default.

An example might be a text box that holds a directory pathname set by the user. The user might put in a different pathname, but when the program is closed, it reverts to the default on reloading. This is irritating for the user, who has to keep inputting the pathname.

The INI file holds this information locally so it can be retrieved when the program is loaded next time.

Two declarations can be used for your INI file. (Other declarations are available for reading and writing to INI files, but you will use these in the example.)

```
Private Declare Function GetPrivateProfileString Lib "kernel32" Alias _
"GetPrivateProfileStringA" (ByVal lpApplicationName As String, ByVal _
lpKeyName As Any, ByVal lpDefault As String, ByVal lpReturnedString As _
String, ByVal nSize As Long, ByVal lpFileName As String) As Long

Private Declare Function WritePrivateProfileString Lib "kernel32" Alias _
"WritePrivateProfileStringA" (ByVal lpApplicationName As String, ByVal _
lpKeyName As Any, ByVal lpString As Any, ByVal lpFileName As String) As _
Long
```

These need to be added into the declarations section of a module (at the top of the module page). They set up references to the kernel32.dll file and describe how the parameters will be passed. You can then use code to pass the parameters and write to the file:

```
Sub Test_INI()
x = WritePrivateProfileString("Parameters", "Path", "C:\temp\", "myini.ini")
s$ = Space$(256)
```

```
x = GetPrivateProfileString("Parameters", "Path", "", s$, 256, "myini.ini")
MsgBox s$
MsgBox x
End Sub
```

The first line writes the INI file. If the file is not already there, it is automatically created. The default location is in the Windows directory, although you can change this by placing a pathname onto the filename.

The first parameter (Parameters) is the section of the INI file into which to write the new string. The second parameter is the keyname or the entry to set—if set to Null, it will delete all keys within this section. The third parameter is the value to write for the key. This is "C:\temp\"—if set to Null, it will delete the existing string for that key. The fourth parameter is the name of the INI file. You can use any suffix; you do not have to use an INI suffix. This is quite useful if you want to hide some settings and wish to disguise your INI file—you can give it a DLL or EXE suffix so it looks like a program file on casual inspection.

This now creates MYINI.INI. If you look in your Windows directory, you will see that the file has been created. If you double-click it, it will be loaded into Notepad because it is a text file, and should look like this:

```
[Parameters]
Path=C:\temp\
```

The next API call reads the path back in. However, before this can happen, you must create a variable for it to be placed in.

The **Space$** command has been used to create a string of 256 spaces. Also, this variable must be specified as a string; otherwise, errors will occur. The return value comes back as a string, so it must be placed into a string variable.

GetPrivateProfileString works in a similar way to **WritePrivateProfileString**, but there are more parameters to pass. The first and second parameters are the same as before and give details of the section and the key to be read. The third parameter has a default value to return if the entry is not found. The fourth parameter contains the variable name to which the result will be passed. The fifth parameter contains the maximum number of characters to load into the variable. The sixth parameter is the filename to search for.

The variable calling the API (**x**) will give the number of characters returned. **S$** will contain the key, terminated by a Null character. If the keyname is left as Null, then all entries in that section will be returned, each terminated with a Null character.

Both these API calls are very forgiving in their operation. If the file is not there, it is created. If the key is not there, it is created. If the file does not exist when you use the read command, then a Null value will be returned.

This method is often used in programs to keep track of user settings so that when the user enters the program subsequently, it is set to that user's personal settings.

Microsoft no longer uses INI files; Windows uses keys in the Registry to record this information.

Reading Keyboard Activity

Another useful purpose of API calls is to read the keyboard and find out if a certain key has been pressed. Events on user forms are used to manage keyboard events, but these only apply to a particular form or a particular control on the form that has the focus at that time.

For example, suppose you write a macro to do a time-consuming task that involves it looping around thousands of times. You may want to give the user a "get out" command to bring it to a halt if it takes too long. You can only do this by checking the keyboard, because the only way you can see a keyboard event is on a UserForm, and this may not have the focus at the time the user presses the "get out" key. You use the API call **GetKeyState** to do this. You must put the following code in the declarations part of a module:

```
Private Declare Function GetKeyState Lib "user32" (ByVal nVirtKey As Long) _
As Integer
```

This will allow you to examine any key while the program is running. You can even differentiate between the left and right SHIFT keys or CTRL keys:

```
Sub Test_Key()
x = 0
Do Until x = 1

        If GetKeyState(&H9) < 0 Then x = 1

        DoEvents

Loop
MsgBox "You pressed the TAB key"
End Sub
```

This program effectively runs in an infinite loop and has only been done that way for demonstration purposes. Normally, you would place the API call somewhere within a loop within your own code so the keyboard can be read while other events are happening.

This program sets up a simple Do Until..Loop that keeps running until **x** = 1. This will never happen until the **GetKeyState** line turns up a value for the specified key that is less than 0—that is, it has been pressed. For the purposes of the example, the TAB key is used, which has a value of 09 in hexadecimal. When the TAB key is pressed, **x** changes its value to 1 and exits from the loop. The message box is then displayed.

The **DoEvents** command is very important here. It literally allows the operating system to catch its breath and finish processing all messages before moving onto the next instruction. If you do not use this, then the message from the keyboard will not be processed before the next loop is started, and the keypress will be missed.

Run this code, and it goes into an infinite loop because **x** will never equal 1. Press any key on the keyboard and nothing happens. But press the TAB key, and the program will end with a message box. Of course, it helps if you know the values of the virtual key codes if you want to use other key combinations. They are listed in Table 20-1.

Symbolic Constant Name	Value (Hexadecimal)	Mouse or Keyboard Equivalent
VK_LBUTTON	01	Left mouse button
VK_RBUTTON	02	Right mouse button
VK_CANCEL	03	CTRL+BREAK processing
VK_MBUTTON	04	Middle mouse button (three-button mouse)
—	05–07	Undefined
VK_BACK	08	BACKSPACE
VK_TAB	09	TAB
—	0A–0B	Undefined
VK_CLEAR	0C	CLEAR
VK_RETURN	0D	ENTER
—	0E–0F	Undefined
VK_SHIFT	10	SHIFT
VK_CONTROL	11	CTRL
VK_MENU	12	ALT
VK_PAUSE	13	PAUSE
VK_CAPITAL	14	CAPS LOCK
—	15–19	Reserved for Kanji systems
—	1A	Undefined
VK_ESCAPE	1B	ESC
—	1C–1F	Reserved for Kanji systems
VK_SPACE	20	SPACEBAR
VK_PRIOR	21	PAGE UP
VK_NEXT	22	PAGE DOWN
VK_END	23	END
VK_HOME	24	HOME
VK_LEFT	25	LEFT ARROW
VK_UP	26	UP ARROW
VK_RIGHT	27	RIGHT ARROW
VK_DOWN	28	DOWN ARROW
VK_SELECT	29	SELECT
—	2A	Original equipment manufacturer (OEM)-specific
VK_EXECUTE	2B	EXECUTE
VK_SNAPSHOT	2C	PRINT SCREEN
VK_INSERT	2D	INS

Table 20-1   *Key Combinations*

Symbolic Constant Name	Value (Hexadecimal)	Mouse or Keyboard Equivalent
VK_DELETE	2E	DEL
VK_HELP	2F	HELP
VK_0	30	0
VK_1	31	1
VK_2	32	2
VK_3	33	3
VK_4	34	4
VK_5	35	5
VK_6	36	6
VK_7	37	7
VK_8	38	8
VK_9	39	9
—	3A–40	Undefined
VK_A	41	A
VK_B	42	B
VK_C	43	C
VK_D	44	D
VK_E	45	E
VK_F	46	F
VK_G	47	G
VK_H	48	H
VK_I	49	I
VK_J	4A	J
VK_K	4B	K
VK_L	4C	L
VK_M	4D	M
VK_N	4E	N
VK_O	4F	O
VK_P	50	P
VK_Q	51	Q
VK_R	52	R
VK_S	53	S
VK_T	54	T
VK_U	55	U
VK_V	56	V

Table 20-1   *Key Combinations (Continued)*

Symbolic Constant Name	Value (Hexadecimal)	Mouse or Keyboard Equivalent
VK_W	57	W
VK_X	58	X
VK_Y	59	Y
VK_Z	5A	Z
VK_LWIN	5B	LEFT WINDOWS (Microsoft Natural Keyboard)
VK_RWIN	5C	RIGHT WINDOWS (Microsoft Natural Keyboard)
VK_APPS	5D	APPLICATIONS (Microsoft Natural Keyboard)
—	5E–5F	Undefined
VK_NUMPAD0	60	Numeric keypad 0
VK_NUMPAD1	61	Numeric keypad 1
VK_NUMPAD2	62	Numeric keypad 2
VK_NUMPAD3	63	Numeric keypad 3
VK_NUMPAD4	64	Numeric keypad 4
VK_NUMPAD5	65	Numeric keypad 5
VK_NUMPAD6	66	Numeric keypad 6
VK_NUMPAD7	67	Numeric keypad 7
VK_NUMPAD8	68	Numeric keypad 8
VK_NUMPAD9	69	Numeric keypad 9
VK_MULTIPLY	6A	MULTIPLY
VK_ADD	6B	ADD
VK_SEPARATOR	6C	SEPARATOR
VK_SUBTRACT	6D	SUBTRACT
VK_DECIMAL	6E	DECIMAL
VK_DIVIDE	6F	DIVIDE
VK_F1	70	F1
VK_F2	71	F2
VK_F3	72	F3
VK_F4	73	F4
VK_F5	74	F5
VK_F6	75	F6
VK_F7	76	F7
VK_F8	77	F8
VK_F9	78	F9
VK_F10	79	F10
VK_F11	7A	F11

Table 20-1   *Key Combinations (Continued)*

Symbolic Constant Name	Value (Hexadecimal)	Mouse or Keyboard Equivalent
VK_F12	7B	F12
VK_F13	7C	F13
VK_F14	7D	F14
VK_F15	7E	F15
VK_F16	7F	F16
VK_F17	80	F17
VK_F18	81	F18
VK_F19	82	F19
VK_F20	83	F20
VK_F21	84	F21
VK_F22	85	F22
VK_F23	86	F23
VK_F24	87	F24
—	88–8F	Unassigned
VK_NUMLOCK	90	NUM LOCK
VK_SCROLL	91	SCROLL LOCK
VK_LSHIFT	A0	LEFT SHIFT
VK_RSHIFT	A1	RIGHT SHIFT
VK_LCONTROL	A2	LEFT CTRL
VK_RCONTROL	A3	RIGHT CTRL
VK_LMENU	A4	LEFT MENU
VK_RMENU	A5	RIGHT MENU
—	E7–E8	Unassigned
—	E9–F5	OEM-specific
VK_ATTN	F6	ATTN
VK_CRSEL	F7	CRSEL
VK_EXSEL	F8	EXSEL
VK_EREOF	F9	ERASE EOF
VK_PLAY	FA	PLAY
VK_ZOOM	FB	ZOOM
VK_NONAME	FC	Reserved for future use
VK_PA1	FD	PA1
VK_OEM_CLEAR	FE	CLEAR

Table 20-1   *Key Combinations (Continued)*

Playing Multimedia Sounds

You can also use an API call to play a sound within your code from a WAV file. The old macro programming language had a command to do this, but it has not been included in VBA, or for that matter in Visual Basic itself, which makes it a bit restrictive if you want to play sound files. If you want to use Multimedia functions within your code to play sounds or voice files, then the means to play sound files is very crucial. The declaration goes in the declarations section of a module:

```
Public Declare Function PlaySound Lib "winmm.dll" Alias "PlaySoundA" _
(ByVal lpszName As String, ByVal hModule As Long, ByVal dwFlags As _
Long) As Long
```

You can then play the WAV files within your code:

```
Sub test_sound()
x = PlaySound("c:\windows\media\windows exclamation.wav", 0, 0)
x = PlaySound("c:\windows\media\tada.wav", 0, 0)
End Sub
```

This example plays two standard Windows sounds. Notice that the flags parameter is set to 0 in both cases. This indicates that the sound is played synchronously so that the command is not handed back to the VBA code until the sound has finished playing.

If you have a microphone on your computer, you can record your own sound effects or speech onto a WAV file and play them back in this way.

These examples give some idea of the power of API calls within a program. Many books are available on this subject if you wish to examine the topic further.

Class Modules

A s you program in VBA and insert modules to hold your code, you will notice from the menu that you can also insert what are called class modules. These are different from ordinary modules in that they allow you to create a component object model (COM) of your own.

Class modules cannot be run in the same way as a standard module procedure and must be referenced from your code within a module. This allows you to create your own objects and collections such as the **TableDef** or the **TableDefs** collection. Unfortunately, you cannot create a DLL (dynamic link library) file, which is what you would do if you were programming in full Visual Basic or C++/C#. However, a class module is still part of a database and you can put a reference into your class module database from another database in order to use it. This makes it a component object, and it effectively adds multitier architecture to your applications.

Earlier in this book, you learned that Access is a multitier application because there is a client services layer that has the Access object model and other object models sitting beneath it, and the data services layer sits under that. The class modules allow you to place another layer between the client services layer and the Access object model or between the client services layer and an external data source, such as Oracle or SQL Server.

Your class module database can then be used as a reference to your object in another database. However, other programmers who use it won't see the underlying code and rules you have built into it if you have used a password. As soon as you put a reference to your class module database, the public functions and subroutines can be accessed from other modules within a database, although if you have password-protected it, other programmers will not see the underlying code.

As an example, a **TableDef** is an object. This contains the hierarchy of objects for each table within your database. One of the collections within this object is Fields, which defines all the fields for that table. You can find out the number of fields in a table by using the **Count** property. For example, you could find out the number of fields in the USysRibbons table (see Chapter 11 on how this table is built) by using the following code:

```
MsgBox CurrentDb.TableDefs("USyRribbons").Fields.Count
```

This will return the value of 2 (fields) for USysRibbons. However, the value is read-only and you cannot alter it to create more fields. If you could do this, it would create tremendous confusion and break the integrity of the table.

The designers of the Access object module have written rules saying, "You can view the number of fields in a table but you cannot change the number directly." In the same way, you can design your own objects and set the rules accordingly about what can be done with those objects—which properties and methods there will be and whether a collection can be changed or whether it is read-only.

In the following example, you will create an object of names taken from cells in a spreadsheet. The object collection will be called **PNames**, and it will be a collection of **PName** objects. The names could be the names of people or the names of places.

Creating a Data Services Layer

You must first create a separate Access database to act as the Data Service Layer for your object model. Open a blank database, calling it **MyData**, and create a new table by clicking Create in the Access menu bar. Then, click the Table Design icon in the Tables group of the ribbon. Create a field called **MyName** and save the table with the name of MyTable. Enter some data into the table to create a few records.

You could also use SQL Server or Oracle as the Data Service Layer, but for the purpose of this example an Access database is used.

It is important to keep the Data Service Layer separate from the Object model you are going to create, otherwise this will lead to locking problems.

Inserting a Class Module

Select Insert | Class Module from the VBE menu to create a class module called Class1. You must change the name immediately, because this will be the name of the object you create, and Class1 is somewhat meaningless because it does not reflect the functionality of that class. You use this name within your code to refer to the object, and it will become tedious if you have to keep referring to Class1.

Change the name in the Properties window. To view the Properties window, select View | Properties Window on the VBE menu, or press F4.

Select the name field and overtype it with **MyPName**. This represents the individual objects within a collection. Double-click the class module within the tree view to display it.

Change the **Instancing** property to PublicNotCreatable. This makes your object visible to other applications.

Creating an Object

You need to set up the actual object for items within the collection first because this has to be used in the construction of the **Collections** object. The **MyPName** object will have one property, the name of the object called **PName**. Remember that a property holds a value for something within that object—in this case, the actual name.

You first need to create a variable to hold the property value, which you do in the declarations section of the module:

```
Private mPname As String
```

This sets up a string variable called **mPname**. Notice that it is private and cannot be seen as part of the object. This is because it is a working variable within the class module and is not for use by the user. Also, the name must be different from the actual property name the user can see, which is why the *m* is added at the front.

Next, you need to set up code to control access to the property. You need a **Property Let** statement and a **Property Get** statement, and the statements must be public—otherwise, you will not be able to view them within the object. These statements effectively read and write values to the property you are setting up:

```
Public Property Let Pname(vdata As String)
      mPname = vdata
End Property
```

The parameter **vdata** represents the value being passed to the property within the **Let** statement.

```
Public Property Get Pname() As String
      Pname = mPname
End Property
```

It is very important that the **Let** and **Get** property statements have the same name; otherwise, you will be able to read a property (**Get**) but not write back to it (**Let**), or you will be able to write to it (**Let**) but not read it back (**Get**).

The **Let** property uses a string variable to transfer the data into your **mPname** variable. The **Get** property sets the property value to whatever is held in your **mPname** variable.

You can use Insert | Procedure from the code menu to create a code skeleton for a property, which opens the Add Procedure dialog shown in Figure 21-1. This automatically writes the **Let** and **Get** property statements and ensures that they both have the same name.

You have now set up an object called **Pname**. This object sits in a collection called **PNames**, just as the **Worksheet** object sits in a collection called **Worksheets**. The **MyPNames** collection is created in the next section.

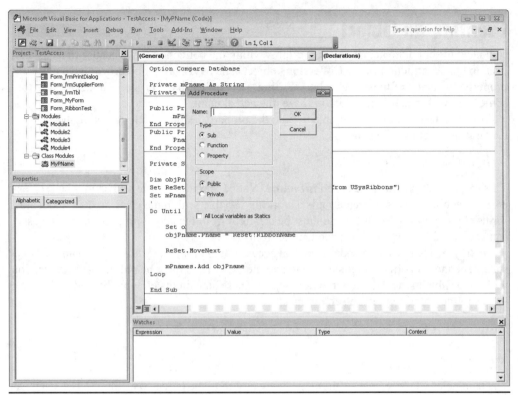

Figure 21-1 *Using the Add Procedure dialog to enter a property*

Creating a Collection

The next stage is to create the **Collection** object to hold the individual **MyPName** objects. Insert another class module using Insert | Class Module from the VBE menu bar. Change the name to **MyPNames** on the property window and double-click the class module to enter it. Change the Instancing property to PublicNotCreatable. This makes your object visible to other applications.

The first thing to do is define a private variable to act as the **Collection** object in the same way you defined a private variable to act as the property for the **MyPName** object. This needs to be placed in the declarations section of the class module:

```
Private mPnames As Collection
```

This must have a unique name, so an *m* is placed in front of the collection name. The letter *m* distinguishes the variable as a member variable.

Next, select the **Class_Initialize** subroutine. This routine runs when you first use the class and determines what the contents will be. To run it, click the Class section in the top-left drop-down and click Initialize in the top-right drop-down. Enter the following code:

```
Private Sub Class_Initialize()

Dim objPname As New MyPName
Dim MyConn As New ADODB.Connection, ReSet As New ADODB.Recordset
Dim ConStr As String
ConStr = "Driver={Microsoft Access Driver (*.mdb, *.accdb)};" & _
                "Dbq=MyTable.accdb;" & _
                "DefaultDir=C:\MyPath\;" & _
                "Uid=Admin;Pwd=;"


MyConn.ConnectionString = ConStr
MyConn.Open
Set ReSet = MyConn.Execute("select * from MyTable")
Set mPnames = New Collection

Do Until ReSet.EOF

    Set objPname = New MyPName
    objPname.Pname = ReSet!MyName

    ReSet.MoveNext

    mPnames.Add objPname
Loop
End Sub
```

First, you define an object called **objPname** based on the object you created called **MyPName**. Notice that the objects **MyPName** and **MyPNames** now appear in the drop-down list as you type the code in. As we are using ADO to communicate with the data services layer, we also define objects for the ADO connection and the recordset (see Chapter 19 for more details on working with external databases). We are using ADO here because it provides an efficient way of connecting to an external database using a class module. If you use linked tables and DSNs, there is a problem that these will have to be set up on whichever computer this example is being run on.

A connection string called ConStr is created. This provides details of the driver to be used, the name, and the location of the database. You can also include a user ID and password, although in the case of your Access database, this is optional.

You then set the local variable, **mPNames**, as a new **Collection** object. At this point, it is empty.

The Do Until loop adds the objects into the collection from a source of data. This could be an external database, or it could just be a local array holding the information. In this example, it is a simple query onto the table you created earlier called MyTable.

The variable **objPname**, which was defined as our **MyPName** object, is set to a new **Pname** for each loop, based on the field in the recordset called MyName. This means create a new instance of **MyPName** that can hold data and be added to the **MyPNames** collection.

The object **objPname** is then added to the **MyPnames** collection. At the end of this loop, all the data in the recordset has been added into the MyPNames collection. You also need to add a public function called **Item** so you can refer to individual objects within the collection by their index number. Enter this into the same class module as the rest of the code:

```
Public Function Item(Index As Integer) As Pname

    Set Item = mPnames.Item(Index)


End Function
```

This defines **Item** as a function of the object **MyPnames** and sets **Item** to point to the **mPnames** collection based on the index number given. Because **mPnames** was defined as a **Collection** object, it already has the **Item** function built into it. This function provides a "mirror" of what is going on in the **mPnames** collection in the background.

You will need to add a property called **Count** so your code can establish how many **MyPName** objects there are in the **MyPNames** collection:

```
Public Property Get Count() As Long
    Count = mPnames.Count
End Property
```

In this case, you only need a property **Get** because this is a read-only property, and it gets updated by the **Class_Initialize** routine adding in the source data. This acts again as "a mirror" against the **mPnames** object, which is defined as a collection and already has the **Count** property built into it.

You have now set up a collection called **MyPNames** of objects called **MyPName**, which simply refers to a recordset based on the table USysRibbons. The collection has a **Count** property and an **Item** method.

Using the PNames Collection

You can now use your **Collection** object **MyPNames** within standard code just as you would any other object. Use the following code within a standard Access VBA module:

```
Sub test_class()
Dim pn As New MyPNames, n As Integer
MsgBox pn.Count
For n = 1 To pn.Count
```

```
    MsgBox pn.Item(n).Pname
Next n
End Sub
```

This creates a new instance of the **MyPnames** object. When this procedure is run, the first thing it does is **initialize** the class module, which means it picks up the data from the spreadsheet and adds the objects to the collection.

The variable **n**, used in the For..Next loop, is defined as an **integer** because it was defined in the **Item** function in the collection as an **integer** (index). An integer was used because this is ideal for a For..Next loop variable. If you do not do this, you will get a Type Mismatch error when the code is run.

You then set up a For..Next loop to work through each object in the collection. This is based on the **Count** function of the object. Note that as you type the code in, the function **Item** and the property **Count** appear in list boxes, just as they do for built-in Access objects.

Using the **Collection** object, you can now use the **Item** function and the variable **n** to reference each object in the collection. The property **Pname** is used to display each name. This is all wrapped into a message box statement so that each name will be displayed in turn.

Run the code in your module by clicking the cursor anywhere in the code and pressing F5 and you will get a message box with the value of the number of objects you entered into the collection, followed by each name in turn. Next, try changing a value in MyTable, which is the source for this collection, and then rerun the code.

The name in the collection will also change because when you create the **MyPnames** object (**pn**) on the first line of the code, it reinitializes and takes the new values. If you made the **Collection**'s object **Static**, it would not reinitialize but would keep the old values of the collection:

```
Sub test_class()
Static pn As New MyPNames, n As Integer
MsgBox pn.Count
For n = 1 To pn.Count

    MsgBox pn.Item(n).Pname
Next n
End Sub
```

Finally, password-protect your object model code. Right-click your project name in the Project window of the VBE and click the project properties. Click the Protection tab of the pop-up window and check the box for Lock Project Viewing. Provide a password (make sure that you remember it!) and click OK.

Using the PNames Collection as a Multitier Application

Having created a working object model based on your data services layer, you can now make use of this in a further Access database that becomes the User Interface Application.

Create a new blank Access database. Open the VBE window by pressing ALT+F11. Use Tools | References on the VBE menu and browse to the object model database you created earlier. Your database will not appear in the list since it is not a DLL or OCX file. Instead, use the Browse button to locate your database. Click OK and then check the box for your reference. Click OK and then click Save on the VBE menu.

Close the database and then re-open it. When you enter the VBE window, you will now see your object model in the Project window.

Insert a module using Insert | Module on the VBE menu. Enter the following code:

```
Sub test_class()

Dim pn As MyPnames, n As Integer

Set pn = New MyPnames

MsgBox pn.Count
For n = 1 To pn.Count

    MsgBox pn.Item(n).Pname
Next n
End Sub
```

Run this code and you will see message boxes giving you the number of records in the collection and the Pname property for each record. This is working back through your object model to the data services layer you created earlier in this chapter.

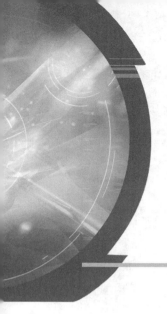

CHAPTER
22

Animation

Believe it or not, it is possible to animate objects in Access. By taking this possibility to an extreme, you can write a complete arcade game in Access—all the tools to do this are there. Serious users of Access would probably not be very impressed to find Space Invaders appearing in their database, but it can be done. However, for the purposes of this book, you will simply move a label object about on a form so it bounces around the borders of the form. This is rather reminiscent of the famous arcade game Breakout.

You first need to create a form for the purpose of a container for your animation. Click Create in the Access menu bar and then click the blank form icon in the Forms group of the ribbon. Close the Field List pane that appears on the right-hand side of the window and click the View drop-down in the Views group of the ribbon.

Change the view to Design View by clicking Design View on the drop-down. Next, click the Label icon on the Controls group of the ribbon. Move your cursor anywhere on the form and hold the left mouse button down to drag a label shape. Once you have dragged your label shape onto the form, right-click the Label control and select Properties in the pop-up menu.

Change the **Name** property to My Label and the **Caption** property to something you wish to display, such as **My Text**. Change the **FontSize** property to 18 (enlarging the Label box to accept this if necessary).

Your form in Design view should look like Figure 22-1.

Click your cursor anywhere on your form (not on the Label box) and right-click the mouse. Select Build Event and choose Code Builder to take you into the VBE window for your form. Add the following code:

```
Private Sub Form_Open(Cancel As Integer)
Dim VIncr As Long, HIncr As Long, Spd As Integer
Spd = 15
VIncr = Spd
```

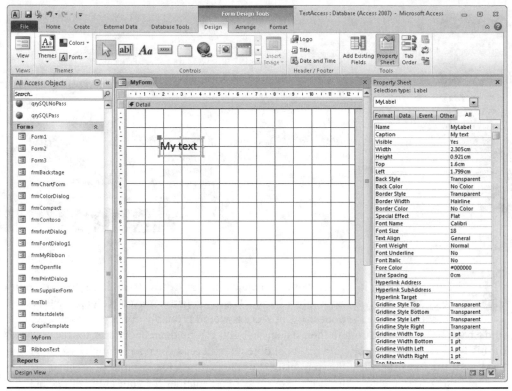

Figure 22-1 *Setting up a form for an animation*

```
HIncr = Spd
Do Until 1 = 2
    If Me.MyLabel.Left + HIncr < 0 Then HIncr = Spd
    If Me.MyLabel.Left > Me.InsideWidth - Me.MyLabel.Width Then HIncr = -Spd
    If Me.MyLabel.Top + VIncr < 0 Then VIncr = Spd
    If Me.MyLabel.Top > Me.InsideHeight - Me.MyLabel.Height Then VIncr = -Spd


    Me.MyLabel.Left = Me.MyLabel.Left + HIncr
    Me.MyLabel.Top = Me.MyLabel.Top + VIncr

    Me.Repaint

Loop
End Sub
```

Bear in mind that when this code runs, it will keep looping continuously forever until you press CTRL+BREAK, or until you write code within the loop to stop it after a set period of time, or some event happens, such as the form is closed.

The code is attached to the Form Open event so it is fired off as soon as the form is opened. Variables are set up to hold a horizontal increment value (HIncr), a vertical increment value (VIncr), and a speed value (Spd) to determine how fast the label will move about. By using this in the code as both a positive and negative value, it will also determine the direction of movement.

HIncr and VIncr are initially set to the value of Spd. This is followed by a looping process that will only end when 1 = 2, which will never happen, of course. A different condition can be used here so that the animation only runs for a set period of time.

The code then checks if the label box has reached a border of the form (top, bottom, left, or right). If it has reached a border, then the code changes the value of HIncr or VIncr, as appropriate, to reverse the direction of the label box.

Notice that the Me object is used as a representation of the current form.

For example, in the first **If** statement, if the left property plus the horizontal increment value are less than 0, then the label box has reached the left-hand side of the form and so the horizontal increment needs to change to a positive value to make the label box move from left to right.

Notice that the properties of **InsideWidth** and **InsideHeight** are used to determine the bottom and right limits of the form. The width and height properties of the label box are also used in the calculation. This is to prevent the label box from disappearing momentarily when it gets to the bottom of the form or the border of its right-hand side.

For example, in the second **If** statement, if the **Left** property of the label box is greater than the inside width of the form, less the width of the label box, then the label box has reached the right-hand side of the form and the horizontal increment needs to change to a negative value to make it move from right to left.

Now that the new values of HIncr and VIncr have been calculated, the **Left** and **Top** properties of your label box are incremented by these values. Finally, the form is repainted so that the changes in the label box properties take effect.

To run the code, all you need to do is click Design in the Access menu bar and then click the Form View icon in the Views group of the ribbon. Your text box will be seen bouncing around your form until you press CTRL+BREAK or the form is closed.

You can easily use this as a splash screen for your Access application or as a window to display while a lengthy query or process is running. You can also substitute a picture control for the label box to use a graphic image.

Access VBA in Action

The purpose of this section is to show the reader the worked examples of how they can apply the VBA code that they have learned in previous chapters to practical situations.

It is very easy to learn the theory on something, but I have always found it very necessary to apply the knowledge to a practical situation in order to learn how to use it fully.

Getting the Login ID

Access applications are multiuser and you can have several users loading your
application at once. If your application is deployed to a server in your organization
and has no protection on it, then anyone who comes across the file can load it up
and start using it. This would pose huge problems in the areas of data security and confidentiality.

You can protect your database by saving it with a password so that every user must know
the password, but the problem here is that people may circulate the password to unauthorized
users, and you would have absolutely no check as to who is using the application and what
they are doing.

Users may also find it irritating to input a password when they have already logged on to
their PC, and the system already knows who they are.

Using a simple API call (see Chapter 20 for more details on API calls), you can find out
the identity of each user as they load up your application.

Create a new module by clicking Insert | Module on the VBE menu. Enter the following
declaration into the General area at the top of the module:

```
Public Declare Function GetUserName Lib "advapi32.dll" Alias _
"GetUserNameA" (ByVal lpBuffer As String, nSize As Long) As Long
```

This sets up a link to the function GetUserName in the dynamic link library advapi32
(which is supplied as part of the Windows operating system).

Next, enter a function to return the user name. Enter the following code in the same module:

```
Public Function ReturnUserName()
Dim strUser As String, X As Integer
strUser = Space$(256)

X = GetUserName(strUser, 256)
strUser = RTrim(strUser)
ReturnUserName = Left(strUser, Len(strUser) - 1)
End Function
```

The code sets up variables to hold a string buffer to accept the user name and to hold the return value from the API call (true or false according to success or failure).

The **Spaces$** function is then used to create a string buffer of 256 characters, which is the maximum size for a Windows user name. The API **GetUserName** is then called, which loads the user name into the buffer **strUser**.

The RTrim function is used to remove all the trailing spaces in the buffer. Because the buffer is made up of 256 spaces, and in my experience Windows user names are generally under ten characters, there will be many spaces left over that will need removing.

Finally, the last character of the remaining string is removed. This is because the API call returns the string with a carriage return delimiter. The next logical step is to check that this user should be entering your application and to do that you do not need the carriage return.

To make use of this function, create a new form (see Chapter 9 on how to do this) or use an existing one and add the following code to the form open event:

```
MsgBox ReturnUserName()
```

You can find the form open event by right-clicking the form and selecting Build Event from the pop-up menu. Select Code Builder, which will open the VBE window for the form. Select Form from the top-left drop-down and choose Open from the top-right drop-down of the window.

Open the form in View mode by clicking the View icon in the View group of the ribbon. Your user name will then appear as a message box. If you ask a colleague to run the application on their PC, the message box will display their user name.

By placing the call to your function in the startup form for your application (refer to Chapter 9 for more information), you have a very reliable means of instantly discovering who is entering your application.

This can, of course, be easily circumvented by the user holding the SHIFT or BYPASS key down when the application is loading. Ways to lock the database and prevent a user from doing this are discussed more thoroughly in Chapter 24.

A Simple Use of the User Name

Now that you have the identity of the user entering your application, you can begin putting it to good use.

The most basic question is "Should this user be in this application?" If they are not an authorized user for this application (perhaps it's someone who has come across it by accident and wonders what it does), you need to deny them access and get them out as fast as possible.

An easy way to do this is to set up a single column table so each record holds a single user name of authorized users. Call the table AuthorizedUsers and the single field UserName. Populate the table with user names (including your own).

You can then use the following code:

```
Sub CheckUser()
Dim RcSet As Recordset
Set RcSet = CurrentDb.OpenRecordset _
("select * from AuthorizedUsers where UserName='" & ReturnUserName & "'")
If RcSet.RecordCount = 0 Then
    MsgBox "You are not authorized to use this application", vbInformation
    DoCmd.Quit
Else
    MsgBox "Welcome to " & ReturnUserName & ",vbInformation"
End If
End Sub
```

The code creates a **Recordset** object called RcSet and opens the recordset as a query on the AuthorizedUsers table, filtering where the UserName field equals the name returned by the **ReturnUserName** function.

If the **RecordCount** property is zero, then an imposter has been detected and a message box displays a suitable warning. The code then quits from the application preventing the user from doing anything more.

If the **RecordCount** property is not zero, then a welcoming message box is displayed and the application stays live.

You can obviously see that, by identifying the user immediately, this opens up a number of interesting possibilities regarding how you control your application with different users. This is discussed fully in Chapter 40.

When entering user names into the AuthorizedUsers table, you need to make sure they are spelled correctly and correspond exactly to the user name string returned by the API call. My own last name, Shepherd, has myriad spelling variations, and it can be extremely frustrating for a valid user to be given the "unauthorized" message and kicked out of the application.

Fortunately, Access is not case-sensitive, so you do not need to worry about upper- and lowercase in the strings.

Not so long ago, I wrote a similar application in Oracle (which is case-sensitive) that had screens to allow users with admin rights to set up new users. Again, it used the Windows user name to determine the validity of the user, but the user name was entered by the admin user.

I found myself frequently fielding calls from irate administrators claiming the application did not work because they had set up a new user who then could not get in. The problem always came down to the spelling of the user name or its case. One of the ways around it was to use the Lower function to convert both strings to lowercase before the comparison, but the spelling issue often was a problem that could not be resolved through code.

Securing Your Database

Once you have created your application, you will want some means of preventing users from changing your application without going through your carefully thought-out user interface.

You certainly do not want them making changes to your code. Thankfully, it is easy to password-protect the code by clicking Tools | <name of database> Properties in the VBE window. Click the Protection tab in the pop-up window, check "Lock Project for Viewing," and enter and reenter your password. Save the project and your code is now protected.

However, as you have already seen, there are other components to your project—such as tables, queries, forms, and reports—and it would be a disaster if a user decided to make a few unauthorized changes! They can delete tables or edit a report, and since the database is multiuser, this affects everyone using it.

You can stop this from happening in a number of ways.

Using an ACCDE File to Protect Your Application

You can save your application as an ACCDE file simply by clicking the File tab in the Access ribbon, clicking Publish to Access Services in the central pane, clicking Save Database As in the File Types pane, and then clicking the Make ACCDE icon in the Save Database As pane.

This will create a compiled file where the user cannot change forms, reports, or VBA code. They can, however, still change tables and queries, and enter new data. This means that your compiled application is still not as safe as you might wish.

Another problem is that you as the developer cannot make changes to forms, reports, or VBA code either. Once you begin writing professional applications in Access, you will find that the users always want to make changes after the application has been rolled out.

I have never seen an application that did not come into this category. One of the difficulties is that until several users start ardently working with your application, various problems may never surface, and so you will find yourself constantly correcting and responding to user requirements.

If the users are building up data in your application and no changes can be made to forms, reports, and VBA, then when a change must be made you will need to use the original ACCDB file that created the ACCDE file. However, it will not be up to date in terms of data and this will need to be imported back in to the original ACCDB tables.

A danger exists of the whole process becoming messy and errors creeping in.

Using VBA to Lock Your Application Down

You can use the database properties to lock your database so users can only do what your user interface lets them do and nothing more. You can also put a custom ribbon on the opening form and subsequent forms (see Chapter 11 for more information on creating ribbons).

For the following example, use a blank database with no data in it. Insert a module into the VBE window using Insert | Module from the menu.

Enter the following code into the module:

```
Sub DisableStartupProperties()
    ChangeProperty "StartupShowDBWindow", dbBoolean, False
    ChangeProperty "StartupShowStatusBar", dbBoolean, False
    ChangeProperty "AllowBuiltinToolbars", dbBoolean, False
    ChangeProperty "AllowFullMenus", dbBoolean, False
    ChangeProperty "AllowBreakIntoCode", dbBoolean, False
    ChangeProperty "AllowSpecialKeys", dbBoolean, False
    ChangeProperty "AllowBypassKey", dbBoolean, False
    ChangeProperty "AllowShortcutMenus", dbBoolean, False
End Sub

Function ChangeProperty(strPropName As String, _
varPropType As Variant, varPropValue As Variant) As Integer
    Dim dbs As Database, prp As Property
    Const conPropNotFoundError = 3270

    Set dbs = CurrentDb
    On Error GoTo Change_Err
    dbs.Properties(strPropName) = varPropValue
    ChangeProperty = True

Change_Bye:
    Exit Function
```

```
Change_Err:
    If Err = conPropNotFoundError Then
        Set prp = dbs.CreateProperty(strPropName, varPropType, varPropValue)
        dbs.Properties.Append prp
        Resume Next
    Else
        ChangeProperty = False
        Resume Change_Bye
    End If
End Function
```

This code includes a function that will change the property value. If the property is not found, it will be created.

When this code is run, it will set the properties shown in the code to False. This prevents, for example, the BREAK key and the BYPASS key (SHIFT) being used to interrupt the database. It also disables shortcut menus (right-click a form or report) and prevents the database navigation window from appearing.

Run this code, but do not exit the database. The property changes have no effect until you exit the database and then reload it.

Next, you need to design a simple ribbon that will remove the existing Access ribbon. To do this, you must first create a table called USysRibbons. You do this by clicking Create in the Access menu bar and then clicking the Table Design icon in the Tables group of the ribbon.

You need to create two fields in the tables. The first is called RibbonName and is a text field. The second is called RibbonXML and is a memo field. Save the table with the name **USysRibbons**.

In the database navigation window, right-click the bar at the top of the navigation pane and click Navigation Options. Check the box for Show System Objects. Because this is a system table, you will not see it or be able to find it unless you do this.

Open the table and type in the value **MyRibbon** in the RibbonName field. Enter the following XML in the RibbonXML field for that record:

```
<customUI
xmlns="http://schemas.microsoft.com/office/2006/01/customui">
<ribbon startFromScratch="true">
</ribbon>
</customUI>
```

Because this uses startFromScratch, it will create a ribbon that displays only the File tab. You can of course add ribbon commands into the XML to suit your application but for this exercise it will just be a simple ribbon that is empty.

You now need to create an opening form for your application using Create on the Access menu bar and clicking the Blank Form icon in the Forms group of the ribbon.

Save the form and give it a name such as Main. Click the File tab in the Access menu and click Options. Click Current Database in the left-hand pane and then use the drop-down for

Display Form to select the form you created. This means that when the database is loaded it will automatically default to your new form.

On the form, you need to view it in Design mode and right-click it to select properties. Select Form in the Selection Type drop-down. You need to set the Ribbon Name property to MyRibbon or whatever you called the custom ribbon.

One further problem exists. All this code and XML will lock the database up completely. At some point, you will need to do maintenance on the database, so how do you get back in?

Currently there is no way to get back in to change anything. What you need is a "back door" that users are unlikely to discover but which will let you in.

Right-click the form you created and select Properties. Choose Form properties on the drop-down and navigate to Key Preview. Set this property to Yes and save the form. This means that keypresses on the form can be picked up by your code.

Return to the module you created and add the following procedure:

```
Sub EnableStartupProperties()
    ChangeProperty "StartupShowDBWindow", dbBoolean, True
    ChangeProperty "StartupShowStatusBar", dbBoolean, True
    ChangeProperty "AllowBuiltinToolbars", dbBoolean, True
    ChangeProperty "AllowFullMenus", dbBoolean, True
    ChangeProperty "AllowBreakIntoCode", dbBoolean, True
    ChangeProperty "AllowSpecialKeys", dbBoolean, True
    ChangeProperty "AllowBypassKey", dbBoolean, True
    ChangeProperty "AllowShortcutMenus", dbBoolean, True
End Sub
```

On the form you created, add the following code to the module for that form:

```
Private Sub Form_KeyDown(KeyCode As Integer, Shift As Integer)
If KeyCode = 191 And Shift = 1 Then
    EnableStartupProperties
    MsgBox "Security Disabled", vbInformation

End If
End Sub
```

In this code, 191 is the ASCII code for a question mark (?). Because it is on the Key Down event for the form, all you need to do is click the form itself and then press SHIFT+?. A message will appear saying security has been disabled. Close the database and load it for the changes to take effect. You will also need to use the File tab to change the ribbon back to the Access default.

You should not use this special key on the live version when doing maintenance, since that will leave it open to everyone. Instead, take a copy and disable the security on the copy. Then make your changes on the copy, which will then replace the live version of the database. This will maintain the data that has been entered.

If you close the database and then reload it, the screen should look like Figure 24-1.

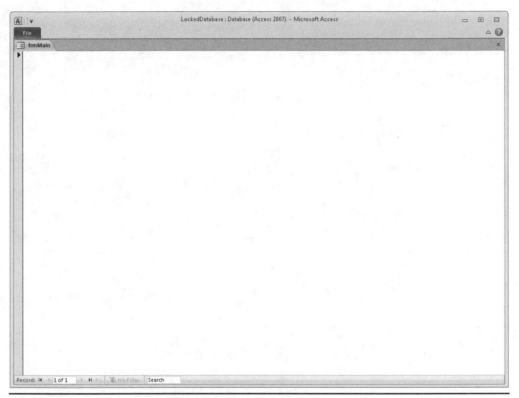

Figure 24-1   *The opening screen for a locked database*

Notice that the File tab now has very limited options. The button for Access Settings is now missing and you cannot customize the Quick Access Toolbar. Your users can do nothing except go where your user interface takes them. However, you still have your special hotkey to gain access.

If you click the displayed form and then press SHIFT+?, you will get the security disabled message box. Close the database and then reload it and you will have access to the objects.

Creating Audit Trails on Tables

E ven the simplest database can end up holding a lot of data, which is constantly changing as users add new records and update and delete existing ones.

The actions of the users may not have huge implications, but let's suppose someone wants to know who made a change and when and what they changed. In the past, I have written applications producing reports for external regulatory bodies, where the need for audit trails was of paramount importance.

A recent feature of Access on memo fields logs a change in terms of date and time but does not tell you who did it or what they changed. To maintain the full story, you need to customize it with VBA.

Who Is the User?

The first fact that must be established is who the user is and who has done the deed. You can use an API call to find out who is actually using your application and altering data.

Create a new module by clicking Insert | Module on the VBE menu. Enter the following declaration into the General area at the top of the module:

```
Public Declare Function GetUserName Lib "advapi32.dll" Alias _
"GetUserNameA" (ByVal lpBuffer As String, nSize As Long) As Long
```

This sets up a link to the function **GetUserName** in the dynamic link library advapi32 (which is supplied as part of the Windows operating system).

Next, enter a function to return the user name. Enter the following code in the same module:

```
Public Function ReturnUserName()
Dim strUser As String, X As Integer
strUser = Space$(256)

X = GetUserName(strUser, 256)
strUser = RTrim(strUser)
ReturnUserName = Left(strUser, Len(strUser) - 1)
End Function
```

The function **ReturnUserName** will always provide the windows login of the current user. Because this is a public function, it can be used in all the form modules.

The Audit Trail on the Table Structure

For the purposes of this example, I am using the Northwind database and the Customers table. You can access the Northwind database by loading Access and clicking Sample in the center Navigation pane (Available Templates) and then clicking the Northwind icon. Add the AuditTrail field to the Customers table.

On each table where you want an audit trail, you must add an extra field to hold the audit trail information. Right-click the table name in the Navigation pane of Access and choose design mode. Add a field as Memo type called **AuditTrail**. Save the table design.

I have chosen a Memo type field so as to demonstrate how you can record every change a user makes to the data. However, this may increase the size of the database too much and you may wish to use a standard text field instead, one that holds less information.

Using Events to Create the Audit Trail

Your table will act as the data feed for a form. In the case of the Customers table, the Customers List form is a convenient one to use. Open this form in Design mode and right-click the form. Click Build Event in the pop-up menu and click Code Builder in the following window.

In the VBE module for the form, click the drop-down in the top-left corner of the module and click Form.

Click the drop-down in the top-right corner and click AfterUpdate. Insert the following code into this event:

```
Dim RecSet As Recordset, Temp As Variant
Set RecSet = CurrentDb.OpenRecordset("select * from Customers where ID=" & Me.ID)
```

```
Temp = RecSet!AuditTrail
Temp = Temp & "Edit" & "|" & ReturnUserName & "|" & Now() & "|"


CurrentDb.Execute ("update Customers set AuditTrail='" & Temp & "' where ID="  _
& Me.ID)
```

This code sets up two variables using the **Dim** statement, one as a **Recordset** object and one as a variant. The reason that variant is used and not string is because initially this object has to be loaded with a null value and a string will not take a null.

The **Recordset** object is then set to point to the Customers table using the current record ID. So long as the ID field is included in the data source for the form, you can refer to it using the **Me** object, even if it is not actually a field on the form.

The existing value of the AuditTrail field is loaded into the variable Temp (this is the point at which it may contain a Null value).

The name of the Action (in this case, Edit), the user name, and the current date and time are all concatenated onto Temp using vertical bars as separators.

Temp now holds the latest details of the audit trail plus the previous details. An **Execute** statement using an update query is then used to write back the new value of the AuditTrail field, and the **RecSet** object is closed.

You also need to add this same procedure to the **BeforeInsert** event. To get to the **BeforeInsert** event, right-click the form and select Build Event. Click Code Builder in the pop-up window and the VBE window for the form will be displayed. Click Form in the top-left drop-down of the module window and click BeforeInsert in the top-right drop-down of the code module. Change the action in the concatenated string to Insert instead of Edit.

Open the Customer List form in View mode and make a few changes to the data. Open the Customers table and look at the AuditTrail field. You will see that the information is starting to build up as to who did what and when.

You will now see why a memo field was used for the AuditTrail field and not text. Text only allows 255 characters and this would soon be exhausted in a database with plenty of updates. If you find you have to use a text field for the AuditTrail, do not concatenate with the previous value—only store the current value:

```
Dim Temp As Variant
Temp = Temp & "Edit" & "|" & ReturnUserName & "|" & Now() & "|"

CurrentDb.Execute ("update Customers set AuditTrail='" & Temp & "' where ID="  _
& Me.ID)
```

One of the problems you may have noticed is that if the user deletes a record, then all of your wonderful audit trail disappears together with the record. The way around this is not to allow users to delete records by setting the form property "Allow Deletions" to No.

Instead, you add another field of Boolean type (Yes/No) to the underlying table called Deleted. You then put your own Delete button on the form and execute a SQL update statement to set the Deleted field to No:

```
CurrentDb.Execute ("update Customers set Deleted=True where ID="  _
&  Me.ID)
```

This statement picks up the current ID using the **Me** object for the form.

You will need to change your form query so that records are only included where the Deleted field is False.

You also need to include the audit trail code from earlier on the Delete button, changing the action from Edit to Delete in the concatenation.

Enhancing the Audit Trail

You can also add more granularity to your audit trail field by adding in the values of fields on the form so that the audit trail shows a snapshot of what the user changed the values to:

```
Private Sub Form_AfterUpdate()
Dim RecSet As Recordset, Temp As Variant
Set RecSet = CurrentDb.OpenRecordset("select * from Customers where ID=" & Me.ID)
Temp = RecSet!AuditTrail
Temp = Temp & "Edit" & "|" & ReturnUserName & "|" _
& Now() & "|" & Me.First_Name & "|" & Me.Last_Name & "|" & Me.E_mail_Address


CurrentDb.Execute ("update Customers set AuditTrail='" & Temp & "' where ID=" _
& Me.ID)

End Sub
```

This can get messy if many fields are displayed on the form, but it does allow you to see exactly what each user has done within the form. For some applications, you do need this level of granularity.

Creating and Editing Queries in VBA

SQL queries in Access are an essential tool for allowing the user to view and update data. In a relational database, it is very rare to obtain meaningful data from a single table. Queries join tables together, or they can be used to update, delete, or append records.

When a form is being used, it is sometimes useful to either create a new query to do something specific or to change the SQL to adapt to changes that the user is making.

Creating a New Query

VBA allows you to easily add a new query to the **QueryDefs** collection using the following code. This example is based on the Orders table of the Northwind database. To access this database, load Access and then click Sample in the left-hand Navigation pane of the opening screen. Double-click the Northwind icon.

```
Sub CreateQuery()
Dim Qd As New QueryDef, Qds As QueryDefs

Set Qds = CurrentDb.QueryDefs

Qd.Name = "MyNewQuery"
Qd.SQL = "Select * from orders"
```

```
Qds.Append Qd

Application.RefreshDatabaseWindow
Set Qd = Nothing
Set Qds = Nothing

End Sub
```

This example assumes you do not already have a query set up called MyNewQuery. This code can be run from any module within Access.

This code sets up two objects using the **Dim** statement: **Qd** to hold the new query definition, and **Qds** to represent the **QueryDefs** collection for the database.

The **QueryDef** name is set to MyNewQuery, and a simple SQL statement is added based on the Orders table.

The new query definition is appended to the **QueryDefs** collection and the Database window is refreshed so that the new query shows in the Navigation pane.

If you look at the list of queries, you will see that your new query is now set up and available for use.

Deleting an Existing Query

You can also use VBA to delete queries from the **QueryDefs** collection. You can see what is in this collection by looking at your queries within the Navigation pane of Access. The **QueryDefs** collection reflects exactly what appears in the pane. There are no warning messages when this happens, so beware of the use of this code:

```
Sub RemoveQuery()
CurrentDb.QueryDefs.Delete "MyNewQuery"
Application.RefreshDatabaseWindow
End Sub
```

This code simply deletes the query you created in the previous section and then refreshes the database window so the query no longer shows in the Navigation pane.

Updating a SQL Query

You can easily change the SQL in an Access query by using the SQL property of the query definition. You can effectively change the query type depending on what the SQL does:

```
Sub ChangeQuery()
CurrentDb.QueryDefs("MyNewQuery").SQL = _
"update orders set customer ='Company Unknown' where
customer='Company D'"
Application.RefreshDatabaseWindow
End Sub
```

This code can be run from any module within Access.

If you look in the Navigation pane for your query, you will now see that it has an update icon against it and it has changed its type.

Similarly, you could also change the query to a Delete query:

```
Sub ChangeQuery()
CurrentDb.QueryDefs("MyNewQuery").SQL = _
"delete * from orders where customer='Customer D'"
Application.RefreshDatabaseWindow
End Sub
```

In the Navigation pane, notice that your query now has a delete icon against it.

You can also change the ODBC **timeout** property in this way. The **timeout** property sets the time limit when a query will end if no data is received. It can be a problem if you are using external tables and the external server is running slow (possibly due to the load from other users). The property value default is set to 60 (60 seconds), but you may wish to increase it:

```
Sub SetTimeout()
CurrentDb.QueryDefs("MyNewQuery").ODBCTimeout = 120

End Sub
```

Search and Replace in Queries

S tructures of queries in large Access applications can become very complicated, particularly when queries are layered on top of each other. There may be over one hundred queries in a database and it is difficult to keep track of which tables or subqueries they use.

If a table name or field name is changed, which is a strong possibility if you are linking to external tables, it can be a nightmare finding the queries that this affects. Tables in an Access database can also become redundant due to changes in the user requirements of an application. Which queries do they affect and which queries is it safe to make redundant?

As a developer, you can write some VBA utilities to help you search queries.

Searching for a Specific String Within All Queries

You will frequently come across situations where you need to find all the queries that use a specific table, subquery, or field name.

Run this code on the Northwind database. You can access this database by loading Access and then clicking Sample in the Navigation pane on the left-hand side of the opening screen. Double-click the Northwind icon.

First you need to create a small table to hold the results, since in some applications this can cover many query names.

Click Create in the Access menu and then click the Table Design icon in the Table group of the ribbon. Create a single text field called **QueryName**. Save this as **tblSearchResults**. You do not need a primary key since it will only be used to hold the results of your search.

Add the following code to a module:

```
Sub SearchQueries()
Dim RecSet As Recordset, Qdef As QueryDef, SearchStr As String
CurrentDb.Execute "delete * from tblSearchResults"
Set RecSet = CurrentDb.OpenRecordset("tblSearchResults")
SearchStr = "orders"

For Each Qdef In CurrentDb.QueryDefs
    If InStr(Qdef.SQL, SearchStr) Then
        RecSet.AddNew
        RecSet!QueryName = Qdef.Name
        RecSet.Update

    End If

Next Qdef
Set RecSet = Nothing
Set Qdef = Nothing
End Sub
```

This code sets up objects for a recordset, a query definition, and a string using the **Dim** statement. The tblSearchResults table is cleared out of any previous results using an **Execute** statement.

The **Recordset** object is then set to point to the table tblSearchResults and the SearchStr is loaded with the word "orders". This search word could be anything, such as a table name, query name, or field name. Here you place whatever you want to search for within the query collection.

This particular example will search for any query containing the word "orders". In Access, this is not case-sensitive, so "orders" will still return results in spite of the fact that the orders table is called Orders.

The code then iterates through the query collection and uses the **Instr** function to test the SQL for each query to see if the search string is present. If it is present, it then adds a new record to the table tblSearchResults and sets the QueryName field in the table to the name of the current query.

Run this code and then open the table tblSearchResults. This holds the names of all the queries that contain your search string. You can now print the list out and work through it deciding what action to take.

One word of warning: It is very dangerous in an Access application to delete a query or table, no matter how sure you are that it is now redundant. It could have unforeseen repercussions that you had not noticed and could cause immense problems in your application—especially if you have to reinstate it on very short notice when an angry user starts shouting.

A far better way is to rename the query or table as "zz" followed by the name of the table or query. For example, the query qryMyQuery would thus be renamed zzqryMyQuery. All the potential deletions then move to the end of the query list. Afterward, you should wait a suitable period of time, such as a month, to make sure this has not caused any problems in the operation of your application.

If a user runs into problems, you can reinstate the query quickly simply by removing the "zz" from the name. If nothing untoward has happened over a period of time, you can delete the query fully.

Search and Replace in a Query

Search and replace should only be run on one query at a time, since a blanket replacement can create horrendous problems for your application if it goes wrong.

You will sometimes need to change queries if any field names are changed in linked table queries, or if you have copied a query and wish to use it on a different set of tables.

One way to do this is to copy the entire SQL statement into a Word document using Copy and Paste. You then use the Find and Replace function in Word, and then copy and paste the SQL statement back into the query.

Since this can be time-consuming, you can write a small VBA utility to do it instead. Add the following code into a module in the Northwind database. This code assumes you already have a query set up called MyNewQuery.

```
Sub SearchReplaceQueries()
Dim QName As String, SearchStr As String, ReplaceStr As String
Dim Temp As String
QName = "MyNewQuery"
SearchStr = "Company D"
ReplaceStr = "Company B"
Temp = CurrentDb.QueryDefs(QName).SQL
For n = 1 To Len(Temp)
    X = InStr(n, Temp, SearchStr)
    If X Then
        Temp = Left(Temp, X - 1) & ReplaceStr & Mid(Temp, X + Len(ReplaceStr))

    End If
Next n

CurrentDb.QueryDefs(QName).SQL = Temp

End Sub
```

Before this code is run, it is advisable to make a copy of the query that will be changed.

The code sets up strings to hold the name of the query and the search and replace information. These are then loaded with the relevant strings. The variable Temp is loaded with the SQL statement for the target query.

A For..Next loop is used to iterate through the SQL statement. The **Instr** function is usually employed to check whether the search string has been found, but in this case a movable start position is used, defined by n from the For..Next loop.

If the search string has been found, the replacement string is inserted at the correct point into the variable Temp. The value n is then incremented by the For..Next loop and another iteration is performed.

This ensures that every instance of the search string will be changed to the replace string, no matter how many are in the SQL statement.

This provides a far quicker and better way of making changes to queries than trying to do it manually. It is very easy to make a mistake on a manual basis, particularly if the query is long and complicated.

Using the DateAdd Function

A ccess provides a useful function that allows a time or date interval to be added or subtracted to an existing date and time, giving the new date and time.

Suppose your users need a report over a specified time interval. They want to be able to pick a month and a year as the start point and then pull out all the data for the next *n* months (where *n* is a variable supplied by the users) from the first day of that month.

Some complex processing is required to sort this out. Therefore, you need to know how many days are in each month in order to know what to add to the starting point, which basically means a lookup table of some sort.

However, **DateAdd** provides the functionality to easily work out the end date based on the starting date and the number of months to increment.

Enter the following VBA code into a module:

```
Function TestDateAdd(Target, Months As Integer)

Dim Temp As String
If IsDate(Target) = False Then
    TestDateAdd = "Invalid date"
    Exit Function
End If
Temp = Right(Target, 2)
If Temp <= 29 Then
    Temp = "20" & Temp
```

```
Else
    Temp = "19" & Temp
End If




Target = Month(Target) & "/" & Temp

TestDateAdd = DateAdd("m", Months + 1, Target)
TestDateAdd = DateAdd("d", -1, TestDateAdd)

End Function
```

This function accepts the parameters of a date and the number of months to increase it by. Notice that the Target parameter is not defined as a date but as a variant. This is because your users may enter a date in a format that VBA cannot understand. If we define Target as a date, there will be a type mismatch error before the function even begins to run, and thus no opportunity for error trapping.

First, there is a procedure using the **IsDate** function to test whether a valid date has been passed across. For example, if Target contains "Next week", it will fail at this point and exit the function, returning the string "Invalid Date".

However, interestingly enough, if the user puts in 31-Nov-09, the **IsDate** function will consider this a valid date! The only problem is that it will interpret the year incorrectly. If the user enters 31-Nov-2009 (with a four-digit year), then **IsDate** will correctly interpret that the date is invalid.

Because Access VBA has problems interpreting dates with two-digit years, a procedure can be used to change the date to a four-digit year. The procedure tests the two right-hand characters of target to see if they are less than or equal to 29. If this is true, then the year is made a four-digit year commencing with "20", otherwise it becomes a four-digit year beginning with "19".

The Target string is then set to the month and the four-digit year. For the purposes of the **DateAdd** function, the day will default to the first day, so long as a four-digit year is used.

The **DateAdd** function is used to add the number of months parameter to the start date. The "m" means add in months, and the number of months plus 1 is added to the target date.

The reason we add an extra month is because we are trying to find the last day of the final month. You can do this by adding an extra month, which takes the calculation to the first day of the next month. The same methodology is used to subtract one day, taking it back to the final day of the last month.

Regardless of your locale, as long as you enter a date in your local format, this will return the last day of the month *n* months ahead.

Even if you enter "31-Nov-09", it will still be interpreted as "01-Nov-2009" and will return "28-Feb-2010" if the months parameter is set to 3.

You can use the following parameters for the interval:

Setting	Description
Yyyy	Year
Q	Quarter
M	Month
Y	Day of Year
D	Day
W	Weekday
Ww	Week
H	Hour
M	Minute
S	Second

Using DateAdd to Pause Your Code

Use the **DateAdd** function to create a function to pause your code for a few seconds. You may need to do this for operational reasons or to display a splash screen for a brief moment.

Enter the following code into a module:

```
Function AccessWait(Target As Long)

TimeWait = DateAdd("s", Target, Time)
Do Until Time >= TimeWait

Loop


End Function
```

You can call this from VBA code by using the following code:

```
X = AccessWait(10)
```

This will stop processing for 10 seconds.

This function has one parameter passed to it, which is the number of seconds to wait. It uses the **DateAdd** function to add the number of target seconds to the current time and puts the result into a variable called TimeWait.

It then uses a Do..Until Loop to hold all processing until the current time is greater than or equal to the variable TimeWait.

This is a simple but effective methodology to pause processing for a set period of time.

Monitoring Table Statistics

In large complex Access applications, it is difficult to keep track of what is actually going on within the database. Tables grow and change in size, particularly if large amounts of data are being imported from external sources.

By seeing how table sizes are changing according to what is going on, developers and some users often get a feel for whether the application is running correctly or not. They often know, for example, how many records they are going to receive from an external data source, so they will expect a particular table receiving this import to grow in size by exactly this number.

Many people refer to these as "sanity" or "health" checks on the database. They use this kind of data for reconciling the tables and checking that no extraneous data is appearing or that records are disappearing unexpectedly.

You can monitor tables quite easily by way of VBA procedures. In this example, we will use the Northwind database. You can find this by loading Access and clicking Sample in the left-hand Navigation pane of the opening window. Double-click the Northwind icon.

You first need to create a table to hold the table statistics. Click Create on the Access menu and then click the Table Design icon in the Tables group of the ribbon.

Create a table with three fields in it:

▶ **TableName**   Text (255 characters)
▶ **TableSize**   Number (Long Integer)
▶ **TimeStamp**   Date/Time

No primary key is required since this is an internal table for information only. Save the table with the name **tblTableStatistics**.

Enter the following code into a module:

```
Sub TableStatistics()
Dim RecSet As Recordset, RecSet1 As Recordset, TDef As TableDef
CurrentDb.Execute "delete * from tblTableStatistics" 'Optional
Set RecSet = CurrentDb.OpenRecordset("tblTableStatistics")
For Each TDef In CurrentDb.TableDefs

    Set RecSet1 = CurrentDb.OpenRecordset(TDef.Name)
    RecSet.AddNew
    RecSet!TableName = TDef.Name
    RecSet!TableSize = RecSet1.RecordCount
    RecSet!TimeStamp = Now()
    RecSet.Update

Next TDef
Set RecSet = Nothing
Set RecSet1 = Nothing
End Sub
```

This code uses the **Dim** statement to set up objects for two recordsets and a table definition object. A **Delete** statement is used to clear previous data from the table. This statement is optional in that the table could keep accumulating statistical data on the tables. Since there is a **Date/Time** field, all you would then need to do is query on a specific range of date/time to find out what the state of the database was at that point.

The process iterates through all the **TableDefs** in the **TableDefs** collection of the database. Using the current **TableDef** name, a second recordset is opened in order to get the number of records for that table definition.

A new record is added to the tblTableStatistics recordset and the TableName, TableSize, and TimeStamp fields are populated and updated.

If you run this and then open the table tblTableStatistics, you will see details for all tables within the database at a particular date and time.

Coupled with Chapter 25, this provides a very useful tool to keep track of exactly what is going on in the application. You could set it on a timer on the opening form so it is fired off every hour, and also fire it off immediately before and after any data import.

I have found this methodology very useful for convincing the most doubtful manager about the integrity of the database!

Handling Large
Text Files

I n an Access application, you frequently have to either import text files or link to them. This is often because they are generated from an external database and the database owner does not want you linking your application to their database either because of security issues or because your application link may cause performance issues on the host database.

Generally, it is easy enough to import or link to a text file, but what if the text file is too big for Access to handle? I recently had to deal with a 4GB text file and Access completely refused to cooperate with it. I could not even view the data in the file using the Access Text File Wizard.

Trying to view the data in Notepad or WordPad was also a non-starter since the file took too long to load.

This was where VBA came to the rescue. The first thing I needed to do was find out the structure of the file, what the delimiters were, and what the data looked like, since I knew nothing about the contents of the file.

The following code creates a file containing the first ten rows of the monster text file:

```
Sub CreateTenRows()
Dim temp As String
fnum = FreeFile
Open "C:\MyLargeFile.txt" For Input As fnum
fnum1 = FreeFile
Open "c:\FirstTenRows.txt" For Output As fnum1
```

```
   For n = 1 To 10
      Line Input #fnum, temp

      Print #fnum1, temp
   Next n

Close fnum
Close fnum1


End Sub
```

This code opened the 4GB file (MyLargeFile) for input so it could be read, and also created an output file called FirstTenRows.

Using a For..Next loop, a row was read into the variable temp and then written out to the output file. This iterated ten times and produced a sample file of manageable size that could easily be viewed in Notepad.

On viewing the sample file, the deliminators were tilde characters (~) and there were also single quote text qualifiers ('). Access does not work well with tilde deliminators and the text qualifiers are not actually necessary for the purpose of linking the text file into Access.

With a small file, the issue of text qualifiers would not matter, but with a 4GB file, the text qualifiers take up a considerable amount of space.

The following code opens the big file and iterates through it changing tilde characters to commas and removing single quote marks.

```
Sub GetMyBigFile()
Dim temp As String, temp1 As String

fnum = FreeFile
Open "C:\MyBigFile.txt" For Input As fnum
fnum1 = FreeFile
Open "c:\MySmallFile.txt" For Output As fnum1


Do While Not EOF(fnum)

   Line Input #fnum, temp
   temp1 = ""
   For m = 1 To Len(temp)
      If Mid(temp, m, 1) = "~" Then
         temp1 = temp1 & ","
      ElseIf Mid(temp, m, 1) = "'" Then
```

```
        Else
            temp1 = temp1 & Mid(temp, m, 1)

        End If


    Next m


    Print #fnum1, temp1

Loop
Close fnum
Close fnum1


End Sub
```

This code opens up the big file as an input file and opens an output file. It then iterates through the entire big file, reading each row into the variable temp. It then moves through the file, temp character by temp character. If it finds a tilde (~), it replaces it with a comma (,). If it finds a single quote mark ('), it does nothing, so the character disappears. If it is any other character, it just concatenates it to the new string that is being created for that row (temp1).

It then writes the string temp1 to the output file and loops back around.

If you are removing single quote marks, you may run into problems if there is text with a quote mark that is meant to be housed there. An example might be a person's name, such as O'Leary.

This procedure took me about 90 minutes to run, but at the end of it, I had a CSV (Comma Separated Values) file with no text qualifiers in it. Access is far more at home with CSV files, and I was able to get a working link to my new text file. However, using a simple query on the linked file still caused problems.

The answer was to split the file into two files and have two linked files on my Access database. I could create a query for each one to pull out the relevant data and then use a union query to join the two outputs together. See Chapter 12 for more information on SQL queries.

My code to create the output file was modified to the following:

```
Sub CreateSplitFiles()
Dim temp As String, temp1 As String, temp2 As String, n As Long

n = 1
fnum = FreeFile

Open "C:\MyBigFile.txt" For Input As fnum
fnum1 = FreeFile
```

```
Open "c:\SmallFile1.txt" For Output As fnum1
fnum2 = FreeFile
Open "c:\SmallFile2.txt" For Output As fnum2

Do While Not EOF(fnum)

    Line Input #fnum, temp
    temp1 = ""
    For m = 1 To Len(temp)
        If Mid(temp, m, 1) = "~" Then
            temp1 = temp1 & ","
        ElseIf Mid(temp, m, 1) = "'" Then

        Else
            temp1 = temp1 & Mid(temp, m, 1)

        End If


    Next m
    If n = 1 Then

        Print #fnum2, temp1
    End If


    If n < 3500000 Then
        Print #fnum1, temp1
    Else
        Print #fnum2, temp1
    End If

    n = n + 1

Loop
Close fnum
Close fnum1
Close Fnum2


End Sub
```

This example works the same way as the previous one in terms of replacing characters in the file, but there are now two output files (SmallFile1 and SmallFile2). It also has a counter (n) to keep track of the number of rows.

When n=1, the first row of the big file is written to both output files. This is because it was a header row containing field names and needed to be the first row in both output files. The process keeps writing rows to Smallfile1 until it reaches 3,500,000 rows. At this point, it begins writing rows to SmallFile2.

The result was two CSV files of a more manageable size that contained all the data of the original big file. The files were linked into the Access database and the union query worked successfully.

The point at which the output procedure changes from one file to the other is arbitrary, so it takes a bit of guesswork to decide where best to set this.

Create and Change Table Structures

As your Access application is running, there may be a need to create a table on-the-fly or amend a table structure. For example, you may be importing data into a table from a text file. If for any reason the data in the field in the text file is too large for the field in your table, it will be truncated and data will be lost.

You may also wish to create a table for a specific operation, do that operation, and then delete the table.

You can also change the properties of each individual field, such as whether it is a required field or whether it is indexed.

Creating a Table

Use this VBA code to create a simple table:

```
Sub CreateTable()
Dim MyTable As TableDef

Set MyTable = CurrentDb.CreateTableDef("NewTable")

MyTable.Fields.Append MyTable.CreateField("TextField", dbText, 100)
MyTable.Fields.Append MyTable.CreateField("LongIntegerField", dbLong)
MyTable.Fields.Append MyTable.CreateField("MemoField", dbMemo)
MyTable.Fields.Append MyTable.CreateField("YesNoField", dbBoolean)
MyTable.Fields.Append MyTable.CreateField("DateTimeField", dbDate)
```

```
MyTable.Fields.Append MyTable.CreateField("IntegerField", dbInteger)
MyTable.Fields.Append MyTable.CreateField("SingleNumberField", dbSingle)
MyTable.Fields.Append MyTable.CreateField("DoubleNumberField", dbDouble)

CurrentDb.TableDefs.Append MyTable

Application.RefreshDatabaseWindow

End Sub
```

This code uses the **Dim** statement to create an object to hold the Table Definition. It then sets this object to a newly created table definition called NewTable. New fields are then created in the table by using the **Append** method of the **Fields** collection for the new table definition.

The field is created using the **CreateField** method and then appended to the Fields collection. The create field method requires a field name (e.g., TextField) and a field type parameter (e.g., dbText). Notice that it is only the text field that uses the optional size parameter. If this is omitted, then the size is set to the default of 255 characters.

Finally, the new **TableDef** object is appended to the **TableDefs** collection and the database window is refreshed so you can see your new table in the Navigation pane.

If you run this code and then open the table NewTable in Design mode, you will see all the fields of different type that have been created.

Deleting a Table or a Field

You can easily delete a table (providing it is not in use) by using:

```
CurrentDb.TableDefs.Delete "NewTable"
```

To delete a single field in the table, use:

```
CurrentDb.TableDefs("NewTable").Fields.Delete "TextField"
```

This deletes the field TextField in the table NewTable and deletes all the data in that field at the same time.

No warning messages are given for either of these methods, so beware. You could easily lose much data.

Editing Field Properties

You can also edit field properties on-the-fly (providing that the table is not open). Here are some examples:

```
CurrentDb.TableDefs("NewTable").Fields("MemoField").DefaultValue = "abc"

CurrentDb.TableDefs("NewTable").Fields("MemoField").Required = True

CurrentDb.TableDefs("NewTable").Fields("MemoField").AllowZeroLength = False
```

These VBA statements act on the field MemoField in the table NewTable, and set the default value to abc, the **Required** property to True, and the **AllowZeroLength** property to False.

Creating Indexes

You can use VBA to create indexes on tables. These are usually placed on key fields within a tables so as to speed up the queries on those tables. The downside of this is that the more indexed fields you have on a table, the longer it takes to insert records because the indexes must be updated each time.

The easiest way to put an index onto a table is to use a SQL statement:

```
CurrentDb.Execute "create index NewIndex on NewTable(TextField)"
```

This creates an index called NewIndex on the table NewTable, specifying the field YesNoField.

You can delete the index by using:

```
CurrentDb.Execute ("drop index NewIndex on NewTable")
```

Use VBA objects to create indexes:

```
Sub CreateIndex()
Dim TDef As TableDef, Idx As Index
Dim db As Database
Set db = CurrentDb()

Set TDef = db.TableDefs("NewTable")


Set Idx = TDef.CreateIndex("MyIndex")
Idx.Fields.Append Idx.CreateField("LongIntegerField")
Idx.Primary = True
Idx.Required = True
Idx.Unique = True
```

```
TDef.Indexes.Append Idx

End Sub
```

This code sets up the relevant objects using the **Dim** statement. Note that you must create a database object. You cannot refer directly to the **CurrentDb** object.

The table definition object is set to point to the table NewTable that you created earlier. The index object is used to create an index on that table definition called MyIndex.

A field called LongIntegerField is then created in the index. This relates to a field already created in the table. Note that this creates the field in the index, not in the table.

Properties for Primary (making it the key field), Required, and Unique are set to True. The index is then appended to the index collection for that table definition.

Run this code and then view the table NewTable in Design mode. You will see that the field LongIntegerField is now a key field and is indexed according to the properties stated earlier.

To remove the index from the table, use the command:

```
CurrentDb.TableDefs("NewTable").Indexes.Delete "MyIndex"
```

Create an Objects
Inventory

Access applications can become extremely complex with large numbers of tables, queries, forms, reports, and modules. You can view these in the left-hand Navigation pane of the Access window, but you will have no idea when they were created and last modified unless you examine each one individually.

From Access 2007 onwards, new objects such as AllTables allow you to interrogate the database objects using VBA and build up a table that will show you at a glance what is happening with the database objects.

You first need to create a table to store the results of the inventory. Click Create in the Access menu and click the Table Design icon in the Tables group of the ribbon. Add the following fields:

- ▶ **ObjectName**   Text field, 255 characters
- ▶ **ObjectType**   Text field, 10 characters
- ▶ **DateCreated**   Date/Time field
- ▶ **DateModified**   Date/Time field

Since this is an internal table, you do not need a primary key for it. Save the table with the name **TblObjectInventory**.

You can now add the following code into a module:

```
Sub Inventory()
Dim Obj As AccessObject, Dbs As Object, RecSet As Recordset
CurrentDb.Execute "delete * from tblObjectInventory"
Set RecSet = CurrentDb.OpenRecordset("tblObjectInventory")

Set Dbs = Application.CurrentData

For Each Obj In Dbs.AllTables
        RecSet.AddNew
        RecSet!ObjectName = Obj.Name
        RecSet!ObjectType = "Table"
        RecSet!DateCreated = Obj.DateCreated
        RecSet!DateModified = Obj.DateModified
        RecSet.Update

Next Obj

For Each Obj In Dbs.AllQueries
        RecSet.AddNew
        RecSet!ObjectName = Obj.Name
        RecSet!ObjectType = "Query"
        RecSet!DateCreated = Obj.DateCreated
        RecSet!DateModified = Obj.DateModified
        RecSet.Update

Next Obj
For Each Obj In CurrentProject.AllForms
        RecSet.AddNew
        RecSet!ObjectName = Obj.Name
        RecSet!ObjectType = "Form"
        RecSet!DateCreated = Obj.DateCreated
        RecSet!DateModified = Obj.DateModified
        RecSet.Update

Next Obj
For Each Obj In CurrentProject.AllReports
        RecSet.AddNew
        RecSet!ObjectName = Obj.Name
        RecSet!ObjectType = "Report"
        RecSet!DateCreated = Obj.DateCreated
        RecSet!DateModified = Obj.DateModified
        RecSet.Update
```

```
Next Obj
For Each Obj In CurrentProject.AllMacros
        RecSet.AddNew
        RecSet!ObjectName = Obj.Name
        RecSet!ObjectType = "Macro"
        RecSet!DateCreated = Obj.DateCreated
        RecSet!DateModified = Obj.DateModified
        RecSet.Update

Next Obj
For Each Obj In CurrentProject.AllModules
        RecSet.AddNew
        RecSet!ObjectName = Obj.Name
        RecSet!ObjectType = "Module"
        RecSet!DateCreated = Obj.DateCreated
        RecSet!DateModified = Obj.DateModified
        RecSet.Update

Next Obj
Set Dbs = Nothing
Set Obj = Nothing
Set RecSet = Nothing


End Sub
```

This code uses the **Dim** statement to set up objects and a **Recordset** object. The table tblObjectInventory is cleared out using a **Delete** statement.

The Dbs object is set to point to the application's current data. This is used for queries and tables. The code then iterates through each collection (AllTables, AllQueries, AllForms, AllReports, AllMacros, and AllModules) and creates new records in the table tblObjectInventory.

Run this code and then open the table tblObjectsInventory. You will see all the details of the database objects, detailing when each object was created and last modified.

Manipulate Chart Colors

When using charts within your application, you will often get requests from users to change the colors of the chart elements, whether it be pie chart segments or bars on a bar chart. This is easily done on the chart itself. But what if the colors need to be changed dynamically?

Some time ago, I had a complicated request from my users. The application in question produced reports on foreign exchange transactions for various customers and contained a pie chart for each customer detailing a summary of the currencies that had been traded.

The problem was that the customers all traded different currencies. One customer might trade U.S. dollars, GB pounds, and euros, while another might trade Australian dollars, euros, and Hong Kong dollars.

The problem was that the chart always represented the colors according to the order of the record source. For one customer, U.S. dollars would come out blue on the pie chart, and for another customer they would come out red. The users found this very confusing and wanted a solution whereby each currency had its own fixed color regardless of the mix of currencies.

To see this code in action, you need a form with a chart object on it. The chart must have a two-column table as the source, detailing the currency indicator and value.

The first step is to create a simple table in Access by clicking Create on the Access menu and then clicking the Table Design icon in the Tables group of the ribbon. Create the following fields:

▶ **Currency**   Text
▶ **Val**   Number, Double

Populate the table as shown in Table 33-1.

Currency	Value
USD	1627.89
GBP	4533.21
EUR	3445.67
AUD	3289.45
HKD	3345.56

Table 33-1 *Currency Table Values*

Save the table as **tblCurrency**. On your blank form, drag a chart object onto the form. Make your currency table the row source for the chart. Select a pie chart as the chart type. Right-click the chart and select Chart Object and then Edit on the pop-up menu. Right-click the chart object and select Chart Options on the pop-up menu.

Click the Data Labels tab in the pop-up window and check the box for Category Name in the Label Contains section. Your pie chart should now show the currency indicator on the appropriate segment.

You will need to add a reference into the Chart Object library. In the VBE window, use Tools | References from the menu and select Microsoft Graph 12.0 Object Library. Mark the check box and click OK.

Next, add the following code to your form (this goes on the Form Activate event):

```
Private Sub Form_Activate()

Dim ch As Graph.Chart, Temp As String, PointCount As Integer

Set ch = Me.Graph0.Object

PointCount = ch.SeriesCollection(1).Points.Count
For n = 1 To PointCount
    Select Case ch.SeriesCollection(1).Points(n).DataLabel.Text
        Case "USD"
            ch.SeriesCollection(1).Points(n).Interior.Color = QBColor(9)
        Case "GBP"
            ch.SeriesCollection(1).Points(n).Interior.Color = QBColor(10)
        Case "EUR"
            ch.SeriesCollection(1).Points(n).Interior.Color = QBColor(11)
        Case "AUD"
            ch.SeriesCollection(1).Points(n).Interior.Color = QBColor(12)
        Case "HKD"
            ch.SeriesCollection(1).Points(n).Interior.Color = QBColor(13)
    End Select

Next n
Set ch = Nothing
End Sub
```

Using the **Dim** statement, this code sets up an object for the chart and two variables. The chart object is set to point to the chart on your form (assumed to be called Graph0).

Using a For..Next loop, all the points on the first series of the chart are iterated through. Each point represents a segment of the pie chart, or in the case of a bar chart, each individual bar.

Using a Select Case statement based on the text of the data label for that point, the interior color is set according to the currency indicator in the data label.

Open your form in form View mode and you will see that the colors of the pie chart segment change accordingly. Experiment with changing the currency indicators in the Currency tables and see what effect it has on your chart.

Notice that the currencies may change position in the pie chart, but they will always have the color dictated by your code.

CHAPTER
34

Drill Down on Charts

Recently, I was involved in an Excel application that allowed the user to drill down on a chart. They could view a balloon chart, and then click a particular balloon and a new balloon chart would appear giving the detail on the element that they originally clicked.

This used a class module and the method **GetChartElement**. It was extremely impressive to see it in action and users liked the functionality.

It occurred to me that this ought to be possible in Access as well. The problem is that a different charting engine is used and the **GetChartElement** method does not exist.

However, using API calls and a little lateral thinking, this is still possible.

The first step is to create a simple table in Access by clicking Create on the Access menu and then choosing the Table Design icon in the Tables group of the ribbon. Create the following fields:

▶ **Currency** Text
▶ **Val** Number, Double

Populate the table as shown in Table 34-1.

Save the table as **tblCurrency**. On your blank form, drag a chart object onto the form. Make your currency table the row source for the chart. Select a pie chart as the chart type. Right-click the chart and select Chart Object and then Edit on the pop-up menu. Right-click the chart object and select Chart Options on the pop-up menu.

Click the Data Labels tab in the pop-up window and check the box for Category Name in the Label Contains section. Your pie chart should now show the currency indicator on the appropriate segment.

Currency	Value
USD	1627.89
GBP	4533.21
EUR	3445.67
AUD	3289.45
HKD	3345.56

Table 34-1 *Currency Table Values*

You will need to add a reference in to the Chart Object library. In the VBE window, use Tools | References from the menu and select Microsoft Graph 12.0 Object Library. Mark the check box and click OK.

Enter the module for your form and add the following code to the declarations section at the top of the module:

```
Private Type POINTAPI
    x As Long
    y As Long
End Type
Private Declare Function GetCursorPos Lib "user32" _
        (lpPoint As POINTAPI) As Long

Private Declare Function GetPixel Lib "gdi32" _
(ByVal hdc As Long, ByVal x As Long, ByVal y As Long) As Long
Private Declare Function GetWindowDC Lib "user32" (ByVal hwnd As Long) _
        As Long
```

This will set up a new data type called POINTAPI and generate declarations for three API calls: **GetCursorPos**, **GetPixel**, and **GetWindowDC**.

On the form module, click the drop-down in the top-left corner and select the graph object. Add the following code to the Mouse Down event for the graph:

```
Private Sub Graph0_MouseDown(Button As Integer, Shift As Integer, x As Single, _
y As Single)
Dim cPos As POINTAPI, Temp1 As Long, Temp2 As Long, Pointcount As Integer
Dim ch As Graph.Chart, PCol As Long
Call GetCursorPos(cPos)


Temp = GetWindowDC(0)
Temp1 = cPos.x
Temp2 = cPos.y
```

```
PCol = GetPixel(Temp, Temp1, Temp2)
Set ch = Me.Graph0.Object

Pointcount = ch.SeriesCollection(1).Points.Count

For n = 1 To Pointcount
    If ch.SeriesCollection(1).Points(n).Interior.Color = PCol Then
        MsgBox ch.SeriesCollection(1).Points(n).DataLabel.Text

    End If


Next n

End Sub
```

This code uses the **Dim** statement to set up objects for the cursor coordinates and the chart. The API call **GetCursorPos** is used to find out where the cursor is in terms of pixels. You may wonder why the *x* and *y* coordinates of the Mouse Down event are not used. This is because they are scaled in twips and we need to use pixels.

The API call is used to get the device context of the current object, which in this case is our graph. The device context is necessary for the API call to get the pixel color. The variable PCol is loaded with the pixel color under the cursor by using the API call **GetPixel**.

The chart object **ch** points to our graph on the form. All the points in the series collection are then iterated through using a For..Next loop and the interior color is compared to PCol. If a match is found, then the data label for that segment is displayed in a message box.

Try clicking the pie chart you created earlier. You will find that as you click each segment the appropriate data label will be displayed.

To take this further, all you then need do is change the query in the chart's row source to reflect the data label clicked and to show the detail for it. You can also use a subform below the chart to show the detail making up that particular segment.

Use Excel For Output

U sing VBA to automate Excel spreadsheets for output of data from Access is extremely useful. You have already seen how you can create reports based on data in tables, but very often users want to see the information in something more flexible.

Access reports are very good for presenting your data in a tabular form, but they are very difficult to copy and paste into other applications. Also, users may have a custom format that they wish to see the data in that is not supported by Access reports.

The Northwind database will be used to provide sample data for this chapter. You can access it by loading Access 2010 and then opening the Sample folder in the central pane (Available Templates) of the opening screen.

Using a Recordset to Create a Spreadsheet

Using a recordset in VBA is a very simple way to dump a chunk of data into an Excel spreadsheet. Press ALT+F11 to enter the VBE window and insert a new module using Insert | Module from the VBE menu.

You also need to add a reference to the Excel Object Library. You do this by using Tools | References on the VBE menu. In the pop-up window, scroll down the extensive list of libraries until you see Microsoft Excel 14.0 Object Library. Set the check box to True and then click OK.

Enter the following code into your module:

```
Sub CreateSpreadsheet()
Dim RecSet As Recordset
Dim MyExcel As Excel.Application
Dim MyBook As Workbook
Dim MySheet As Worksheet

Set MyExcel = CreateObject("Excel.Application")
Set MyBook = MyExcel.Workbooks.Add
Set MySheet = MyBook.Worksheets(1)
Set RecSet = CurrentDb.OpenRecordset("customers")
MySheet.Range("a1").CopyFromRecordset RecSet
MyBook.SaveAs ("TestExcel")
MyBook.Close
MyExcel.Quit
Set RecSet = Nothing
Set MyExcel = Nothing
Set MyBook = Nothing
Set MySheet = Nothing

End Sub
```

This code creates an Excel object and opens a new blank workbook. It then creates a **Recordset** object based on the Customers table in the Northwind database and copies this to cell A1 on the first worksheet in the workbook. The new workbook is then saved to the default folder and the Excel application is closed.

Run the code by clicking anywhere on it and pressing F5, or clicking the green triangle (Run) icon on the toolbar. The code will take a few seconds to run since a fair amount of data is being transferred.

If you open the new workbook in Excel, you will find that the orders table has been copied into the first sheet of the workbook, as if you had done a copy and paste from Access. However, you may notice that no column headings have been provided and column widths do not always allow the data to be seen.

Using an Existing Spreadsheet as a Template

A way to make the transfer tidier is to load in an existing spreadsheet that already has the headings and column widths set, but no data in it.

To do this, create a blank spreadsheet in Excel. Open the Customers table in Access in View mode by clicking the View icon in the Views group of the ribbon and selecting the first row.

Make a copy of the row and then go to your Excel spreadsheet. Paste the row into Excel as text.`

This will paste in the single row, but it will also include the column headings. Set the column widths as appropriate, and then delete the data row, leaving the headings only.

Save the spreadsheet as **MyRecSet**. This now provides a blank template to load your data into. Make sure you close this file, otherwise it will have a lock on it.

Copy the following code into the module you created earlier in this chapter.

```
Sub CreateSpreadsheet1()
Dim RecSet As Recordset
Dim MyExcel As Excel.Application
Dim MyBook As Workbook
Dim MySheet As Worksheet

Set MyExcel = CreateObject("Excel.Application")

Set MyBook = MyExcel.Workbooks.Open("MyRecSet", , True)
Set MySheet = MyBook.Worksheets(1)
Set RecSet = CurrentDb.OpenRecordset("customers")
MySheet.Range("a2").CopyFromRecordset RecSet
On Error Resume Next
Kill "TestExcel.xlsx"
On Error GoTo 0
MyBook.SaveAs ("TestExcel")
MyBook.Close
MyExcel.Quit
Set RecSet = Nothing
Set MyExcel = Nothing
Set MyBook = Nothing
Set MySheet = Nothing

End Sub
```

This code works similar to the earlier example in that it creates an Excel application, but this time it loads in your Excel file called MyRecSet as a read-only file. The recordset is now copied to cell A2 to allow for the column headings. A further enhancement is that the Kill command is used to delete the previously saved file.

Run the code by clicking anywhere on it and pressing F5, or clicking the green triangle (Run) icon on the toolbar. The code will take a few seconds to run since a fair amount of data is being transferred. Do not forget to make sure you have added a reference to the Excel Object Model, as shown on the first page of this chapter.

If you open TestExcel, you will now see that your data is far more user-friendly, with column headings and column widths set correctly. This data could easily form the basis for a pivot table, and all you would need to do is incorporate the pivot table into the Excel file MyRecSet.

Transferring Individual Numbers to Excel

The preceding examples are very good for transferring large chunks of data into Excel, but you may encounter a situation where you only want to transfer specific numbers to Excel. You can do this by iterating through the **Recordset** object instead of copying and pasting it. The reason for this may be that you do not want the data put into the spreadsheet in one contiguous chunk, and you want more control over where the data will appear.

Insert the following VBA code into the module you created earlier in this chapter. Do not forget to make sure you have added a reference to the Excel Object Model, as shown on the first page of this chapter.

```
Sub CreateSpreadsheet2()
Dim RecSet As Recordset
Dim MyExcel As Excel.Application
Dim MyBook As Workbook
Dim MySheet As Worksheet
Dim strTemp As String
Dim Coun As Long
Dim Coun1 As Long
Set MyExcel = CreateObject("Excel.Application")
Set MyBook = MyExcel.Workbooks.Add
Set MySheet = MyBook.Worksheets(1)
strTemp = "SELECT Products.[Product Name], Sum([Unit
Cost]*[quantity]) AS Cost "
strTemp = strTemp & "FROM Products INNER JOIN [Purchase Order
Details] "
strTemp = strTemp & "ON Products.ID = [Purchase Order
Details].[Product ID] "
strTemp = strTemp & "GROUP BY Products.[Product Name];"

Set RecSet = CurrentDb.OpenRecordset(strTemp)
Do Until RecSet.EOF
    Coun = Coun + 1

    MySheet.Range("a" & Coun).Value = RecSet![Product Name]
    MySheet.Range("b" & Coun).Value = RecSet!Cost
    Coun1 = Coun1 + 1
    If Coun1 = 5 Then
        Coun = Coun + 2
        Coun1 = 0
    End If
    RecSet.MoveNext
Loop
```

```
On Error Resume Next
Kill "TestExcel.xlsx"
On Error GoTo 0

MyBook.SaveAs ("TestExcel")
MyBook.Close
MyExcel.Quit
Set RecSet = Nothing
Set MyExcel = Nothing
Set MyBook = Nothing
Set MySheet = Nothing

End Sub
```

This code works similar to the first example in this chapter in that it creates an Excel application and a new workbook in that application. A recordset is then created based on the Products and Purchase Order Details tables to show the product name and the cost.

Notice that the query has been loaded into the variable strTemp in several stages. It could have been done as one continuous string, but this makes the string very difficult to view in its entirety and will create problems for another developer trying to learn your code.

The code iterates through the recordset and transfers the Product Name and Total Cost into columns A and B of the spreadsheet. There is a counter that works out the row each record is placed on.

A second counter increments the first counter by two every time five items are reached. This has the effect of populating the spreadsheet in groups of five items, which could not be done using the **CopyFromRecordset** method.

Allowing Users to Design Their Excel Reports

You can also use VBA code to allow users to design their own Excel reports, provided that they follow a few simple rules. They can use an Excel template, such as MyRecSet that you used earlier in this chapter, and you can provide them with the flexibility to decide where the numbers will appear.

This is particularly useful where the reporting criterion is a moving target each month. Instead of having to rewrite your VBA code to encompass new criteria (and where it is to be shown in the Excel spreadsheet), you can allow the user the freedom to decide.

Open up the original Excel template file that you created earlier, called MyRecSet, and select a cell such as C5. Enter **!Northwind Traders Syrup** into this cell.

The string "Northwind Traders Syrup" is a product within the Northwind database and the exclamation mark (!) is a marker to tell our VBA code that it has to find a number for this product. This would normally be completed by the user and they would use this notation to select different products for reporting on the spreadsheet.

The idea of this is to allow users to design their own Excel reports using a few simple rules. By using the exclamation mark (!), your Access application can pick this up as part of a query and concatenate it into a valid query to supply the number to the Excel cell.

Open the module you created earlier in this chapter and insert the following code. Do not forget to make sure you have added a reference to the Excel Object Model, as shown on the first page of this chapter.

```vba
Sub CreateSpreadsheet3()
Dim RecSet As Recordset
Dim MyExcel As Excel.Application
Dim MyBook As Workbook
Dim MySheet As Worksheet
Dim strTemp As String
Dim strCriteria As String
Set MyExcel = CreateObject("Excel.Application")

Set MyBook = MyExcel.Workbooks.Open("MyRecSet", , True)
Set MySheet = MyBook.Worksheets(1)


For n = 1 To 20
    For m = 1 To 20
        strCriteria = MySheet.Range(Chr(n + 64) & m).Value
        If Left(strCriteria, 1) = "!" Then
            On Error Resume Next
            strCriteria = Mid(strCriteria, 2)
strTemp = "SELECT Products.[Product Name], Sum([Unit
Cost]*[quantity]) AS Cost "
strTemp = strTemp & "FROM Products INNER JOIN [Purchase Order
Details] "
strTemp = strTemp & "ON Products.ID = [Purchase Order
Details].[Product ID] "
strTemp = strTemp & "WHERE [Product Name]='" & strCriteria & "' "
strTemp = strTemp & "GROUP BY Products.[Product Name];"
            Set RecSet = CurrentDb.OpenRecordset(strTemp)
            If RecSet.RecordCount > 0 Then
                MySheet.Range(Chr(n + 64) & m).Value = RecSet!cost
            Else
                MySheet.Range(Chr(n + 64) & m).Value = 0
            End If
        End If


    Next m
Next n
```

```
On Error Resume Next
Kill "TestExcel.xlsx"
On Error GoTo 0
MyBook.SaveAs ("TestExcel")
MyBook.Close
MyExcel.Quit
Set RecSet = Nothing
Set MyExcel = Nothing
Set MyBook = Nothing
Set MySheet = Nothing

End Sub
```

In this example, the SQL statement in the variable strTemp would normally be indented, but this causes display problems for this book.

This code works in a similar way to earlier examples in that it creates an Excel object based on the template spreadsheet MyRecSet. Where it is different is that it then iterates through a 20×20 range of cells, beginning at A1, and looks for any cell with a text string that commences with an exclamation mark (!).

When it finds the exclamation mark, it removes it from the string. It then incorporates the criteria into the SQL string using a WHERE clause. A recordset is created and the value is overwritten into the same cell. If no value is found, then 0 is used. Notice that an "On Error" statement is used in case the user has entered something in the spreadsheet that will cause an error.

The spreadsheet is saved under a different name (so the original criteria are maintained) and the Excel application is closed.

Run the code and the spreadsheet TestExcel will be created.

If you open the spreadsheet TestExcel, you will see there is now a number in cell C5.

Users can also use multiple criteria by employing an AND or OR statement in the spreadsheet string. An example would be ![Product Name]= 'Northwind Traders Syrup' and [Reorder Level]>10. So long as the criteria can be concatenated into the SQL statement within the VBA code, this will still work.

Use FTP in VBA

A ccess applications are all about manipulating and presenting data to the user. Often, this data is held on another server and sometimes you cannot directly connect to that data.

An example might be files of stock exchange closing prices or foreign currency values.

Lack of connectivity may be for a variety of reasons. The data could belong to a third-party organization that does not want you to connect to their network. Database owners in your own organization could have security concerns if they allow you to connect directly. They could also have concerns about the effect on performance of their own database if a number of outside connections are suddenly being made and many time-consuming queries are being executed.

One way around all this is to transfer the data via a text or CSV file, which Access is already well equipped to deal with. However, there is the question of how the file is transferred to your application. It could be e-mailed to you, but this becomes difficult to automate so that your VBA code picks it up.

Many organizations now use FTP (File Transfer Protocol) servers for this purpose. This uses an Internet connection to link to the FTP server, normally employing a user ID and password, and allows you to view and transfer the files on the server as if they were folders on your own PC.

If you open Windows Explorer and type in the address of an FTP server, such as ftp://MyOrg.MyServer.net, into the path window at the top of the screen (providing the required user ID and password when prompted), you will see the available folders and files for that user ID. You will find that you can easily drag these files into your local folders and, if your user ID has permission, drag files from your local folders back to the FTP server.

You may not have an FTP server available to you to experiment on, but if you Google "public ftp servers," you will find many available that allow public access. When experimenting, stick with sample text files that you have uploaded yourself. Anything that contains code coming from a public source could be dangerous to your PC.

Using VBA Code to Transfer Files

You can see how easy it is to move files between the FTP server and your PC. Even if the FTP server is on the other side of the world, the process is still very fast, depending on the size of file being transferred.

However, you may require a VBA procedure to transfer files from an FTP server either at a user's request or at a set time, such as an overnight job.

You can use VBA to do this by using API calls. See Chapter 20 for more information on what API calls are and what they can do for you.

Open a new module by clicking Insert | Module on the VBE toolbar. Enter the following code into it:

```
Private Declare Function InternetOpen Lib "wininet.dll" Alias "InternetOpenA" _
(ByVal sAgent As String, ByVal lAccessType As Long, ByVal sProxyName  _
As String, _
ByVal sProxyBypass As String, ByVal lFlags As Long) As Long


Private Declare Function InternetConnect Lib "wininet.dll"  _
Alias "InternetConnectA" _
(ByVal hInternetSession As Long, ByVal sServerName As String, _
ByVal nServerPort As Integer, ByVal sUsername As String, _
ByVal sPassword As String, ByVal lService As Long, _
ByVal lFlags As Long, ByVal lContext As Long) As Long


Private Declare Function FTPGETFile Lib "wininet.dll" Alias "FtpGetFileA" _
(ByVal hFtpSession As Long, ByVal lpszRemoteFile As String, _
ByVal lpszNewFile As String, ByVal fFailIfExists As Boolean, _
ByVal dwFlagsAndAttributes As Long, ByVal dwFlags As Long, _
ByVal dwContext As Long) As Boolean


Private Declare Function FtpPutFile Lib "wininet.dll" Alias "FtpPutFileA" _
(ByVal hFtpSession As Long, ByVal lpszLocalFile As String, _
ByVal lpszRemoteFile As String, ByVal dwFlags As Long, _
ByVal dwContext As Long) As Boolean

Private Declare Function InternetCloseHandle Lib "wininet.dll" _
(ByVal hInet As Long) As Integer
```

These statements set up declarations in the General section of your module to use FTP commands in the wininet.dll dynamic link library (which is supplied as part of Windows).

Next, set up a subroutine to transfer a file from your chosen FTP server to your local PC:

```
Sub GetFile()
Dim MyConn, MyINet, Chk As Boolean

Chk = False
MyINet = InternetOpen("MyFTP", 1, vbNullString, vbNullString, 0)
If MyINet > 0 Then

    MyConn = InternetConnect(MyINet, "MyOrg.MyServer.net", 21, _
"MyUserID", _ "MyPassword", 1, 0, 0)

    If MyConn > 0 Then

        Chk = FTPGETFile(MyConn, "MyFolder/MyFileName.txt", _
CurrentProject.Path & "\MyFileName.txt", 0, 0, 1, 0)
        InternetCloseHandle MyConn
    End If
    InternetCloseHandle MyINet
End If

If (Chk) Then

    MsgBox "File downloaded"
Else
    MsgBox "FTP Error"
End If

End Sub
```

This code first of all creates variables MyConn, MyInet, and Chk. Notice that MyConn and MyInet are set to the default type of Variant. Chk is to hold a value to show that there has been success in transferring the file. It is set to False initially to show a fail.

The **InternetOpen** API is then used to open the Internet (similar to the Internet browser window being initially opened). This returns a value into the variable MyINet on success.

If a handle has been returned (value is not 0), then the API call **InternetConnect** is used to establish a connection to the FTP server using the user ID and password required. If no user ID and password are required, then use empty quotes (""). Notice that the name of the FTP server does not include ftp://. The value of 21 is the default port for FTP.

This then returns another handle. If it is non-zero, then the API call **FTPGEtFile** is used to transfer the file. The parameter MyFolder/MyFileName.txt is the path and name of the file on the FTP server and the parameter CurrentProject.Path & "\MyFileName.txt" is the local path and name of the file. CurrentProject.Path picks up the path of the Access database and ensures that the file is downloaded to the same path.

A true or false value is placed in the variable Chk by this process. If Chk is true, then the file download was a success and the appropriate message is displayed. Otherwise, a failure message is shown.

The Internet connections are closed using the API call **InternetCloseHandle**.

By using the API call **FTPPutFile**, files can be transferred from the local PC to the FTP server, provided that your user ID has the necessary permissions. Here is the modified code:

```
Sub PutFile()
Dim MyConn, MyINet, Chk As Boolean

Chk = False
MyINet = InternetOpen("MyFTP", 1, vbNullString, vbNullString, 0)
If MyINet > 0 Then

    MyConn = InternetConnect(MyINet, "MyOrg.MyServer.net", 21, _
"MyUserID", _ "MyPassword", 1, 0, 0)

    If MyConn > 0 Then

        Chk = FtpPutFile(MyConn, CurrentProject.Path & \test.txt", _
" MyFolder/MyFileName.txt", 1, 0)
    InternetCloseHandle MyConn
    End If
    InternetCloseHandle MyINet
End If

If (Chk) Then

    MsgBox "File uploaded"
Else
    MsgBox "FTP Error"
End If

End Sub
```

Use of Semaphore Files

In applications that use FTP code to transfer files, the files are often very large and can take many minutes to transfer. The problem here is that the next stage of the process does not know when the file is complete. If you use the FTP process to transfer a big file over, when you look at the folder you will see the file is there almost immediately but with a very small length. This then increases in size as the FTP transfer takes place.

If you use an automated process to transfer a large file onto an FTP server (possibly as an overnight job), there may be a process on the FTP server polling once a minute to check for your file.

You could also have the situation in reverse. You may have written a procedure to poll the FTP server once a minute for a file that you wish to download. The problem in both cases is how does the procedure know that the file is fully complete? If the procedure opens the partially complete file, errors will occur.

In cases like this, semaphore files are used to indicate the completion of the file being built. These are small text files of a few bytes in length, usually with the same name as the file you wish to download, and with an SMP suffix.

The procedure that generates the file then generates the semaphore file when the transfer file is complete. The transfer procedure polls the server for the semaphore file at minute intervals instead of the real transfer file. When it finds the semaphore file, it is guaranteed that the transfer file is complete and ready to be processed.

What Happens When the 2-GB Limit Is Reached

Access 2010 still has a 2-GB limit in terms of file size. The database cannot grow beyond this. I think this is because Microsoft would rather you purchase SQL Server once you get to a database of this size!

If you are importing loads of data from text files, and many applications that I have worked on do have loads of data, it is very easy to reach this limit. Even if you are deleting old data, the memory is not released until you compact the database.

However, once your database size goes through the 2-GB limit, you are in serious trouble. This can easily happen if a user imports a text file that pushes the database over the limit. The text file can have a problem with it in that someone may choose to extract a week's worth of data instead of one day's worth, but users don't always look at file sizes when importing data, and they certainly have no idea of the consequences!

Once over the 2-GB limit, your database will not run at all. Anything you try will prompt the error message "invalid argument," which is not very helpful in informing you what is wrong. Even if you try to compact and repair the database, you will still get this error message.

In short, your application is trashed and totally useless. Hopefully, your application will have been backed up every night and your latest backup copy can be used as a fallback. However, if you do not have this luxury, how do you get out of this situation?

It is a situation that I have been in on more than one occasion. The solution is to first create a new blank database. You then size the application window so only the Navigation pane is showing. You also size the application window for your trashed database so only the Navigation pane is showing.

Place the two windows on your screen so they sit side by side. Right-click the Navigation pane in each database, select Category on the pop-up menu, and then select Object Type, so all the objects are shown in type order.

Your screen should now look like Figure 37-1.

If you are fortunate enough to have a double screen on your computer, you can set each database to each window without having to resize them.

Now that you have the two databases side by side, all you need to do now is drag and drop all the database objects from the trashed database to the blank database. You have to do this one at a time, which is fairly time consuming, but it *is* a solution to recovering your application.

Make sure you pull across all the objects—tables, queries, forms, reports, macros, and modules. Linked tables can also be brought across in this way. Once everything has been transferred to the new database, make sure you do a compact and repair on the new database to make sure it is as small as possible.

You now have a fully working copy of your original database, complete with the most recent users' data, and your reputation has been saved!

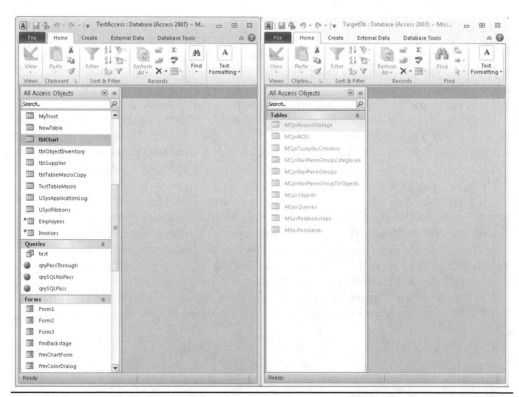

Figure 37-1   *Host and target databases shown*

Creating Menu
Structures with the Ribbon

Back in Chapter 11 of this book, you learned how to create custom ribbons for use on forms and reports. But what if you wanted to create a full menu structure for your application with trees of drop-down menus similar to versions before Access 2007? This is still possible within the XML structure of the ribbon. As before you need to create a system table called USysRibbons if you do not have it already. You need to create two fields in this new table. The first is called RibbonName and is a text field to hold the name you give to your custom ribbon. The second field is called RibbonXML and needs to be set to a memo field.

As before, you will also need the 2007 Custom UI Editor for Microsoft Office, which can be downloaded for free from www.openxmldeveloper.org/articles/CustomUIeditor.aspx.

Load a blank Excel XML file into the Custom UI Editor by choosing File | Open from the menu. Enter the following XML into the Custom UI Editor:

```
<customUI xmlns="http://schemas.microsoft.com/office/2009/07/customui" >

<ribbon startFromScratch="true">

<tabs>
```

```
    <tab id="customTab" label="MyMenu" >


    <group id="customGroup" label="My New Menu Structure">
<box id="box1" boxStyle="horizontal">

<menu id="Group1" label="Group1" >
<button id="id1" label="Option1" onAction="Action1"/>
<menuSeparator id="sep1"  />
<button id="id2" label="Option2" onAction="Action2"/>
<button id="id3" label="Option3" onAction="Action3"/>
</menu>
<button id="SP1" label="    " enabled="false"/>
<menu id="Group2" label="Group2"  >
<button id="id4" label="Option4" onAction="Action4"/>
<button id="id5" label="Option5" onAction="Action5"/>
<menuSeparator id="sep2"  />
<menu id="Group3" label="Group3"  >
<button id="id7" label="Option7" onAction="Action7"/>
<button id="id8" label="Option8" onAction="Action8"/>
</menu>


<button id="id6" label="Option6" onAction="Action6"/>
</menu>
</box>
</group>


    </tab>

  </tabs>
 </ribbon>
</customUI>
```

Use the validate option in the Custom UI Editor to ensure that your XML code has been entered correctly and has no errors. To do this, click the red tick mark in the toolbar (third icon from the left).

Use Copy and Paste to copy the XML into the USysRibbons table. Copy the XML shown earlier into the field RibbonXML and enter the name **MyRibbon** in the RibbonName field.

Close the Access database and re-open it. Create a new form by clicking Create in the Access menu and clicking the Forms Design icon in the Forms group of the ribbon. Right-click the form in Design mode and select Properties. Click Form in the drop-down at the top of the Properties sheet. Scroll down the Properties list to Ribbon Name and use the drop-down for this property to select your new ribbon.

Save the form and then open it in View mode. You will see your new menu tab (MyMenu) and a tree of menu options underneath. Your screen should look like Figure 38-1.

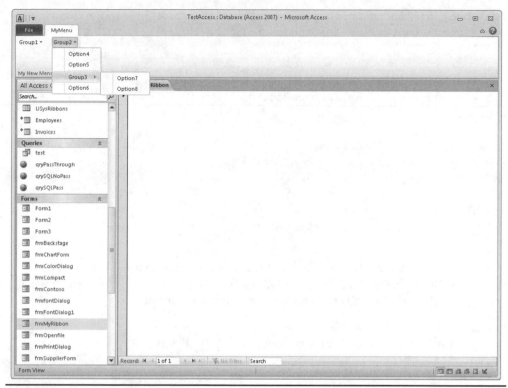

Figure 38-1   *The MyMenu ribbon*

Notice how the menu separators have been used and how Group3 forms a submenu of Group2. Also, notice that a disabled button with a label made up of spaces has been placed between Group1 and Group2 to provide a spacer. This makes the menu structure look better.

Currently, there is no code for all your actions, so none of the menu items will do anything except produce errors.

You can use the Custom UI Editor to generate your callback code. In the Editor, click the Generate Callbacks icon on the right-hand side of the toolbar. This will generate the following VBA code:

```
'Callback for id1 onAction
Sub Action1(control as IRibbonControl)
End Sub


'Callback for id2 onAction
Sub Action2(control as IRibbonControl)
End Sub
```

```
'Callback for id3 onAction
Sub Action3(control as IRibbonControl)
End Sub

'Callback for id4 onAction
Sub Action4(control as IRibbonControl)
End Sub

'Callback for id5 onAction
Sub Action5(control as IRibbonControl)
End Sub

'Callback for id6 onAction
Sub Action6(control as IRibbonControl)
End Sub
```

Enter the VBE window by pressing ALT+F11 and insert a module using Insert | Module from the VBE menu. Copy and paste the callback code into your new module. You can now enter your VBA code for the various actions. An example might be:

```
'Callback for id1 onAction
Sub Action1(control as IRibbonControl)
MsgBox "You selected Option1"
End Sub
```

Make Controls
on Forms Interactive

You can use VBA very effectively to make the controls on a form interactive. For example, a user may make a selection in one drop-down on your form that then dictates the selection in another drop-down. You could also have the situation that if a certain selection is made in a drop-down, then other controls are not visible or are disabled for input.

If done properly, it has the additional advantage that as the user browses through records on your form, the controls automatically react.

Here is a very simple example of how to do this.

Creating a Simple Table

As an example, we will use a simple table of supplier names and sizes of supplier. Create a table by clicking Create in the Access menu and then clicking the Table Design icon in the Tables group of the ribbon. Add in three text fields: SupplierName, SupplierSize, and SupplierRef.

Your table design window should now look like Figure 39-1.

Save the table as **tblSupplier**. There is no need for a primary key. Populate the table with some data—the SupplierSize field should be Small, Medium, or Large. Your data for the table should resemble Figure 39-2.

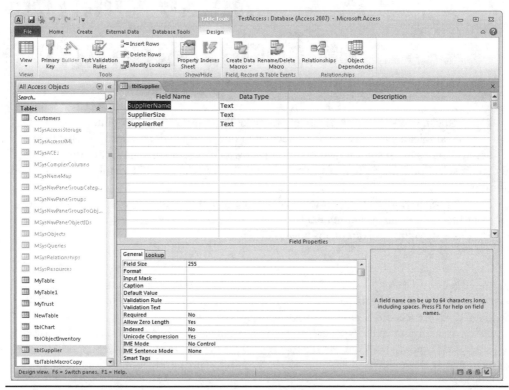

Figure 39-1   *The table design window for the supplier table*

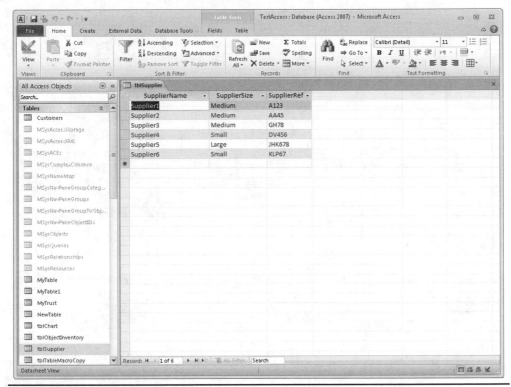

Figure 39-2   *Data for the supplier table*

Creating a Form for the Table

Create a form based on the Suppliers table by clicking Create in the Access menu and clicking the Form Design icon in the Forms group of the ribbon. Right-click the form in Design mode and select Properties. On the Property Sheet, select Form in the drop-down at the top and set the Record Source property to tblSupplier.

Add on to the form two drop-down (combo) boxes and one text box. Go to the property sheet for each control and set the Control Source property for the first drop-down to SupplierSize and the second drop-down to SupplierName. Set the Control Source property for the text box to SupplierRef.

Set the Row Source property for the SupplierSize drop-down to the SQL statement:

```
SELECT DISTINCT SupplierSize FROM tblSupplier;
```

Your form should now look like Figure 39-3.

You can now add some VBA code to your form to make it interactive. Right-click the SupplierSize drop-down and select Build Event. Select Code Builder in the pop-up box and you will be taken to the VBE window for the form. For the Combo0 control (assuming that

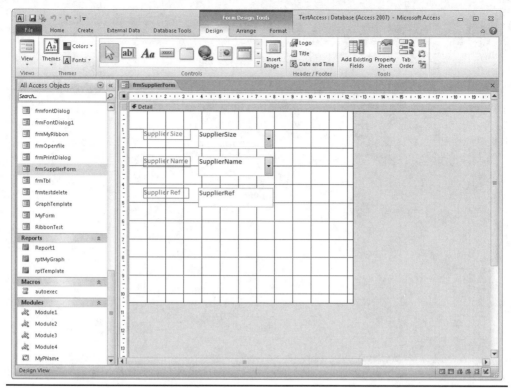

Figure 39-3 *The supplier form in Design mode*

the SupplierSize drop-down is called Combo0), select the Change event in the drop-down in the top-right corner of the code window. Enter the following code:

```
Private Sub Combo0_Change()
Dim strTemp As String
Me.Combo0.SetFocus
strTemp = Me.Combo0.text
Me.Combo2.SetFocus
Me.Combo2.RowSource = _
"select distinct SupplierName from tblSupplier where SupplierSize='" _
& strTemp & "'"

If strTemp = "Small" Then
    Me.Text4.Visible = False
Else
    Me.Text4.Visible = True
End If
```

```
Me.Combo0.SetFocus
End Sub
```

This code assumes that the two drop-down boxes you created are called Combo0 and combo2, and the text box is called Text4. These are the default names given as the controls are created.

This code is called when the SupplierSize drop-down is changed. The value of the SupplierSize drop-down is captured into a string variable and then the row source for the SupplierName drop-down is altered according to the SupplierSize chosen. Also, if the SupplierSize is "Small", then the SupplierRef text box is not visible.

In the code window, select Form in the drop-down at the top-left corner and choose the Current event in the drop-down in the top-right corner of the window.

Enter the following code:

```
Private Sub Form_Current()

Combo0_Change

End Sub
```

This ensures that as the user browses through the records in tblSupplier, the form is updated according to what SupplierSize is showing.

Save the form and then load it in Form view.

As you move through the records, you will see that the controls on the form automatically change to suit the SupplierSize field. If you click the SupplierName drop-down, you will see this is populated according to what the SupplierSize control is showing.

If you change the SupplierSize field, then the drop-down for SupplierName will also automatically change.

Set Up Levels
of User Security

Because your application is likely to be multiuser, you will need some kind of security over who can do what in your database and what they are allowed to see.

You may have users who can only see very basic information, users who can see more but cannot change records, users who can change records, and administrators who can create new users and change privileges.

You can use VBA to do all of this, but you first need to set up a table of users. Click Create on the Access menu and then click the Table Design icon in the Tables group of the ribbon. Create two text fields: **UserName** and **UserLevel**. Save the table as **tblUserRights**.

Populate the table with the user name of each user (their Windows login ID) and their user level. The levels can be administrator, expert, novice, and basic.

Create a new module by clicking Insert | Module on the VBE menu. Enter the following declaration into the General area at the top of the module:

```
Public Declare Function GetUserName Lib "advapi32.dll" Alias _
"GetUserNameA" (ByVal lpBuffer As String, nSize As Long) As Long
```

This API call will allow you to get the user name (as discussed in Chapter 23).
You also need to add in a public function to get the user level:

```
Public Function ReturnUserLevel()
Dim strUser As String, X As Integer, RecSet as Recordset
strUser = Space$(256)
```

```
X = GetUserName(strUser, 256)
strUser = RTrim(strUser)
strUser = Left(strUser, Len(strUser) - 1)
Set RecSet = CurrentDb.OpenRecordset _
("select * tblUserRights where UserName='" & strUser & "'")
If RecSet.RecordCount Then
        ReturnUserLevel = RecSet!UserLevel
Else
        ReturnUserLevel = "unknown"
End If
Set RecSet = Nothing

End Function
```

This public function uses the API call **GetUserName** to return the Windows login ID of the current user. It then opens a **Recordset** object based on the table tblUserRights, where the UserName field is equal to the login ID and returns the user level. If no record is found, it returns "unknown".

You can now set up rules on your forms as to how they will work in relation to the user level.

For example, if the form will be one that only administrators can use, such as for setting up new users, then you would put the following code on the form activate event:

```
If ReturnUserLevel <> "administrator" Then
    MsgBox "You are not authorized to view this screen", vbCritical
    DoCmd.Close
End If
```

Similarly, you can use the following code on a form if you want "basic" users to have read-only access, and all other user types to be able to change records:

```
If ReturnUserLevel = "unknown" then DoCmd.Close
If ReturnUserLevel = "basic" Then
    Me.AllowAdditions = False
    Me.AllowEdits = False
    Me.AllowDeletions = False
Else
    Me.AllowAdditions = True
    Me.AllowEdits = True
    Me.AllowDeletions = True

End If
```

Notice that there is an option for an unknown level that closes the form, although in theory an unknown level user should not get this far.

If you only want certain users to be able to see some of the controls, you can easily hide and unhide individual controls according to the user level:

```
If ReturnUserLevel = "unknown" then DoCmd.Close
If ReturnUserLevel = "basic" Or ReturnUserLevel = "novice" Then
      Me.Text1.Visible = False
      Me.Label2.Visible = False
Else
      Me.Text1.Visible = True
      Me.Label2.Visible = True

End If
```

Do not forget that when hiding controls this way you also need to hide the attendant label for that control.

This methodology provides a very good way of restricting users as to where they can go and what they can do. Combined with Chapter 24, it provides a discipline over your application.

ASCII Character Codes

This appendix is a listing of the 255 ASCII (American Standard Code for Information Interchange) character codes that Access uses. They work in conjunction with the functions **Asc** and **Chr**. **Asc** will give the ASCII number of a character, and **Chr** will give the character based on an ASCII number.

All these characters can be used to produce text strings by using the **Chr** function (see Chapter 5). The following example will produce the string "ABC":

```
MsgBox Chr(65) & Chr(66) & Chr(67)
```

You can also insert carriage return and line feed characters to make your text wrap at the correct point.

In the table, the _ symbol indicates no displayable character exists.

Beyond character 128, Access uses an extended character set (which is not real ASCII) that partially depends on the locale of the user and the PC being used. For example, =CHAR(153) will give a ™ (trademark) symbol. However, you may need to experiment with these beyond character 128.

ASCII Code	Character	ASCII Code	Character
1	_	8	_
2	_	9	Horizontal tab
3	_	10	Line feed
4	_	11	Vertical tab
5	_	12	Form feed
6	_	13	Carriage return
7	_	14	_

ASCII Code	Character	ASCII Code	Character
15	_	52	4
16	_	53	5
17	_	54	6
18	_	55	7
19	_	56	8
20	_	57	9
21	_	58	:
22	_	59	;
23	_	60	<
24	_	61	=
25	_	62	>
26	_	63	?
27	_	64	@
28	_	65	A
29	_	66	B
30	_	67	C
31	_	68	D
32	Space	69	E
33	!	70	F
34	"	71	G
35	#	72	H
36	$	73	I
37	%	74	J
38	&	75	K
39	'	76	L
40	(	77	M
41	)	78	N
42	*	79	O
43	+	80	P
44	,	81	Q
45	-	82	R
46	.	83	S
47	/	84	T
48	0	85	U
49	1	86	V
50	2	87	W
51	3	88	X

ASCII Code	Character
89	Y
90	Z
91	[
92	\
93	]
94	^
95	_
96	`
97	a
98	b
99	c
100	d
101	e
102	f
103	g
104	h
105	i
106	j
107	k
108	l
109	m
110	n
111	o
112	p
113	q
114	r
115	s
116	t
117	u
118	v
119	w
120	x
121	y
122	z
123	{
124	|
125	}

ASCII Code	Character
126	~
127	_
128	„
129	_
130	,
131	ƒ
132	„
133	…
134	†
135	‡
136	ˆ
137	‰
138	Š
139	‹
140	Œ
141	_
142	Ž
143	_
144	_
145	'
146	'
147	"
148	"
149	•
150	–
151	—
152	~
153	™
154	š
155	›
156	œ
157	_
158	ž
159	Ÿ
160	
161	¡
162	¢

ASCII Code	Character	ASCII Code	Character
163	£	200	È
164	¤	201	É
165	¥	202	Ê
166	¦	203	Ë
167	§	204	Ì
168	¨	205	Í
169	©	206	Î
170	ª	207	Ï
171	<<	208	Ð
172	¬	209	Ñ
173	–	210	Ò
174	®	211	Ó
175	¯	212	Ô
176	°	213	Õ
177	±	214	Ö
178	²	215	×
179	³	216	Ø
180	´	217	Ù
181	µ	218	Ú
182	¶	219	Û
183	·	220	Ü
184	¸	221	Ý
185	¹	222	Þ
186	º	223	ß
187	>>	224	À
188	¼	225	Á
189	½	226	Â
190	¾	227	Ã
191	¿	228	Ä
192	À	229	Å
193	Á	230	Æ
194	Â	231	Ç
195	Ã	232	È
196	Ä	233	É
197	Å	234	Ê
198	Æ	235	Ë
199	Ç	236	Ì

ASCII Code	Character
237	Í
238	Î
239	Ï
240	Đ
241	Ñ
242	Ò
243	Ó
244	Ô
245	Õ
246	Ö

ASCII Code	Character
247	÷
248	Ø
249	Ù
250	Ú
251	Û
252	Ü
253	Ý
254	Þ
255	Ÿ

Index